Gender and warfare

in the twentieth century

Published in our
centenary year
～ **2004** ❦
MANCHESTER
UNIVERSITY
PRESS

Gender and warfare in the twentieth century

Textual representations

edited by Angela K. Smith

Manchester University Press

Manchester and New York

distributed exclusively in the USA by Palgrave

Published by Manchester University Press
Oxford Road, Manchester M13 9NR, UK
and Room 400, 175 Fifth Avenue, New York, NY 10010, USA
www.manchesteruniversitypress.co.uk

Distributed exclusively in the USA by
Palgrave, 175 Fifth Avenue, New York,
NY 10010, USA

Distributed exclusively in Canada by
UBC Press, University of British Columbia, 2029 West Mall,
Vancouver, BC, Canada V6T 1Z2

British Library Cataloguing-in-Publication Data
A catalogue record for this book is available from the British Library

Library of Congress Cataloging-in-Publication Data applied for

ISBN   0 7190 6574 7 hardback

First published 2004

13 12 11 10 09 08 07 06 05 04   10 9 8 7 6 5 4 3 2 1

Designed and typeset in Monotype Joanna
by Illuminati, Grosmont

Printed in Great Britain
by Bell and Bain Limited, Glasgow

Contents

Notes on contributors   vii

Acknowledgements   ix

Introduction   1

1   'What part have I now that you have come together?'
    Richard Aldington on war, gender and textual
    representation   12
    Caroline Zilboorg

2   Shell-shocked in Somerville: Vera Brittain's
    post-traumatic stress disorder   33
    Andrea Peterson

3   Gender, war and writing in Aldous Huxley's
    'Farcical History of Richard Greenow'   53
    Erik Svarny

4   How gender serves Trotskyism: the Spanish Civil War
    in Ken Loach's *Land and Freedom*   76
    Alan Munton

5   Clothes and uniform in the theatre of fascism:
    Clemence Dane and Virginia Woolf   96
    Jenny Hartley

6   Women and the battle of the Atlantic 1939–45:
    contemporary texts, propaganda, and life writing   111
    G. H. Bennett

7   'The best disguise': performing femininities for
    clandestine purposes during the Second World War   132
    Juliette Pattinson

8   The war at home: family, gender and post-colonial issues
    in three Vietnam War texts   154
    Marion Gibson

9   Chicken or hawk? Heroism, masculinity and violence
    in Vietnam War narratives   174
    Angela K. Smith

10 Elite women warriors and dog soldiers:
    gender adaptations in modern war films   195
    Jeffrey Walsh

    Select bibliography   216

    Index   221

Notes on contributors

Dr G. H. Bennett is Head of American Studies and a Lecturer in History at the University of Plymouth. He is also the editor of the *European Journal of American Culture* and is the author of four books.

Dr Marion Gibson lectures in English Literature at Exeter University, and is programme leader of the University's B.A. in English degree at Truro College, Cornwall. Her main area of research interest is the English Renaissance, especially the supernatural, but she has also written on twentieth-century film and political biography.

Jenny Hartley is Principal Lecturer in the School of English and Modern Languages at the University of Surrey, Roehampton. She has published books on women's writing from the Second World War with Virago Press; her most recent book is *The Reading Groups Book, 2002–2003* (Oxford University Press, 2002).

Alan Munton published *English Fiction of the Second World War* with Faber in 1989, and has since written on the war experience of Wyndham Lewis, Edgell Rickword and Louis MacNeice. He has interests in modern and contemporary poetry, and is writing a book on Wyndham Lewis and the twentieth century. He teaches English Literature at the University of Plymouth.

Juliette Pattinson is a lecturer in History at the University of Wales, Bangor. She is the author of *Secret War: A Pictorial History of the Special Operations Executive* (Caxton, 2001).

Andrea Peterson is Lecturer in English at the University of Birmingham. She has published various articles and essays on feminism, women's writing and Vera Brittain. She is currently writing a book on Vera Brittain.

Angela K. Smith is Senior Lecturer in English Literature at the University of Plymouth. She is the author of *The Second Battlefield:Women, Modernism and the First World War* (Manchester University Press, 2000) and editor of *Women's Writing of the First World War: An Anthology* (Manchester University Press, 2000). She is currently writing on the First World War and the Suffrage movement.

Erik Svarny teaches English Literature at the University of Surrey, Roehampton. He is the author of *Men of 1914:T. S. Eliot and Early Modernism* (Open University Press, 1988).

Jeff Walsh is Principal Lecturer at Manchester Metropolitan University. He has published widely in literary and cultural studies. His books include: *American War Literature: 1914 to Vietnam, Tell Me Lies About Vietnam: Cultural Battles For The Meaning of War, Vietnam Images:War and Representation, The Gulf War Did Not Happen: Politics, Culture and Warfare Post-Vietnam* (ed.) (Arena Press, 1995).

Dr Caroline Zilboorg is a member of Clare Hall and the Faculty of English at Cambridge University. She has edited the Richard Aldington–H. D. letters and has written a biography of Mary Renault. She is currently working on a historical novel featuring H. D., Richard Aldington and their modernist circle during the First World War. She divides her time between Cambridge and Brittany.

Acknowledgements

The idea for this book had been growing for some time before I finally got round to inviting contributions. I had become increasingly aware of the need for this subject to be tackled while teaching gender and warfare to undergraduates, and I am grateful to all at Manchester University Press for giving me the opportunity to offer students a coherent, generic guide to the twentieth century. I would like to thank all the contributors for offering such diverse, interesting and high-quality chapters. Thanks must also go to Harry Bennett and Dafydd Moore for much technical and moral support and to Mary Jacobs for such intelligent critical readings of my work. I am forever grateful to Jim and Ben Sargent for their tireless love and support.

Introduction

War is not an occasional interruption of a normalty called peace; it is the climate in which we live.[1]

We are at war now. Even in the infant years of the new millennium, war surrounds us. The twenty-first century has begun in just the same way as the twentieth ended. As I write, the media are filled with stories of the 'war against terror' and American and British troops occupy an unstable Iraq. And these stories create apprehension in all of us – that is, the general public, the civilian population – because we know that we could be the primary targets, the people in the front line, in any major war.

At the beginning of the twentieth century this was not so. The average man and woman on the street did not feel threatened by the prospect of war. Indeed as the new century dawned Britain was at war, fighting for the Empire in South Africa, and it was a war that the general public appeared to support, even relish. But it was in South Africa. Few people outside the combat troops involved had any notion of the realities of the Boer War. The majority of public opinion supported it because public opinion endorsed the 'greatness' of Britain. Confidence of victory, together with the enormous geographical distance, acted as an effective buffer between the ordinary civilian and the battle front.

The twentieth century changed all that. Today there is a strong movement within public opinion that opposed the war against Iraq. And 'terror' strikes at the very heart of our culture. In short, in the

space of one hundred years the nature of warfare has changed, dras-
tically and irreversibly. It began, of course, with the First World War.
Veterans of the Boer and other colonial wars served on the Western
and other fronts, but they were joined by hundreds, by thousands,
of others: civilian conscripts, who were to die in sufficient numbers
to shock the world into re-thinking warfare. Those who survived
returned to 'normal' life bearing wounds, both mental and physical, that would not heal and thus altered public perceptions of the
legacy of war for all time.

Yet a mere twenty years later the world was back at it again.
This is not to suggest that these had been twenty years of peace,
far from it. Even Europe was racked by war during this period, in
Russia, in Spain, in Greece, in Ireland, through its colonies. But the
Second World War, of course, brought with it a whole new set of
military processes. The civilian population, mostly male, had been
decimated in 1914–18, but generally speaking these men had been
put in uniform first, and only 5 per cent of all casualties were of-
ficially civilian. In the Second World War this figure rose to 75 per
cent. One needs only to think of the Blitz, the Holocaust, the atomic
bomb. And in the multiple wars of the 1990s civilians, very often
women and children, made up 90 per cent of the casualty lists.[2]
We have, it seems, good reason to be afraid.

This shift in the structure and make-up of warfare during the
course of the twentieth century disrupts expectations, many of
them gender-based, that have altered little for generations. War has
always been a man's game. This, of course, has equally always been
a problematic notion and women have been involved in warfare on
multiple levels since the earliest civilisations. But historically, the
distinction is clear: men are the ones who fight and die. The ability to do so, to defend one's community, to demonstrate courage
and prowess in battle, has been intrinsically linked with Western
constructions of masculinity for centuries. The battlefield presents
the ultimate location for 'being a man'. If alterations in the format
of war shift the battlefield into the midst of civilian society, age-
old understandings of gender difference may be problematised, if
not destroyed.

The changes in warfare during the twentieth century could be
addressed from a variety of perspectives, political, cultural, national.
So why choose to focus on gender? Trudi Tate and Suzanne Raitt
have argued:

Important work remains to be done if we are to understand how gender is constructed, especially in relation to significant historical events such as war. And perhaps we need to start asking why gender has become a critical orthodoxy; why critics rarely feel the need to justify an analysis of gender, especially in writing by women, to the exclusion of many other issues. For to focus exclusively on gender can produce a curiously depoliticized reading of our culture, its history, and its writing.[3]

In some ways they are right and this collection hopes to address the issue of how gender is constructed by exploring a range of historical events. But the collection also asserts that a focus on gender, rather than producing a depoliticised reading of our culture, offers instead an informed debate on a range of political issues. Alan Munton links gender with politics directly in his examination of textual representations of the Spanish Civil War. The 'theatre of fascism' identified by Jenny Hartley gives telling insight into 1930s' perceptions of international political developments. The notions of nationhood explored by Munton, Marion Gibson and Angela K. Smith suggest that issues of gender are intimately bound up with ideas of national identity and patriotism. The social and cultural processes illustrated in the textual investigations of Caroline Zilboorg, Erik Svarny, Juliette Pattinson and Jeff Walsh indicate the versatility of gender as a central theme.

A great deal has been written in the past decade concerning the relationship between women and warfare, triggered not only by the increased participation of women in war but also by the growth of a feminist critical orthodoxy intent on highlighting the roles played by women in all aspects of twentieth-century life. Books such as Claire Tylee's *The Great War and Women's Consciousness*,[4] Sharon Oudit's *Fighting Forces, Writing Women*,[5] Jenny Hartley's *Millions Like Us*[6] and Gill Plain's *Women's Fiction of the Second World War: Gender, Power and Resistance*[7] explore gendered female responses to various wars through the medium of the literary text. The First World War, in part because of the wealth of literature produced by both men and women, inspired the greatest response. Writing by trench soldiers such as Siegfried Sassoon, Wilfred Owen and Robert Graves has been so instrumental in creating a male-dominated impression of war writing, that it was here, perhaps, that redress was most urgently needed. These books and edited collections of women's writing[8] attempt to deconstruct the canon by demonstrating how much valuable writing by women was produced, and how it can alter our perceptions of conflict.

This body of work complements that which has been produced simultaneously by feminist historians such as Gail Braybon and Penny Summerfield,[9] Angela Woollacott[10] and Sayre P. Sheldon, among many others, documenting publicly the multiple and extended roles played by women in twentieth-century wars. In turn, these books argue against the male-dominated history books, those that have for decades delineated warfare as an entirely 'masculine' enterprise.

It is interesting to look at this literature survey. There are so many books looking at the experience and testimony of women through the gendered consciousness of the 'other'. Women have been *excluded* because of their gender. Equally there are many books exploring the combat experience and testimony of men. But they have not been *included* because of their gender, simply because they are perceived to be the essence of warfare. The titles give it all away: *Gendering War Talk*,[11] *Behind the Lines: Gender and Two World Wars*,[12] *Writing War: Fiction Gender and Memory*.[13] To write about women in war is to write about gender – about what it means to be constructed as 'feminine' in time of war. But for men this is not an issue. Fussell's *The Great War and Modern Memory*[14] does not mention or acknowledge women, but equally does not explore constructions of gender either. Samuel Hynes' *The Soldiers' Tale*[15] finds only men on its list of witnesses. There is no need to justify this because masculine identity is synonymous with war. To be a soldier is to be 'a man'; to be anything else, no matter how involved in the combat, is to be 'other'. There is no need to extrapolate masculinity from man – in the soldier they become one.

For women it is different. To participate in war, on many levels, they need to break traditional codes of femininity. Even as victims and casualties they trespass into a male arena – historically women have been kept away from the battlefield. Although there have always small numbers of women within various national militaries, they have rarely been encouraged into the line of fire.[16] Yet 80 per cent of the world's refugees are women and children,[17] displaced as the battle front comes in from the field and invades their domestic space. Their vulnerability, their 'femininity', so often exacerbates their victim status.

This volume attempts to unravel these complications of gender constructions through the exploration of a variety of discourses and representations. A number of the chapters explore the impact of warfare on women whose civilian or quasi-military roles resulted in their exile or self-exile to the role of 'other'. In Chapter 1, Caroline Zilboorg's interpretation of a marriage in wartime draws upon a number of genres to use Richard Aldington and H. D. (the poet Hilda Doolittle), to understand the social and cultural implications of warfare for both parties in a relationship. Zilboorg explores notions of identity and gender through a close examination of the Aldingtons' relationship as the war impacted on it. Aldington's letters to his wife reveal a complex dynamic, a search for self that conversely locates him as poet, as 'other', as frustrated by his inability to write as a result of the war as H. D., exiled as she was to the more conventional 'other' role, as non-combatant, as woman. Zilboorg also considers poetry produced by the couple, as well as a range of their post-war writings and fiction, to explore the relationship between war and writing and gender for these unusual individuals. The traumatic influence of the war may have been commonplace; this artistic response to it is unique.

In Chapter 2, Andrea Peterson examines the intricate gender assumptions that surround the condition of 'shell shock' through a detailed exploration of the life and work of Vera Brittain. Peterson deconstructs the tangled web of mental illness, locating Brittain's nervous collapse of the early 1920s within the boundaries of war-related neurosis. In doing so, she raises questions about the psychological effects of warfare on men and women, combatants and non-combatants, challenging conventional thinking on the subject.

Continuing this theme, considering the nature of warfare, the gendered experience of warfare, through the lens of the home front, Erik Svarny, in Chapter 3, discusses the gendered attitudes to the First World War located within Aldous Huxley's novella 'Farcical History of Richard Greenow'. This proves to be an informative debate as Huxley's story appears to address many of the prominent gendered issues of the day from the suffrage campaign to pacifism, from homosexuality to psychoanalysis. Svarny's detailed analysis breaks with earlier readings of this text and offers a cultural and political commentary highlighting a number of ideas that resonate through this collection.

In Chapter 5, Jenny Hartley explores the questioning of war in the 1930s, a period when memories of the First World War remained fresh. Hartley reads gender, politics and war from a feminist perspective through an analysis of the use and interpretations of clothes and uniform in the very different writings of Clemence Dane and Virginia Woolf. She examines the performative aspects of fascism, chillingly presented by these writers through a range of genres, with a particular emphasis on two specific works, Dane's *The Arrogant History of White Ben* and Woolf's *Three Guineas*. Her conclusions regarding the ideology of performance and the psychology of fascism give a fascinating insight into gendered perceptions of war in the 1930s.

What is of course noticeable about the twentieth century is the growth of women's active participation in the military. This was not just in quasi-military organisations such as the FANY[18] or the WAAC,[19] or the involvement of women in the SOE,[20] as discussed by Juliette Pattinson in Chapter 7. Instead there was actual participation on the field of battle – in killing. The First World War provides a handful of examples: the Russian Women's Battalion of Death[21] and Flora Sandes, the only British woman to see active service as a soldier in the Serbian army.[22] As Alan Munton points out in Chapter 4, women did fight in the early stages of the Spanish Civil War for various militia groups, but were moved from the front line during the course of the multifaceted political wranglings that he discusses. Munton's exploration of the Trotskyist politics of Ken Loach's 1995 film *Land and Freedom* illustrates the movement of women from soldier status towards a re-transfiguration as 'other' as a direct result of the politics of this war: women returned to their more traditional roles as nurses or domestics. In this text, Munton argues, politics and gender are inseparable as debates around sexuality, desire and prostitution examine the iconography of woman as symbol of revolution and the problems found therein.

The story for the Second World War is similar, with women soldiers appearing on a small scale, for example in the army of the Soviet Union. Women fought in some branches of the infantry, as in the First World War, and also in the Soviet Air Force: a specialist detachment called the 'night witches' flew out-of-date aircraft on night-time bombing raids.

In this collection, the Second World War focus is on women penetrating the previously male-dominated sphere of front-line warfare, not as soldiers, but in unconventional ways nonetheless. Juliette Pattinson's chapter, '"The best disguise": performing femininities for clandestine purposes during the Second World War' draws upon a wide range of different textual representations in order to explore the practices of performativity and enactment adopted by women in the Special Operations Executive. Pattinson demonstrates how women used a variety of dis/guises of femininity in order to carry out their undercover work in occupied Europe in the Second World War. Her sources include memoir, autobiography, biography, official records and oral testimony, which blend together effectively to create a vivid picture of the roles of these 'para-military' women. She also shows how the constructions of femininity employed by these women often stood in opposition to the reality of their jobs behind enemy lines.

G. H. Bennett, in Chapter 6, also examines women performing very 'unfeminine' roles during the Battle of the Atlantic, and yet argues that femininity is imposed nonetheless for propagandist purposes. The Battle of the Atlantic, Bennett suggests, was a global, rather than a localised affair, involving naval forces, merchant seamen, women and civilians from many different countries. He explores the way in which women's involvement was represented both by the media and by the women themselves drawing on a wide range of textual sources from naval records to personal memoirs, official histories to advertising campaigns. This analysis considers not only the ex-periences of the women at sea, but also those on the home front who constantly felt the impact of the Battle of the Atlantic. Bennett finds women expertly fulfilling the roles of men as engineers and such like, while still retaining the trappings of femininity, enabling them to become ministering angels at times of crisis. And they are the material of propaganda both as patriots and as victims, invoking that perpetual image of the innocent suffering in wartime. These women are not soldiers, although some of the testimonies come from the women's branches of the armed services. But, Bennett argues, military status was not necessary; the Battle of the Atlantic was all-encompassing.

However, in the later years of the twentieth century the numbers of women in the military seem to have grown. Chapter 9 illustrates the confusion often experienced by women in the Vietnam War. They could be soldiers in the armies of either the North or the South, or they could be involved in guerrilla activity. Many suffered as the various armies assumed that they were involved, while they were in fact trying to go about their daily lives. Women, it seems, were often unsure of their place, operating on instinct in the combat situation. Chapter 10 takes up this issue directly through a detailed analysis of the women soldiers of Hollywood.

The debate surrounding the role of women soldiers became very animated in the last years of the twentieth century, following the active participation of many women, particularly Americans, in the Gulf War.[23] Ilene Rose Feinman attempts to represent both sides of this debate in her book *Citizenship Rites: Feminist Soldiers and Feminist Antimilitarists*.[24] She explores the position of feminist soldiers – that is, women who believe that active service in the military is both a right and a duty required by full citizenship. This is an old argument in reverse. It is easy to recall the old *fin de siècle* rhetoric put forward by anti-suffragists, that women were not entitled to equal citizenship *because* they did not fight alongside men on the field of battle. But Feinman favours the feminist anti-militarist stance that opposes women's involvement. She argues:

> Feminist antimilitarist analyses teach us that the military is a deeply masculinist institution. Feminist antimilitarist analyses suggest that motivations for war are lodged in the traditional modalities of economic and political domination and sexual conquest, and the masculinist dynamic of militarist discourse.[25]

In other words, Feinman argues that war fundamentally oppresses women. Her ideas resemble those found in other recent feminist anti-militarist works such as Lois Ann Lorentzen and Jennifer Turpin's recent collection *The Women and War Reader*,[26] which contains a wide range of essays, but has a tendency to focus on woman as victim rather than participant. Such arguments tend to locate women politically within various peace movements and, again, draw on feminist pacifist ideas that originate in the early years of the twentieth century when women campaigners constructed essentialist and biological reasons why they should oppose the First World War.[27] They do not, generally, engage with the point of view and, indeed, the existence of the feminist soldier.

Clearly women continue to oppose war. The protests at Greenham Common in the 1980s provide a vivid contemporary illustration of this. But, equally, the first Gulf War and the recent war with Iraq, in which women were so publicly present and sustained casualties, seems to offer a tangible manifestation of the feminist soldier argument. Perhaps it is not surprising, then, that America's greatest publicity machine, Hollywood, has taken an interest. Jeff Walsh examines cinematic representation of women soldiers in the 1980s and 1990s – representations that ostensibly place 'the other' in the masculine heartland of the military. Walsh considers both the 'masculine' and the 'feminine' in the late twentieth century. Arguably, by the final decades it had become more difficult to consider warfare without looking at both.

Marion Gibson does just this, in Chapter 8, when exploring national gender identities through the iconic roles of the 'mother' and the 'father' in various written and filmic representations of the Vietnam War. Gibson explores the interface between war and familial relationships from a post-colonial perspective, identifying metaphorical patterns imposed on and/or accepted by conflicting nations. She examines Vietnam through the post-colonial observer, J. M. Coetzee; the colonised, Le Ly Hayslip; and the one-time American soldier, Oliver Stone. These narratives each use allegorical representations of the family to delineate war experience in different ways, from a series of binary oppositions to a much more complex family web. This chapter links gender representation with nationhood, reading both through the cultural ideologies of race and identity.

Chapter 9, 'Chicken or hawk? Heroism, masculinity and violence in Vietnam War narratives', invokes the ghosts of Vietnam, male and female, to examine the impact of a war that confuses the traditional relationships between soldiering and masculinities. Through readings of a range of different Vietnam narratives from battle front memoirs to retrospective civilian novels, with a particular focus on representations of violence and sexuality, I consider undermined conventional notions of masculinities and the resultant textual legacy. The roles of men and women, soldiers and civilians, in the works of writers such as Philip Caputo, Bao Ninh, Jayne Anne Phillips and Bobbie Ann Mason can be used to illustrate the complexities of gender in warfare in the second half of the twentieth century.

The collection concludes with Jeff Walsh's study of late-twentieth-century Hollywood, cinematic representations of both men and women on the front line. Discussing films such as *Courage Under Fire*, *G. I. Jane*, *Sands of Iwo Jima* and *Apocalypse Now*, Walsh makes a critical examination of the masculinities and the femininities of the battlefield informed by race, culture and nationhood, challenging much conventional iconography such as that surrounding the presentation of Eastern women by the West and the notion of woman as victim. By referring to a broad range of films that collectively highlight

numerous issues concerning the representation of gender and warfare, this final chapter brings together many of the themes and ideas
encountered in those that precede it.

There are many ways in which I could have organised the essays in this collection, according to themes or content or discipline.
But for ease of reference I have kept them in general chronological
order, starting with the responses to the First World War and ending as close to the twenty-first century as possible. I hope this will
enhance the coherence of the book as a whole and allow the reader
to make connections between the different significant conflicts of
the twentieth century.

'War is not an occasional interruption of a normality called peace;
it is the climate in which we live...' Since 11 September 2001 warfare
has changed again. It has taken an even more sinister turn, which
locates civilians globally as the primary target for some combatants.
Location in a 'war zone' is no longer necessary. The ongoing 'war
against terror' puts all of us, potentially, in the front line at any
time. War, then, is very much a part of the climate in which we
live. As politicians across the globe talk about war, there is none of
the hysteria or the excitement of 1914. There are voices that speak
out, very often in opposition, but it is questionable whether or not
anyone will listen to them. The real nature of twenty-first century
warfare has yet to be determined. But whatever form it takes, however it affects all our lives, doubtless there will be people, writers,
artists, film-makers who will be prepared to chronicle it – our own
testimony for future generations.

Notes

1 Samuel Hynes, Introduction, *The Soldiers' Tale* (London: Pimlico, 1998), p. xii.
2 Sayre P. Sheldon (ed.), Preface, *Her War Story: Twentieth Century Women Write About War* (Carbondale and Edwardsville: Southern Illinois University Press, 1999) xi.
3 Suzanne Raitt and Trudi Tate (eds.), *Women's Fiction and the Great War* (Oxford: Oxford University Press, 1997), p. 3.
4 Claire Tylee, *The Great War and Women's Consciousness* (London: Macmillan, 1990).
5 Sharon Ouditt, *Fighting Forces, Writing Women* (London: Routledge, 1994).
6 Jenny Hartley, *Millions Like Us: British Women's Fiction of the Second World War* (London: Virago, 1997). It should be noted that these titles represent a small sample of a growing market.
7 Gill Plain, *Women's Fiction of the Second World War: Gender, Power and Resistance* (Edinburgh: Edinburgh University Press, 1996).
8 See Margaret Higonnet (ed.), *Lines of Fire: Women Writers of World War I* (New York Penguin, 1999); Agnes Cardinal et al. (eds.), *Women's Writing on the First World War*

(Oxford: Oxford University Press, 1999); Claire Tylee (ed.), *War Plays by Women* (London: Routledge, 1999); Angela K. Smith (ed.), *Women's Writing of the First World War: An Anthology* (Manchester: Manchester University Press, 2000).

9   Gail Braybon and Penny Summerfield (eds.), *Out of the Cage: Women's Experiences in Two World Wars* (London: Pandora, 1987).

10   Angela Woollacott, *On Her Their Lives Depend: Munitions Workers in the Great War* (London, Berkeley and Los Angeles: University of California Press, 1994).

11   M. Cooke and A. Woollacott (eds.), *Gendering War Talk* (Princeton, NJ: Princeton University Press, 1993).

12   M. R. Higonnet, J. Jenson, S. Micel and M. C. Weitz (eds.), *Behind the Lines: Gender and the Two World Wars* (Newhaven, CT and London: Yale University Press, 1987).

13   L. Hanley, *Writing War: Fiction, Gender and Memory* (Amherst, MA: University of Massachusetts Press, 1991).

14   Paul Fussell, *The Great War and Modern Memory* (Oxford: Oxford University Press. 1977).

15   Hynes.

16   For information on exceptions to this role, see Julie Wheelwright, *Amazons and Military Maids* (London: Pandora, 1989).

17   Sheldon, Preface, p. xi.

18   First Aid Nursing Yeomanry.

19   Women's Army Auxiliary Corps.

20   Special Operations Executive.

21   See Wheelwright and accounts related in Higonnet (ed.).

22   See Wheelwright and Sandes own accounts of her experiences in *An English Woman-Sergeant in the Serbian Army* (London, New York and Toronto, Hodder & Stoughton, 1916) and in *The Autobiography of a Woman Soldier: A Brief Record of Adventures with the Serbian Army 1916–1919* (London: H. F. & G. Witherby, 1927).

23   'In the Gulf War, nearly 40,000 US women participated – 6% of the US forces deployed … About a dozen women soldiers died, of whom five were killed by hostile forces.' See Joshua S. Goldstein *War and Gender* (Cambridge: Cambridge University Press, 2001) p. 94.

24   Ilene Rose Feinman, *Citizenship Rites: Feminist Soldiers and Feminist Antimilitarists* (New York and London: New York University Press, 2000).

25   Feinman, p. 2.

26   Lois Ann Lorentzen and Jennifer Turpin (eds.), *The Women and War Reader* (New York and London: New York University Press, 1998).

27   See, for example, Margaret Kemester and Jo Vellacott (eds.), *Militarism versus Feminism* (London: Virago, 1987).

'What part have I now that you have come together?' Richard Aldington on war, gender and textual representation

Caroline Zilboorg

The English poet Richard Aldington and his wife, the American poet
H. D. (Hilda Doolittle), became modernist writers who in different
ways explored the boundaries of both identity and textual representation. H. D. is known for her formalist experiments; Aldington, in a
more obviously realistic tradition, has an international reputation not
only as a poet and novelist but as an editor, translator and biographer.
Although H. D. was initially marginalised in the canon because of
her gender, her work, like that of Joyce or Eliot or Pound, falls into
the privileged mode of high literary modernism. Aldington's writing
is more experimental than he has been given credit for, while his
very versatility calls into question the parameters of genre (Are his
novels a form of biography? Are his biographies about their osten-
sible subjects – Voltaire, D. H. Lawrence, Lawrence of Arabia – or
about himself?) Specifically, the issue of textual representation is a
central concern for both writers, but while feminist scholars over
the last twenty years have stressed H. D.'s attention to gender in her
work, Aldington's attitudes towards both textuality and sexuality are
generally misrepresented as conventional and fixed. Nothing could
be further from the case.

I

In Cornwall in late July of 1918 H. D. wrote to her husband that she
was fairly certain she was pregnant. Aldington, a first lieutenant in
the Signal Corps fighting with the Ninth Royal Sussex in northern

France, had not been in England since mid-April, and both of them knew that the child was not his.

Commissioned in November of 1917, Aldington had begun a passionate affair with Arabella Yorke during a month's leave that included the Christmas holidays. Living with H. D. in London until he returned to the army after the new year, he fully expected to be sent immediately to the front where he had already served for sixth months as a corporal in 1917. As it turned out, technology in the last months of the war raced ahead of even the long-anticipated and fast-approaching 'Big Push', and Aldington was kept in southern England for week after week, attending one course after another, being trained in increasingly sophisticated communications. The Great War, after all, had begun by relying on young officers who conveyed the whereabouts of troops and hills and trenches by means of flags. By the time Aldington crossed the Lens–La Bassée front in October of 1918, he was laying telephone lines over the craters of what had been no man's land, navigating into Belgium and telephoning information back to his battalion headquarters, to which he was attached as an acting captain in early November. Throughout the winter and early spring of 1918, however, he was never far from London and enjoyed the poignant privilege of frequent weekend leaves, during which he saw Arabella and H. D., made love to both of them, then left each woman over and over again for what every time seemed the last time they might ever see one another.[1]

Aldington experienced a conflict of roles which could scarcely have been more acute. Was he husband or lover? Soldier or poet? Free or caught? Even before his earliest days in the trenches, Aldington tried to configure himself as other – elsewhere, in another time or place, someone or something different from the automaton common life in early-twentieth-century Britain often appeared to him to require. Indeed, H. D.'s Hellenism was fostered not only by her readings with Pound in the first days of their courtship (1905–10) but by her relationship with Aldington, who by the time they met in 1911 had already come to see the past as 'another country', an alternative space in which he could realise himself in ways contemporary England increasingly worked against.[2] For Aldington, the key to this past, this other space – and eventually to this and his modernism – was language and languages, especially Greek but also Latin, Italian and French. Even as an adolescent, he had begun translating fluently and independently, creating versions of texts which were at once his own and a displacement of the past into the present, the present into the past.

When Aldington and H. D. launched The Poets' Translation Series in 1915, he stated in the introduction what he hoped the project would achieve: the translators – like good Imagist poets – would 'endeavour to give the words of these Greek and Latin authors as simply and clearly as may be'; the resulting translations would give readers access to beautiful and emotionally powerful works otherwise inaccessible to them.[3] The poet's job was, Aldington felt, to link the past with the present, the sublime with daily life, to serve as a bridge between the two, to communicate lofty ideas and feelings to an audience that could be persuaded by beauty to share them. In this vein, during the summer of 1918, Aldington struggled in his letters to H. D. to define the man and poet he wanted to be – a matter at once of politics, aesthetics, history, and gender. On 1 July he wrote that 'keeping in touch with common humanity' was not exactly what he meant, and admitted that 'The attitude I am getting at is very hard to define.' He continued: 'Why is it Ezra, for instance, seems to us so utterly dead? Just because he has cut himself off from this common humanity – which is fundamentally the same that Christ walked with and Plato talked with & Villon played the scoundrel with.' He cautioned, 'Don't mistake me; I am a thousand miles from the philanthropic man, the man who wants to reform the world, the democrate.' Rather, Aldington wanted 'to avoid the dead-egotism of Pound, the very foolish paltryness of Chelsea, the ridiculous splurging of Chicago, the diseased strength of the Cubists, and the mere belly-worship of the bourgeois, the mere struggle with poverty of the poor.'

Aldington then attempted to include in his idea of the poet what many young officers felt in their relationships with the ordinary men they led into battle:

> Oh, yes, books are good and it is good to know all about Gothic churches & the philosophy of Lucretius – but it is good too to know how a soldier puts together his marching order, how a blacksmith shoes a horse & why we do not grow as much wheat in the west of England as in the east. And beyond all this knowledge one should be sincerely interested in common lives, realise I mean what these people do.

Aldington concluded that while he did not see poets as Shelley's 'unacknowledged legislators', he felt that poets, among which he counted himself and H. D., had the responsibility of 'a kind of unauthorised priesthood'; they were called to serve as 'the go-betweens of the spirit and the flesh'. He concluded: 'We interpret humanity to itself, & ourselves.' For Aldington, being a poet was a heavy responsibility, and he took seriously the struggle to define and embody and enact his calling amid the demands of life at the front. 'I am trying', he wrote to H. D. on 1 July 1918, 'to approach it obliquely, through little prose poems, feeling my way & waiting for illumination which may or may not come.'

Together with H. D., Aldington had from his youth immersed himself in Hellenism as an idealised alterity. Thus, for instance, in H. D.'s *Sea Garden* (1916), numerous poems explore the tensions between male and female figures negotiating a difficult relationship in a raw and rocky Attic space. Other, more obviously personal, poems of the period reveal a similar displacement: Aldington is Adonis to H. D.'s Venus (in 'Adonis', 48–9); Pygmalion to her statue (in 'Pygmalion', 48–50); Apollo to her Evadne (in 'Evadne', 132). More explicitly and autobiographically still, H. D. and Aldington are configured as nameless, competitive but collaborating poets in both 'Heliodora' (151–4) and 'Nossis' (155–7).[4] For his part, drawing on Greek and Latin pastoral traditions, Aldington figured himself repeatedly as a faun in an Arcadian space simultaneously threatened by modern violence. He addresses H. D. in many of his later war letters as 'Astraea', his starry lover, and as his beloved 'Dryad', and on 8 July 1918 he recalls earlier letters, dating from his first tour at the front, when he had portrayed himself as her faun, concluding 'The Faun sends kisses to his dear Dryad.' Included in this letter was Aldington's poem 'The Faun Captive', in which he portrays himself as an imprisoned animal, taken from 'under Zeus-holy oaks', 'snared and bound', 'dragged ... for their uncouth mirth/ ... coarsely derided'. 'I am weary for the freedom of free things', the faun declares in the penultimate stanza. Then he grows briefly threatening: 'one night I shall break these things/ And kill, kill, kill in sharp revenge.' Escaping his nameless captors – who are clearly military figures embodying the materialism of contemporary culture – the faun flees 'Out to the unploughed lands no foot oppresses,/ The lands that are free, being free of man.' While the faun is clearly male (he flees as well 'To the wild-rose kisses of the deathless girls/ Who laugh and flash among the trees'), he is no powerful stag, no Minotaur or Nemean lion; there is indeed finally something delicate and diminutive about Aldington's faun, something winningly feminine about Aldington-as-faun, turning his frustration upon himself, nearly biting 'the brown flesh of my arms and hands for shame and grief', as caged he longs to romp with those girls in the 'lush pastures' and 'foot-hills'.[5]

Aldington's struggle to define himself (the soldier caught in the maelstrom, the poet struggling for agency) was complicated by his cross-identification with his wife and by hers with him: most obviously, she was the poet writing as he could not while in the trenches; he was the soldier fighting in a war that she as a woman could not participate in directly. H. D.'s confession of her pregnancy in the summer of 1918 intensified these conflicts of role and gender and identity that Aldington's experiences at the front made it impossible for either of them to resolve.

The Aldingtons had always led a Bohemian life, and both of them were committed to free love, an open marriage. Indeed, Aldington was having an affair with Brigit Patmore, an older, married woman, when he and H. D. met in late 1911, an affair that seems to have continued intermittently throughout the first year of their courtship, although it is unlikely that H. D. was aware of it at the time. Aldington and H. D. probably slept with no one but each other from the moment they became lovers in Paris in the summer of 1912 until the spring of 1916 when Aldington, anxiously awaiting conscription, began a brief affair with Florence Fallas, the wife of a close friend. There was little duplicity in these affairs: Aldington was apparently open with H. D., who knew of his attraction to other women and agreed with him that both of them should be free to act on their physical desires. Aldington told her about his affair with Flo Fallas, and insisted sincerely, despite his affection for Flo, on his deep and lasting love for H. D.

For her part, H. D. was extremely upset, experiencing emotions she had not anticipated. Although she had consented intellectually in each case, and would insist throughout her life on Aldington's right to take lovers, she was quickly uncomfortable with the women he chose, even if she had at first liked them. Ultimately, she would find all of his 'other' women shallow, superficial, unworthy, even faintly ridiculous – and not surprisingly she invariably saw them as competitors, a threat to her, to her marriage, and to Aldington's nevertheless enduring love for her.

H. D. herself had been engaged to Ezra Pound before she left America for Europe in June of 1911, and certainly Pound continued to feel proprietary not only when she arrived in London in August but during the summer before the Aldingtons' marriage in 1913 and even at the time of H. D.'s daughter's birth in March of 1919. While Pound and H. D. had never slept together, they had certainly kissed and petted during the earliest stages of their courtship (1906–10), but in 1910–11 H. D. had experienced a passionate and fully physical relationship with Frances Gregg, the woman who became her first lover. H. D. would continue throughout her life to be sexually attracted to women as well as to men. Despite H. D.'s love for Aldington and Frances's marriage to Louis Wilkinson in 1912, H. D. impulsively decided to accept Frances's invitation to accompany her friend on what was in fact a honeymoon, and was only dissuaded by Pound, who had himself courted Gregg at the time of H. D.'s involvement with her.

In other words, H. D. was no stranger to overlapping relationships, conflicting desires and the crosscurrents of high emotion. Indeed, she herself was deeply attracted to D. H. Lawrence during the fraught Christmas when Aldington and Arabella began their affair. H. D. evidently knew of their attraction and even agreed to its consummation, despite her ensuing resentment and deep distress once the affair had started. In the event, it was not Lawrence whom H. D. accompanied to Cornwall in March of 1918, but Cecil Gray, a volatile young musician who had been Frieda Lawrence's lover until she tired of him that winter.

Such tangled relationships undermined numerous conventions. Baldly chronicled (as here) they appear faintly absurd and certainly foolish. Passionately experienced by the participants, these relationships were the result of a radical and modernist rethinking of 'Victorian' values and behaviour; they were both the result of and in turn themselves produced an instability not only (and perhaps not surprisingly) in the Aldingtons' marriage but in their notions of gender and gender roles and in their ideas of what sexual activity was and meant.

Aldington's affair with Yorke was a result of a great many factors, not the least of which was the common sense of *carpe diem* experienced by many soldiers during the Great War. When Aldington published two volumes of poetry in 1919, he entitled one *Images of Love* and the other *Images of War*. It is often difficult to know why particular poems made it into one book rather than the other, for all the poems can be classed as 'war poems'; most of them seem to one degree or another 'love poems' as well.[6] In fact, the war was as interpenetrating when added to the heady mix of passions in Aldington's bohemian life as any of the many overlapping relationships both he and H. D. were experiencing. He wrote of his feelings in 'Before Parting' (1919). 'Give me, O Love, your love for this last brief season,' the speaker pleads,

> though the whole earth rock
> With the shattering roar of the guns' booming,
> Though in that horror of din and flame and murder
> All men's blood grows faint and their limbs as water,
> Though I return once more to battle,
> Though perhaps I be lost to you forever— [7]

This destabilising of conventional roles reached its zenith in Aldington's reaction to H. D.'s confession in August of 1918.

Perhaps most obviously, H. D.'s pregnancy threatened to redefine her a second time as a mother. While she and Aldington had not wanted a child at the time of her first pregnancy in 1915, by the time of their baby's birth they had welcomed the notion of parenthood; both were then devastated when, as Aldington wrote to Amy Lowell, the 'beautiful child … wouldn't breathe'.[8] Set, despite the war, to take on the traditional roles of father and mother, Aldington and H. D. suddenly found themselves alone together, painfully struggling to re-establish themselves as husband and wife. Both fearful of another pregnancy, their sexual relationship became fraught. The increasing tensions of the war period made any realistic planning for the future impossible as conscription laws made their way through Parliament, laws which would propel Aldington into military service because of his gender and age (twenty four) whether or not he wanted to go. Indeed, he seriously considered conscientious objection – a difficult choice with the imputations of cowardliness, effeminacy and even homosexuality with which it was associated – then decided to assert what minimal agency he had in the matter and signed up with his friend Carl Fallas in Devon in May 1916. Thus Aldington went in with a 'pal' and exercised some choice over the regiment in which he would serve. While the stillbirth caused Aldington and

H. D. to re-evaluate their union – as possible parents, as husband and wife, as lovers – the war further strained the partnership they had renegotiated as intimate companions, fellow poets, uneasy but nonetheless passionate lovers. Finally, their decisions to take other lovers made their relationship even less conventional or clear.

On 24 July, just before he received her confession, Aldington responded to H. D.'s apparent concern about her identity as a woman and a poet, as an American who had left America, as a woman who was attracted to both men and women: 'You must never feel discouraged because the social order of to-day has apparently no niche to offer you, because you appear to be a sort of outcast, "deracinée" as you like to call it.' He continued, 'You lay too much stress on nationality – a thing invented by politicians.' He then offered reassurance: 'You speak of not having a body – you are wrong; you have a beautiful and passionate body. I knew that the last times we were together.' Finally, leaving rational discourse aside, Aldington insisted, 'My dear, dear beautiful child-wife … I know you must love me as inevitably as I must love you. You have never looked into anyone else's eyes as you have looked into mine & I have never looked into anyone else's eyes as I have looked into yours.' But H. D.'s pregnancy in the summer of 1918 called into question all of the delicate definitions she and Aldington were struggling to establish through their letters.

Aldington's response on 4 August reveals his efforts to redefine even the very words 'husband' and 'wife', terms he attempts to delineate rationally even as he is emotionally rocked by H. D.'s news. He tries to structure a rational response, discussing his thoughts under 'two main headings: Natural and Social':

> We assume, do we not, that each man & woman is free to live his own life, to ignore any ordinary rules of conduct when he so chooses. We assume also that men & women are at liberty to use this freedom in matters of sex … But in sexual relationships a woman's part is curious and difficult (so is a man's). That is to say a man has one 'mate' & many mistresses; a woman one 'mate' & many lovers. But there is a difference here somehow, for a man only loves eternally his spiritual mate, whereas a woman's 'mate' is the man to whom she bears children.

The implications of his argument here are acutely distressing for Aldington:

> Formally I stood first with you & remained first however many lovers
> you might have had. But doesn't this event cause a sort of volte-face?
> Gray becomes your husband & I merely your lover; because the emo-
> tions that bind lovers together are exquisite & sterile [pure], like poetry,
> but a child is a more ponderous link than any beauty.

Socially, Aldington theorises, 'Two lovers meet, kiss, love & part;
there is no contract socially, no bond is formed. They are free. But
two lovers meet & there is a child – then there is a bond, the first
social unit is formed, it is ruthless and iron.' But the agony of
Aldington's emotions rupture his rational discourse:

> Every moment that child is growing within you makes you go further
> from me & nearer to Gray. Inevitably, you must come to love him
> more – is he not the father of your child? Inevitably, he must come
> to love you more – are you not the mother of his child? Inevitably,
> I must drift further from you both – what part have I now that you
> have come together?'

Aldington's efforts to say what words ('husband', 'wife', 'mate')
mean here offer a different and deeply disturbing view of what
it might mean 'to make it new': nothing, including conventional
gender roles and language itself, could mean what they had once
been assumed to mean, what they were conventionally accepted to
mean; the losses of war would include not only the physical losses
on thousands of miles of the battlefields, but the loss of former
certainties, the loss of pre-war duties and roles, even the erasure
of self as previously conceived.

   Notwithstanding Aldington's radical attitudes towards sexual relationships in his letters to H. D., there is something Victorian in his
efforts in August of 1918 to set matters straight, to sort things out
rationally for him and H. D. (as if things could be sorted out, as
if love or sex or war could be rationally ordered and then coped
with). Notwithstanding her having taken a lover and confided in her
unusually sympathetic husband, there is evidently something equally
Victorian in H. D.'s apparent confidence that her husband, engaged
in bitter trench warfare hundreds of miles away, could at least address if not resolve her present difficulty. We cannot know, however
– except from Aldington's responses and from evidence textualised
in her war novel, Bid Me to Live (1960) – what H. D. actually wrote
to him, for her side of the correspondence, her contemporary and

immediate war text, has not survived. Indeed, her letters became a casualty of war, burnt by Aldington in 1920 as too painful for him to reread, painful not because of what many men of the time might have seen as her betrayal, but because her letters testified to the tremendously disturbing losses that he came to see as occasioned by, even represented by, the war itself. Indeed, the pressing question for Aldington from this point on in the war, from this point on in his marriage, from this point on in his career as a writer, became exactly the one he voiced to H. D. on 4 August: what part could he now play?

II

Richard Aldington prefaces his important war novel *Death of a Hero* (1929) with an open letter to his friend, the popular playwright Hal Glover. He indicates that he first began the work 'almost immediately after the Armistice in a little Belgian cottage – my billet. I remember the landscape was buried deep in snow, and that we had very little fuel. Then came demobilization, and the effort of readjustment cost my manuscript its life.' Here Aldington identifies himself with his novel, situating its composition within biographical space but also joining the original manuscript, whose life was lost in the readjustment after demobilisation, with his own life, which was constantly at risk in the trenches and transformed if not literally destroyed by the war. He simultaneously blurs the distinction between the post-war period – which makes textual representation, the representation of war, masculinity, death and heroism so difficult – with the war itself, which Aldington is aware of having survived by mere chance. He then goes on in his preface to discuss the issue of genre, a matter at the heart of the problem of textual representation:

> This book is not the work of a professional novelist. It is, apparently, not a novel at all. Certain conventions of form and method in the novel have been erected, I gather, into immutable laws, and are looked at with quite superstitious reverence. They are entirely disregarded here. To me the excuse for the novel is that one can do any damn thing one pleases. I am told I have done things as terrible as if you introduced asides and soliloquies into your plays, and came onto the stage in the middle of a scene to take part in the action.

Indeed, Aldington's novel is at once a fiction and a personal dramatic text which the writer enters in the middle so as 'to take
part in the action'. In his preface Aldington struggles to categorise
Death of a Hero, calling it 'a jazz novel', 'a threnody', 'a memorial ...
to a generation which hoped much, strove honestly, and suffered
deeply.' He does not call it autobiography or history or memoir;
and while he suspects that some readers may find it an example
of 'Expressionism or Super-realism', he insists that he has written
only 'what appears to be the truth'.[9]

Aldington cannot define his text, indeed sets up a text which
resists definition. The preface is itself preceded by a quotation from
Horace Walpole about England as a country with many old fools
and few young ones and followed by a 'Prologue' of twenty-eight
pages in which an unnamed first-person speaker recounts the fact
and aftermath of the death of Acting Captain George Winterbourne
on 4 November 1918. The prologue is subtitled in French 'Morte
d'un Eröe' and its pace indicated as 'allegretto', as if it were a piece
of music.

The main body of the text consists of three parts. Part I, whose
pace is indicated as 'vivace', is made up of five short chapters and
covers George's parents' unhappy marriage and his own birth, youth
and adolescence in the countryside near Dover. The section ends with
George's decision to leave home: through mismanagement, his father
has lost the family's money, and George moves to London, to support himself with a part-time job as a reporter. Part II, whose pace
is 'andante cantabile', covers the period from 1912 through the first
years of the war. It includes an account of George's bohemian life,
his courtship of and modern marriage to the superficial Elizabeth
as well as the beginning of his affair with the equally superficial
Fanny, and concludes in the seventh chapter with George's enlist-
ment. In Part III, which begins three-fifths of the way through the
book, Aldington finally starts to write about the war. The pace of
this section is indicated as 'adagio'; it comprises thirteen chapters,
and contains the most compelling writing of the entire work.
The narrator, who has been increasingly less of a presence in the
text, almost completely drops out here, and while the narrative
remains in the third person, the reader is given intimate access to
George's thoughts, feelings and individual actions. Part III ends with
George's death; Aldington writes, 'Something seemed to break in
Winterbourne's head. He felt he was going mad, and sprang to his

feet. The line of bullets smashed across his chest like a savage steel whip. The universe exploded darkly into oblivion.'[10]

Two more brief sections conclude the volume. On a separate page following Part III Aldington quotes General Foch's official statement, dated 12 November 1918, in which he praises the officers and men of the allied armies of which he was Commander-in-Chief − a statement of course ironic in the context which Aldington has established for it. *Death of a Hero* concludes with an epilogue, specifically with a poem explicitly entitled 'Epilogue', reprinted in Aldington's collected poems in 1948 as 'Epilogue to *Death of a Hero*'. The poem is set eleven years after the fall of Troy. The first-person speaker, a former soldier, thinks of the war's destruction, 'the beauty of many young men now dust,/ And the long agony, and how useless it all was.' Overhearing his fellow combatants as they recall their experiences, he parallels their conversation with the war itself: the old men's talk 'clashes' futilely about him, 'like the meeting of blade and blade'. A young man and woman dismiss the discussion as dull and irrelevant, and walk away, kissing and laughing. At the end of the poem, the speaker also moves off, 'in an agony', Aldington writes, 'of helpless grief and pity'.[11]

Text and subtext here shift back and forth like those optical illusions of rabbits and vases and women's faces. The tripartite narrative of George Winterbourne's life is at once the main text of the novel, the 'story', and the subtext for the final poem, for a particular understanding of General Foch's statement (not at all ironic when it was first published the day after the Armistice), for the title of the book, for the prologue in which the narrator calls George's death 'a symbol', something for which we have to atone. The book's three central sections can be seen, in fact, as an effort at that atonement, and the narrator's account of George's life and death, Aldington's act of writing his war novel, serve, in Aldington's words, as 'a desperate effort to wipe off the blood-guiltiness', to expiate a culpability in which narrator, author and reader, too, are involved.[12]

Alternatively, Part III, the most powerful section of the work, the one that seems to come most directly from Aldington's own experiences first as a corporal and then as a commissioned officer in the front line, can be seen as the significant text, the section upon which everything else in the book is predicated. One feels, for instance, that it is Part III that justifies all the other bits, that it is Part III that inspired the author, that made him want to write the book, and that it is Part III that readers remember long-est and admire most. If Part III is the text, then everything else becomes subtext. Or perhaps the subtext is merely the symphonic form to which Aldington calls attention through his use of Italian musical terms. Or perhaps the subtext is the five-part Greek drama in twenty-five chapters: the Prologue, three − as it were − 'acts', and the Epilogue. Or perhaps the subtext, related to the text in more complicated ways than most scholars have as yet explored, is biography. George's life − if not his death − is in outline more or less Aldington's, although George's selfish wife is emphatically not H. D.; nor is George's mistress Arabella Yorke. A number of characters in the novel are satirised *à clef*: the painter Frank Upjohn is to a degree Ezra Pound; Herr Shobbe is in some measure Ford Madox Ford and Mr Jeames is Harold Monro; in turn, Mr. Bobbe is D. H. Lawrence and Waldo Tubbe is T. S. Eliot. George's death, however, belongs at least in date to Wilfred Owen, and the narrator comes closer to being Aldington in values and attitudes than the hapless George ever does. As pastiche, as burlesque, *Death of a Hero* draws on specific events and people taken from life, but the novel is neither autobiography nor memoir nor history. Perhaps the entire text is a sort of letter, the narrator's biography of George as an epistle to the reader; or perhaps the book is, as Aldington says, a threnody, a death dirge, a lamentation.

From its very first page, H. D.'s own war novel, *Bid Me to Live* (1960), also addresses the issue of form, the problem of genre, and the difficulties of identity and textual expression are, in fact, the novel's central subject.[13] The conflict on which H. D. focuses is at once the Great War and the war between the sexes, while the problem of female utterance stems both from the war which defines her through marginalisation and loss and from the oppres-sion inherent in the relations between men and women during the war period.

H. D. takes her title from the first line of Robert Herrick's 'To Anthea', which she includes as a kind of prologue or preface − or indeed a subtext − for her novel. Herrick's speaker (whose gender is not specifically defined in the poem, although most readers might assume him to be male) declares his love for Anthea, telling her that he will do whatever she bids, in fact, as he implores her to define his behaviour, he depends on her will for his very existence. He says, 'Bid me to live, and I will live', then goes on to vary his plea:

'Or bid me love'; 'Bid me to weep'; 'Bid me despair'; and finally, 'bid me die'. The poem concludes:

> Thou art my life, my love, my heart,
> The very eyes of me:
> And hast command of every part,
> To live and die for thee.

Thus H. D.'s novel, whose title may initially strike us as affirmative in contrast to Aldington's use of 'Death' in his, contains similar ironic overtones, ironies carried not only by the implication of the title itself (what if the speaker is not bid to live?) and by Herrick's poem (what if the speaker is bid to die?) but by the book's first section, at the end of which H. D., having asserted the difficulties of self-definition in a time of tremendous change, declares about her characters that 'What was left of them was the war-generation, not the lost generation, but lost actually in fact, doomed by the stars in their courses, an actuality, holocaust to Mars, not blighted, not anaemic, but wounded, but dying, but dead.'[14]

Bid Me to Live is more autobiographical than Aldington's novel, more transparently a sustained roman-à-clef. The central character and narrator is Julia Ashton, whose very name echoes the author's, Hilda Aldington, who is married to Rafe (Richard Aldington). Rafe has an affair with Bella (Arabella Yorke), while Julia and Fredrico or Rico (a character based on D. H. Lawrence, often called 'Lorenzo' by his friends) are drawn to each other. Rico's German wife, Elsa, has been involved with Vane (Cecil Gray), to whose Cornwall cottage Julia goes when Rafe leaves as an officer for the front. The novel falls into two parts: in the first, set primarily in Julia's London flat in Queen's Square, Julia looks back on her life between 1914 and 1918 and specifically on her struggle to write and on her marriage to Rafe and relationship with Rico. In the second part, set in Cornwall, Julia continues to reflect on her life in an account which finally becomes a kind of letter to Rico. Characters tend to blur into one another: Rafe is both himself and not himself, both the young poet-husband Julia first loved and the philandering and coarse soldier-in-uniform whom she must reject, while Rico, whose name parallels Rafe's, is in some ways a substitute for him, the recipient of the novel-as-letter, letter-as-novel, that Julia writes.

Early in the novel, it is Rafe to whom Julia writes. She remembers what Rafe has told her: that he is kept alive at the front by the

knowledge that she is alive in London, in fact by the letters she
sends to him.[15] As soon as he leaves for his second tour of duty
in France, she begins a letter to him, mentions that she has their
earlier correspondence with her, all of his early letters from the
trenches and all of her letters to him, which he has brought back
from France and given to her for safekeeping. Julia writes to him,
'I won't read them. I know that what I am writing is written in all
those ... I've got on your dressing gown.'[16] Here Julia/H. D. fuses
'what I am writing' – that is, Julia's letter to Rafe – with the novel
itself, which 'is written' already in the letters they have written
to one another; the letters are the novel; the novel is the letters.
Thus the novel, which becomes a letter to Rico, begins as a letter
to Rafe. The novel, which H. D. began in Cornwall in the summer
of 1918 – or even earlier, if we want to think of it as having its
source, its first draft, as it were, in the letters H. D. began to write
Aldington in 1916 – was finally reworked in Switzerland in the
1950s and sent to Aldington for his response at a time when he
and H. D. were once again exchanging frequent letters. As a recast-
ing of material on which Aldington also draws in *Death of a Hero*,
Bid Me to Live is not a corrective to Aldington's 'version' but H. D.'s
own response to personal pain and loss and to the dislocation of
war, to the war which was at once the fighting on the battlefields
and the conflict between femaleness and maleness. In Julia's terms,
as she announces to Rafe, 'I've got on your dressing gown.' As Julia
wears Rafe's bathrobe, H. D. blurs the distinction between herself
and Aldington, between self and other, between female and male.
Julia continues her letter to Rafe: 'Writing letters to you and writing
poetry go along in the same sort of groove'. Eliding the distinction
between her letters and her verse, she quotes Wordsworth, begins to
compose a stream-of-consciousness passage about Italy that in turn
slips into a pastiche of Shakespeare. At the end Julia paraphrases
a fragment of a Bible verse, then signs her letter 'Love, Anthea',[17]
figuring herself as the subject/object of Herrick's poem, as Anthea
to Herrick's pleading speaker, Rafe. Richard Aldington may well
have called H. D. 'Anthea': he addresses his early letters to her as
'Dearest Dooley' and 'Dearest girl' but most often as 'Astraea', the
name which H. D. echoes here.

　　Ivan (based on the Aldingtons' friend John Cournos) writes letters
to Julia from which she quotes; he calls her 'Grey-eyed goddess';
Vane calls Julia, as Gray did H. D. in his correspondence, 'Personne'

– that is, both 'person' (suggesting somebody or anybody) and 'nobody'. As others try to define her, to write and unwrite and rewrite her work and her self, Julia struggles with disturbing and affirming superimpositions (she reflects on Keats's 'Beauty is truth, truth beauty', for example), but her difficulty culminates in the problem Rico poses for her when he insists that men and women are and must be different and separate. Julia eventually counters his limited views with her assertion that there is maleness in femaleness, femaleness in maleness, that she can write about whatever she wants.[18]

For Aldington, writing from the front in 1918 as well as in *Death of a Hero* a decade later, the union that H. D. can insist on in 1960 seems impossible: Winterbourne is a casualty of war from the beginning of the novel; Aldington's response to both his personal and military conflicts is finally self-negation.

III

By the summer of 1918, Aldington could only cope with the war as a liminal space. On 17 May, he recalled for H. D. a poem written a year earlier in almost exactly the same place as he now found himself, with its 'shell-smashed crumbling traverses', heat, and choking, 'evil smells'. 'But', he wrote in 'Reverie', 'these things pass over me, beyond and away from me,/ The voices of the men fade into silence' as the speaker is soothed 'By love, by an unfaltering love'. The disjunction of Aldington's experiences – love and peace and poetry with military experience and the reality of violence; home with the front; his identity as gentle poet-lover with his role as masculine soldier – causes him to imagine an alternative time and place. In 1917 he wishes disconcertingly 'that we were dead, we two,/ Dead centuries upon centuries,/ Forgotten … '. Indeed, he goes so far as to imagine himself dead 'To-morrow' with the guns 'beating madly upon the still air', 'One in a vast field of dead men,/ Unburied, or buried hastily, callously', while in contrast, in an alternative space, 'we two are together, she bending over by the pale flower/ And I beside her:/ We two together in a land of quiet/ Inviolable behind the walls of death.'[19]

When the unimaginable happened and the love between Aldington and H. D. faltered, Aldington – very much still alive in 1918 – could only perceive himself as not himself, as already dead, as sexless and other. One of the pressing practical issues of H. D.'s pregnancy was its social interpretation: what fiction could she and Aldington fabricate to allow people to perceive the child as his? Could he pretend to have been where he was not at a time when he was elsewhere? On 3 August, he wrote to H. D., 'Can you give a guess at the date of conception? ... Let me have as soon as possible the date on which you want me to have been in England.' Hoping that she may not in fact be pregnant, he wrote on 5 August: 'I don't want to lose my Astraea ... I love you & I want you to be happy & have lovers & girl lovers if you want, but I don't want to lose you as I should if this happened.' But H. D. was pregnant, and by 31 August, feeling 'passion' for Arabella as well as 'tenacious devotion' to H. D., Aldington blamed himself: 'I have made a mess of things', he declared, 'the only straight thing is to quit and see neither of you.' He reiterated his position on 1 September: 'I hope you will be happy and I hope Arabella will, and I hope you will both forgive me for having loved too much and now not at all.' Before H. D.'s confession of her pregnancy, Aldington was able to imagine an alternative post-war, meta-war time and space. He wrote to her on 23 July that 'What troubles me nowadays is the semi-drying up of my impulses to work, though I think I would get them again with idleness and tranquillity. But I am very tedious & bored as a child sometimes.' Aldington then adds in an insistent postscript: 'The faun sends kisses to his dear Astraea, and never, never, NEVER forgets her, nor her girl laughter, nor all the sweet parts of her. When the faun is free again she will love him as she used to.' On the following day, 24 July, he asserted that despite their emotional difficulties and the physical war currently separating them, 'Someday you are coming back to be my dear Astraea again and all these mad adventures we have been on will make us the richer for each other, make our love the sweeter & keener.'

By 1 September, however, Aldington was shattered. He informed H. D.: 'My present job is to get on with the war, which I shall do to the best of my ability. Afterwards I shall do what I think best – almost certainly it will not be literature, nor women.' He added, 'Look on me as a sort of eternally absent friend ... I am deeply sorry for you, but I can do no more.' His former confidence, fuelled by his commitment to both love and poetry, to Eros and the desire to write, was now displaced by irony and impotence, by feelings of vacuity and loss. On 27 September, he reiterated his position, writing bluntly to H. D., 'women are not so essential to life as they imagine; and in any case – well, there's no need to be offensive, is there?' He concluded, 'Things can't ever be the same again, so why carry on with something patched-up, a makeshift? ... There is nothing I particularly want.' Back from the line for a period of rest on 13 October, Aldington described the landscape that reflected his own state:

> Strangely enough, the country is not nearly so destroyed as the kind I have known before. The villages are wrecked, it is true; no life, except soldier's, exists over vast tracts, dotted with shell-holes & crosses, pitted with the holes of myriads of field mines, where only the whirr of partridges & the noise of starlings break the silence. Desolation, yet not unpleasant.

The end of the war brought, of course, new hope to a degree and a very changed situation for Aldington. Shortly after her daughter's birth in March of 1919, H. D. took the decision to distance herself from her husband and to make a life with Bryher (Winifred Ellerman), whom she had met in July of 1918. Demobilised in February of 1919, Aldington returned to London and eventually to Arabella, with whom he lived for the following decade in a small cottage in Berkshire. There he turned to reviewing and translating, to pastoral and to his most experimentally modernist work, the long poem 'A Fool i'the Forest' (1925), a precursor to *Death of a Hero*, the book that would signal the end of his career as a poet and the beginning of ten years of novel-writing.

Informed by Freudian notions of identity and by Aldington's own experiences during the war, 'A Fool i'the Forest', a dramatic verse narrative subtitled 'A Phantasmagoria', features three characters: 'I', Mezzetin, and the Conjuror, who are, the author explains in a note, 'one person split into three'. Mezzetin, a figure from the *commedia dell'arte*, embodies 'the imaginative faculties – art, youth, satire, irresponsible gaiety, liberty'. He recalls Aldington-as-faun, Aldington before 1916. The Conjurer is, in contrast, a malicious figure who embodies 'the intellectual faculties – age, science, righteous cant, solemnity, authority'- the very forces that Aldington saw as responsible for and expressed by the war. 'I', shown at 'a moment of crisis', is 'by temperament more fitted for an art than for a scientific civilisation', while the phantasmagoria of the poem is 'the mirror

of his mind's turmoil as he struggles to attain a harmony between
himself and the exterior world'.

'I' becomes transparently Aldington-the-survivor, the post-war
poet who is only a shattered remnant of his former integral self.
When Mezzetin is killed during the war, the speaker intuits what
has happened and realises that 'something vital left me forever', for
Mezzetin 'Was as much to me as life itself;/ I wished a bomb would
fall into my shell-hole,/ For I felt too numb to stand up to the
bullets.' Unlike George Winterbourne, who stands up to oncoming
bullets in an act of suicide, Aldington's speaker here is immobilised
by his loss. The Conjurer, whom the speaker holds responsible for
Mezzetin's death, announces, 'Now he's gone, we'll make a man of
you.' The pre-war self is thus cast as feminine; the Conjurer is in
turn masculinity at its most brazen and unattractive; 'I', as a result
of war, is ironically at the mercy of these male forces which make
his survival possible while rendering him at once conventional and
artistically barren. Impotent, the speaker cannot write an elegy for
Mezzetin ('now he's dead I have no interest in writing'); nor can he
immediately destroy the Conjurer, for, like Aldington, who refused to
carry bullets in his gun, the speaker confesses that he 'never could
face the horror/ Of jabbing a bayonet in a man's belly;/ And, as
usual, my rifle was unloaded.'[20]

IV

Richard Aldington's reputation as an embittered old man – fostered
by those, including Winston Churchill and Robert Graves, outraged
by his *T. E. Lawrence: A Biographical Inquiry* (1955) – appears grossly
undeserved, as does his subsequent reputation as a testosterone-
driven womaniser, a by-product of recent interest in H. D.[21] Often
now omitted from anthologies and studies of war poets, Aldington
is out of favour among those First World War scholars who prefer
to address the currently popular interest in homosexual or women
war writers, the ironies of whose lives may seem in these days
of feminist and queer theory more theoretically interesting. But
Aldington's struggle – as evidenced in his correspondence, his verse
and his fiction – to discover what part he could possibly play, what
'self' he could salvage from the war's destruction, is eloquent testimony to the difficulties of the textual representation of both war
and gender. That Aldington's name is at the head of the alphabetical

list of only sixteen male war poets memorialised in Westminster Abbey is perhaps one of the sharpest ironies of his career, and one whose acerbity would not have been lost on him. He created, after all, the alter ego who 'trembled' with Mezzetin 'in blank darkness' as well as the nameless narrator of Winterbourne's suicide. He had been the young soldier who admitted to H. D. on 9 January 1919, 'I have such extraordinary head-aches these days that I can scarcely write'; who confided on Christmas eve 1918, 'I do hope I can get free soon'; who shared with H. D. on 6 January 1919 his abiding conviction that 'we poets are anachronisms; the world has no place for us ... yet it is impossible for us, by reason of our temperaments, to succeed in any other capacity.'

Notes

1 All biographical information in this chapter, unless otherwise noted, is drawn from a new, revised and expanded edition of correspondence, *Richard Aldington and H. D.: Their Lives in Letters*, ed. Caroline Zilboorg (Manchester: Manchester University Press, 2003). This single paperback volume includes all of the letters and much of my original commentary previously published in *Richard Aldington and H. D.: The Early Years in Letters* (Bloomington: Indiana University Press, 1992) and in *Richard Aldington and H. D.: The Later Years in Letters* (Manchester: Manchester University Press, 1995). All quotations from Aldington's letters are taken from this new volume.

2 H. D.'s Hellenism has received extensive attention from several scholars. See, for example, Eileen Gregory's *H. D. and Hellenism: Classic Lines* (Cambridge: Cambridge University Press, 1998) and Diana Collecott, *H. D. and Sapphic Modernism* (Cambridge: Cambridge University Press, 1999). While both of these books discuss Aldington's Hellenism in passing and in relation to H. D.'s own attitudes, his response to the past – and particularly his own modernism in the context of his attitudes towards ancient Greece and history more generally – has as yet to receive the critical attention it deserves. This situation is especially curious given recent interest in modernism's relation to history, of which Gregory's and Collecott's books are merely two examples. See as well Cassandra Laity, *H. D. and the Victorian Fin de Siècle* (Cambridge: Cambridge University Press, 1997). Pound, for instance, has also been examined in the context of his attitudes towards the past, as in Marianne Korn (ed.), *Ezra Pound and History* (New York: National Poetry Foundation, 1985).

3 Richard Aldington, *The Poems of Anyte* (London: The Egoist Press, 1915), p. 7. I discuss further the issues raised in this paragraph in 'Joint Venture: Richard Aldington, H. D. and the Poets' Translation Series', *Philological Quarterly*, 70:1 (Winter 1991), 67–98.

4 All page references here are to H. D., *Collected Poems: 1912–1944*, ed. Louis Martz (New York: New Directions, 1983). 'Heliodora' and 'Nossis', initially published in *Hymen* in 1924, were clearly written earlier; see my essay '"Soul of My Soul", A Contextual Reading of H. D.'s "Heliodora"', *Sagetrieb*, 10:3 (Winter 1991), 123–38.

5 Richard Aldington, 'The Faun Captive', *The Complete Poems* (London: Allan Wingate, 1948), pp. 69–70.

6 This is a matter discussed at greater length by Michael Copp in his introduction to *An Imagist at War: The Complete War Poems of Richard Aldington* (Madison, NJ: Fairleigh Dickinson University Press, 2002).

7 Richard Aldington, 'Before Parting', in *The Complete Poems*, p. 137.

8 Quoted in *Richard Aldington and H. D.: Their Lives in Letters*, p. xx.

9 Richard Aldington, *Death of a Hero* (London: The Hogarth Press, 1984), pp. 7–8.

10 *Death of a Hero*, p. 372.

11 *Death of a Hero*, pp. 375–6.

12 *Death of a Hero*, p. 36.

13 These are issues I discuss in greater detail in '"The Center of the Cyclone": Gender and Genre in H. D.'s War Novel', in *Dressing Up for War: Transformations of Gender and Genre in the Discourse and Literature of War*, ed. Andrew Monnickendam and Aránzazu Usandizaga (Amsterdam: Rodopi Press, 2002), pp. 27–37.

14 H. D., *Bid Me to Live* (London: Virago, 1984), p. 8.

15 *Bid Me to Live*, p. 42.

16 *Bid Me to Live*, pp. 42–3.

17 *Bid Me to Live*, p. 44.

18 *Bid Me to Live*, p. 62. H. D. quotes Rico as saying, 'Stick to the woman-consciousness', while Julia realises 'This man-, this woman- theory of Rico's was false.' The tension between male patriarchal views of female capacity and H. D.'s assertion that creativity is both female and male, beyond gender and a combination of gendered perspectives, is central to this novel.

19 Richard Aldington, 'Reverie', in *The Complete Poems*, pp. 98–101.

20 Richard Aldington, 'A Fool i'the Forest', in *The Complete Poems*, pp. 189–239.

21 See, for instance, Fred Crawford's excellent study, *Richard Aldington and Lawrence of Arabia* (Carbondale: Southern Illinois University Press, 1998). See also Barbara Guest, *Herself Defined: The Poet H. D. and Her Circle* (New York: Doubleday, 1984).

2

Shell-shocked in Somerville:
Vera Brittain's post-traumatic stress disorder

Andrea Peterson

In her Foreword to *Testament of Youth*, Vera Brittain describes her auto-biographical project as an attempt 'to tell [her] own fairly typical story as truthfully as [she] could against the larger background'; 'to put the life of an ordinary individual into its niche in contemporary history'; and to 'illustrate the influence of world-wide events and movements upon the personal destinies of men and women'.[1] I will argue that Brittain's claim to truthfulness is compromised by the fact that her autobiography portrays her as having suffered a 'nervous breakdown' on her return to Oxford in 1919, when she appears, instead, to have succumbed to 'shell shock', or post-traumatic stress disorder, after being bombed during the Ludendorff offensive in 1918. As a Voluntary Aid Detachment nurse, Brittain was well aware of the symptoms of shell shock; consequently, I will argue that her failure to identify her own breakdown as such is indicative of her belief that shell shock was an exclusively masculine condition that served to hinder the feminist cause.

In *Testament of Youth*, Brittain confesses that she experienced 'the horrible delusion ... that [her] face was changing,' and she 'was ashamed, to the point of agony, of the sinister transformation'. In short, 'throughout 1920', Brittain believed herself to be 'developing a beard' and 'turning into a witch'.[2] Although various critics make reference to this striking revelation, they tend to understate the seriousness of Brittain's illness. Whilst Brittain's beard is the most striking manifestation of her post-war trauma, to focus on this one symptom alone serves to obfuscate her mental state further. A number of causal factors must be considered, along with Brittain's other symptoms.

Brittain was acutely aware that '[t]he myth of female inferiority' was 'rooted in the contention that men die for their country but women do not'.[3] It remains a common misconception that during the First World War women were not asked to die in the service of their country; nevertheless, many women were killed whilst undertaking voluntary war work. Indeed, Brittain had already recorded the fact that

> Many women, young and older, went down in hospital ships; others died on duty in air raids against which they had no defence system of underground tunnels and concrete shelters. The nurses who lost their lives in the bombing of Étaples were buried beneath crosses marked 'Killed in action'; it was perhaps the first time in history that such an inscription had appeared on a woman's grave.[4]

Nevertheless, the bravery of female nurses and drivers close to the front line received very little commemoration. This situation, in which women's suffering went unnoticed, continued after the war. Although both soldiers and nurses experienced a sense of culture shock on their return to civilian life, Brittain astutely observed that women like herself were '[i]solated, as none of the men were isolated, from contemporaries who had shared the common experiences of wartime'.[5]

Women were not welcomed back when they returned from their war service, but were received with hostility. In her first novel, *The Dark Tide*, Brittain commented that the period immediately after the war was 'a very difficult time' because many students were experiencing psychological problems: 'For two years ... Oxford was full of people who were either suffering from reaction, which made them despise work, or from the aftermath of sorrow, which made them despise play.'[6] Indeed, as those 'mature students who had served in the War were coming back to college, old in experience' and 'impatient with scholastic seclusion', Oxford had to endure a 'stormy time of readjustment'.[7]

Back at Somerville and already in mourning, Brittain lost another of her friends, Nina Ruffer, in the summer of 1919. In *Testament of Youth* Brittain explains that she and Ruffer were drawn together by their wartime experiences as her father 'had been drowned in the Mediterranean on the torpedoed *Arcadian* in the spring of 1917, when

[Brittain] was in Malta'. It would seem significant that it was only after Ruffer's death that Brittain 'looked one evening into [her] bedroom glass and thought, with a sense of incommunicable horror, that [she] detected in [her] face the signs of some sinister and peculiar change. A dark shadow seemed to lie across [her] chin' and she feared she was 'beginning to grow a beard, like a witch'.[8]

Along with these hallucinations, Brittain also had to endure nightmares. She writes that 'persistent dreams recurred of Roland [Leighton, her fiancé] and Edward [Brittain, her brother]'.[9] With hindsight, she attributes her 'hallucinations and dreams and insomnia' to 'over-fatigue and excessive strain'; however, she concedes that she waged an 'exhausting battle against *nervous breakdown* ... for eighteen months' and bemoans that 'no one, least of all myself, realised how near I had drifted to the borderland of *craziness*'.[10] As Brittain was experiencing not only hallucinations, but nightmares and insomnia too, I would argue that her symptoms were, in fact, indicative of post-traumatic stress disorder, or shell shock, caused by her experiences as a VAD nurse.

Elaine Showalter suggests that shell shock arose partly from the fact that '[t]he heightened code of masculinity that dominated in wartime was intolerable to surprisingly large numbers of men'.[11] If many men were unable to cope with 'the heightened code of masculinity' within the armed forces, it would seem likely that many women may have struggled to cope with the correspondingly heightened code of femininity applied to them as 'ministering angels' within the nursing profession. Indeed, to push either gender role to its extreme would appear to invite psychological problems; however, the term 'madness' has tended to be ascribed disproportionately because of societal conditioning and female oppression.

The First World War demanded that many men and women adopt distorted gender roles. Men who joined the armed forces expected to adopt an extreme form of masculinity; in fact, the conditions of trench warfare frequently forced them into a state of passivity akin to femininity. Similarly, the role of the male non-combatant (including injured, immobilised combatants) was viewed as passive or feminine. Contemporary propaganda suggests that women who volunteered for active service as nurses were held up as icons of extreme femininity because of their caring role, whilst the equally feminine maternal role was projected onto those women who chose not to undertake any war work. Many men and women must have found it difficult both

to adopt their wartime gender roles and to readjust to their peacetime
gender roles. Indeed, Showalter goes on to observe that for women
as well as men, 'the war continued to be fought in the psyche, and
the period of readjustment precipitated psychological problems'.[12]
Brittain's symptoms seem remarkably similar to the neurasthenic
symptoms commonly exhibited by officers. Indeed, Brittain's male
counterpart was the officer who, because of his upbringing, was accustomed to 'a more "complex and varied" mental life' and, because
of his schooling, had been 'taught ... "successfully to repress, not
only expressions of fear, but also the emotion itself"'.[13] His wartime
role, like Brittain's, involved taking '[r]esponsibility for others and
... keeping up appearances under continual strain or shock' and,
so, would have 'produce[d] "a state of persistent anxiety"'.[9] Had
Brittain been a man, her symptoms would surely have been attrib-
uted to some form of shell shock or war neurosis. However, active
participation in the First World War was still widely perceived as a
male preserve and so too were war neuroses.

It would seem that any form of madness should be considered
in terms of gender. In Testament of Youth, Brittain appears to view shell
shock as a particularly masculine form of madness as she links its
after-effects with the widespread misogyny that generated the hostility experienced by the women at Oxford. According to Brittain, this
'post-war reaction, in which war neurosis had been transformed into
fear ... of incalculable results following from unforeseen causes; fear
of the loss of power by those in possession of it; fear, therefore, of
women' was 'typical' and contributed to 'the disappointing aftermath
of [the] suffragist movement'.[15] Having subscribed to the view that
shell shock was a masculine form of madness that had somehow set
back feminism, Brittain not surprisingly was reluctant to consider
her own psychological problems as a form of shell shock.

Although many cases of neuroses had already been observed
during earlier wars and battles, the First World War was unusual
because 'a remarkably large number of soldiers succumbed to traumatic neuroses ... Of these a greater proportion were from among
the officer ranks. This posed a problem for degeneracy theory.'[16] It
is interesting that even though theories of hereditary degeneration
were quickly undermined, Brittain does not entirely rule them out
of her autobiography. She explains that as a child she was disturbed
by 'irrational fears' and that for this 'perverse unreasonableness' she
was 'scolded for thus "giving way"'.[17] She goes on to describe her

feelings as 'humiliating cowardice' and notes that '[s]ince I thus grew up without having my fears rationalised by explanation, I carried them with me, thrust inward but very little transformed, into adulthood, and was later to have only too good reason to regret that I never learnt to conquer them while still a child'.[18] Indeed, when she returns from active service abroad in 1918, at the insistence of her parents, Brittain is concerned that 'no one in France would believe a domestic difficulty to be so insoluble' as to justify her breaking her contract. She worries that she will 'merely be thought to have "wind-up"' and describes herself as 'a cowardly deserter'.[19] That her 'cowardice' or tendency for 'giving way' to 'windiness' might be hereditary is further suggested when she compares her own childhood with that of her mother. Brittain is thankful that by the time she was born, '[p]arents and nurses had … outgrown the stage of putting children into dark cupboards as a "cure" for … "tiresomeness"', but she goes on to remark that this 'atrocity [was] once perpetuated on [her] mother' and it 'adversely affected her psychology for ever afterwards'.[20] Moreover, although Brittain does not choose to foreground the fact in Testament of Youth, her father had suffered many '[y]ears of acute depression' and had made several 'vague suicide threats' before attempting to gas himself in 1934 and to drown himself in 1935.[21]

It was contemporaneously believed that certain people were predisposed to shell shock. In his 1919 study, The Problem of Nervous Breakdown, Edwin Ash notes that '[n]ervous disorders due to war strain' did 'not differ essentially from those occurring in the breakdowns of ordinary civilian life'.[22] Moreover, there were 'no new nor special nervous disturbance for which such a novel name [was] required'.[23] Correspondingly, Ash argues,

> breakdown on the field of battle … is enormously favoured by certain predisposing conditions … [O]ne is tempted to believe that a complete record of the past life of each man who suffers from a war neurosis would certainly reveal the occurrence of one or other of these [predisposing conditions]. Certain it is that there has been individual or family tendency to nervous instability in a great many instances.[24]

Indeed, Ash explains that 'careful inquiry into the life history of sufferers from nervous disorders very often reveals the fact that from earliest years there have been manifestations of instability'.[25] He states:

nervous children are very sensitive, and ... react abnormally to
conditions that do not bother a normal child. Thus, the morbidly
sensitive youngster dwells unduly on snubs and punishments ... In
this way false ideas of injustice and harsh treatment render the little
victim pitiably miserable ... [S]ensitive children may nurse fears in
their waking hours, leading lives full of terror, never confiding in
their parents or nurses; whilst all the time resultant nerve tension
impoverishes general health ... and hinders their proper physical and
mental development.[26]

In *Testament of Youth*, Brittain divulges that '[a]t the age of thirteen'
she was 'small for [her] years and still very much a child'. That she
seems to have dwelt 'unduly on snubs and punishments' is suggested
by her account of the severe reprimand she received for 'publicly
conversing' with her brother's school friends as a girl. She comments
that this 'small incident ... aroused ... a rebellious resentment that
I have never forgotten'. In addition, she remembers her shame at
being unable 'to restrain [her] tears' when 'badly bullied by two
unpleasant little girls' at school. Importantly, however, Brittain also
lists 'the strange medley of irrational fears which were always waiting to torment' her as a child: 'fears of thunder, of sunsets, of the
full moon, of the dark, of standing under railway arches or cross-
ing bridges over noisy streams, of the end of the world and of the
devil waiting to catch me round the corner'.[27]

Later passages in *Testament of Youth* strongly suggest that Brittain
felt she was less able to cope with the nervous strain of the war
because of her childhood experiences. As a child, Brittain learnt to
carry her fears with her, 'thrust inward but very little transformed'.
During the war, when she realised her brother was 'involved in the
"show" on the [Asiago] Plateau', she became afraid and internalised
her fear: 'there was nothing to do ... but practise that concealment
of fear ... thrusting it inward until one's subconscious became a
regular prison-house of apprehensions and inhibitions which were
later to take their revenge'. Furthermore, she explains: 'A number of
neurotic ancestors, combined with the persistent, unresolved fears
of childhood, had deprived me of the comfortable gift of natural
courage; throughout the War I was warding off panic'.[28] In short,
Brittain, like Ash, seems to give credence to aspects of hereditability
within a person's psychological make-up. Although she calls her later
illness 'nervous breakdown' rather than shell shock, the symptoms
of these two psychological disorders were so similar that, as I have

shown, contemporary psychologists did not deem the inauguration of a new term to be necessary.

It was contemporaneously acknowledged that there were a significant number of cases of civilian war neurosis. The connection between the combatant and the non-combatant would seem to lie in the fact that industrialised warfare demanded they both remain 'passive' in the face of 'mechanized slaughter'.[29] Furthermore, civilians who found themselves under fire frequently exhibited symptoms like those of shell shock. To refer further to Ash:

> All wars necessarily throw an added stress on the nerves of the people at large; thoughts of dear ones at the front, anxieties about general developments, financial worries and the inevitably distressing effects of war-time conditions always react on those left at home. But when the conditions of warfare are such that the army is the nation and the battle-front is from time to time carried to the heart of big cities and to the very threshold of the citizens, the stress becomes very great for many individuals and unbearable for some of nervous temperament … [W]here breakdowns occurred primarily as the result of naval or aerial bombardment, the resulting conditions in many instances resembled those of the shell-shock of the battlefield. After all, the conditions of bombardment with the shock of explosions, the ear-splitting crashes, the emotional strain, and only too often the terrible sights are the same, and must react on human beings in the same way, whether they occur in an actual battle or, say, during an air-raid, and so … after bombardments civilians suffered from such things as loss of voice, paralysis, persistently rapid heart-beat, sleeplessness, terrifying dreams, tremblings, mental depression, and digestive disturbances.[30]

Indeed, in her study *Women's Identities at War*, Susan R. Grayzel records the case of Elizabeth Huntley, who claimed that 'air raid shock' led her to decapitate her daughter.[31] Grayzel concludes, much like Ash, that this case evidences 'the blurring of the line indicating who exactly was under fire'.[32]

Brittain had first seen 'shocked' soldiers on a visit to 'Somerville Hospital' on 15 June 1915. In her diary she wrote: '[Somerville] is really splendid – much better as a Hospital than a College … The [soldiers] suffering from shock go into the little rooms, where there are only two people & sometimes only one … Oh! They are all so, so pathetic! Seeing them filled me with longing to begin nursing right away.'[33] Consequently, Brittain was aware of the effects of war strain on combatants even before she started to nurse. However, she admits that she failed to consider the effects of war strain on non-combatants until much later. In *Testament of Youth* she writes:

> It seemed to me then ... quite inexplicable that the older generation, which had merely looked on at the War, should break under the strain so much more quickly than those of us who had faced death and horror at first hand for months on end. To-day ... I realise how completely I under-estimated the effect upon the civilian population of year upon year of diminishing hope, diminishing food, diminishing light, diminishing heat, of waiting and waiting for news which was nearly always bad when it came. Those older men and women who ... escaped the dreariness of passive submission to wartime circumstances, the colonels ... [and] the Matrons ... had a far better chance of surviving with nerves unimpaired than those who played exclusively the apprehensive rôle of parents.[34]

Although this statement acknowledges the passivity of civilian life, it fails to mention the physical danger of bombardment faced by soldiers, nurses and civilians alike. This omission is striking, as by the time she wrote *Testament of Youth* Brittain had learnt that Winifred Holtby had been bombed in Scarborough as a girl, had been made aware that the Leightons moved from Lowestoft to Keymer in 1915 because of Zeppelin raids, and had herself been bombed on many occasions.

As a nurse, Brittain had to contend with exhaustion, emotional repression, and the 'chronic conditions of fear, tension, horror, disgust, and grief' familiar to officers.[35] She was also in the line of fire. For example, of her time at the 24 General Hospital in Étaples, Brittain writes:

> mutilated men and exhausted women ... [were] further oppressed by the series of nocturnal air-raids which for over a month supplied ... periodic intimations of the less pleasing characteristics of a front-line trench ... After days of continuous heavy duty ... our nerves were none too reliable, and I don't suppose I was the only member of staff whose teeth chattered with sheer terror ... Hope Milroy and I, thinking that we might as well be killed together, sat glassy-eyed in her small, pitch-black room ... One young sister ... lost her nerve and rushed screaming through the Mess ... I knew that I was more frightened than I had ever been in my life, yet all the time a tense, triumphant pride that I was not revealing my fear to the others held me to the semblance of self-control.[36]

Brittain had effectively experienced trench warfare. Like those civilians who were bombed, and like the many soldiers and officers in the trenches, Brittain was expected to face death calmly and passively.

In short, Brittain would seem to have experienced all of the conditions that precipitated war neuroses in both soldiers and civilians. She certainly satisfied the criteria listed by Ash as the cause of shell shock in a person who, having been 'under bombardment', has 'come through with his entire physical system apparently undamaged', yet later succumbs to a 'disorder of his nervous system which has resulted from the mental strain he has undergone'.[37] Ash explains this phenomenon, thus: 'the shock of the attack, the horror of seeing others struck, the fear about self, friends, and comrades, anticipation of more intense bombardment, near explosions and the excitement … have combined to produce a volume of mental stress that has proved too much for his [sic] nervous system'.[38]

As I have already noted, according to the emphasis she places on her various symptoms in Testament of Youth, Brittain would seem not to have suffered from neurosis until her return to Oxford in 1919. It is usually argued that these post-war neuroses were slightly different to their wartime counterparts, although they were no less common. Neurotic diseases brought about by the war did not simply disappear. In Testament of Youth, Brittain notes that although she put on civilian clothes and looked to her parents very much like the attractive young woman known throughout Somerville for her fashionable attire, she felt alienated:

> I threw off my dilapidated garments and jumped into a hot bath, while my mother hurried my holdall and my much-travelled uniform out of the newly decorated flat … because of fleas … It was delicious after the bath to slip into clean underclothes, and to appear before my family gorgeously wrapped in the scarlet silk kimono that I had made so perseveringly on night-duty … After supper I settled down luxuriously to smoke … and to talk to my father … [A]fter twenty continuous months of Army service I was almost a stranger.[39]

Brittain's Testament of Youth clearly shows her also to have been disillusioned, angry and very bitter on her return to Oxford after the war.

The men most susceptible to delayed, post-war neuroses experienced the end of the war as an anticlimax that destroyed their sense of identity: 'But where was the triumph, where was the rejoicing?

... For the soldiers ... the end [of the war] was an unravelling of order in their lives ... For four years, war had given their lives meaning and direction; now it was over, *who were they*'?[40] Hence, the way soldiers describe the end of the war often indicates a 'sense of loss', which is clearly 'an uncomfortable feeling for men who know that they *ought* to rejoice'.[41] For example, in *Goodbye to All That*, Robert Graves confesses, 'Siegfried [Sassoon]'s famous poem celebrating the Armistice began: *Everybody suddenly burst out singing,/ And I was filled with such delight/ As prisoned birds must find in freedom* ... But "everybody" did not include me'.[42] Similarly, in *Testament of Youth*, Brittain writes:

> When the sound of victorious guns burst over London at 11 a.m. on November 11th, 1918, the men and women who looked incredulously into each other's faces did not cry jubilantly: 'We've won the War!' They only said: 'The War is over.'
>
> From [Queen Alexandra's Hospital] Millbank I heard the maroons ... and, like a sleeper who is determined to go on dreaming after being told to wake up, I went on automatically washing the dressing bowls ... Deeply buried beneath my consciousness there stirred the vague memory of a letter that I had written to Roland ... when I was still at Oxford ... '... I wonder if I shall be one of those who take a happy part in the triumph − or if I shall listen to the merriment with a heart that breaks and ears that try to keep out the mirthful sounds.'
>
> And as I dried the bowls I thought: 'It's come too late for me. Somehow I knew, even at Oxford, that it would ...' ... [O]n Armistice Day not even a lonely survivor drowning in black waves of memory could be left alone with her thoughts ... I stood there, stupidly rigid ... listening ... to the wild noise of a world released from nightmare ... Already this was a different world from the one that I had known during four life-long years, a world in which people would be light-hearted and forgetful ... And in that brightly lit, alien world I should have no part.[43]

Brittain's wartime role might be described as more masculine than feminine, in that her experiences were often closer to those of the combatant than those of the civilian. On her return to Oxford, contemporary ideology informed her that she was adopting another masculine role. Consequently, Sharon Ouditt suggests, since Brittain 'had always been conscious of her own "chocolate-box prettiness"', or femininity, 'the effects of the horrors of war ate into the most obvious elements of her gendered identification' and made her see a bearded or masculine face when she looked in the mirror.[44] If, as I have argued, Brittain's hallucinations were symptomatic of a form of war neurosis or post-traumatic stress disorder, then another reading of the 'beard' becomes possible. In her study *Trauma and Survival: Post-Traumatic and Dissociative Disorders in Women*, Elizabeth A. Waites notes that 'hallucination remains a commonly observed and not well explained feature of the most debilitating mental disorders', although hallucinations 'are now … a recognized feature of post-traumatic and dissociative disorders'.[45] An individual who has experienced some great trauma is subject to 'pathological forms of identification' and these 'might contribute to the hallucination of significant figures', such as a figure of 'authority'.[46] Brittain's beard, therefore, might simply have been a metaphor for patriarchal authority – the authority responsible for the deaths of her fiancé, her brother, and her friends, and for her own post-traumatic stress disorder.

As I have already noted, Brittain's symptoms of post-traumatic stress disorder included not only hallucinations but also insomnia and nightmares. In *Testament of Youth*, she writes that 'persistent dreams recurred of Roland and Edward – the one missing and purposely hiding his identity because facially mutilated, the other suffering some odd psychological complex which made him turn against us all and keep silence'.[47] Freud suggests that most dreams are dreams of 'wish-fulfilment'.[48] He observes that many 'dreams … can be understood only as wish-fulfilments' and they 'present their content without concealment'.[49] Although Brittain has omitted to record her dreams in detail in *Testament of Youth*, from her brief descriptions they would seem, superficially, to convey her wish that her fiancé and her brother had sustained horrific injuries. However, if Leighton were 'facially mutilated' and Edward Brittain psychologically disturbed, Vera Brittain would still suffer a great deal of emotional pain, so it is difficult to interpret her dreams as simple wish-fulfilment. In such cases, Freud suggests that we 'compare and contrast the *manifest* and the *latent dream-content*' in order to facilitate interpretation.[50] Freud acknowledges that 'there are dreams the manifest content of which is of the most painful nature. But … there is always the possibility that even our painful and terrifying dreams may, upon interpretation, prove to be wish-fulfilments'.[51] In this case, the latent content of Brittain's dreams has been distorted. Although their manifest content is distressing, the latent content of Brittain's dreams would seem to be that both her fiancé and her brother were still alive.

Brittain was troubled by dreams of 'the griefs and losses of the past' 'for ten years'. In fact, her nightmares began not in 1919, but in 1915. Significantly, the last of these dreams occurred in 1925, whilst she was 'preoccupied by the psychological stress of approaching marriage [to Gordon Catlin], and too uncertain whether [she] was glad about it or not'. Brittain writes:

> as though my subconscious were determined to make one final protest against my belief that the worst phase of the War was all but over ... I dreamed that while [Gordon] was in America, regarding me as his future wife, news came that Roland had never really died, but had only been missing with a lost memory, and now, after indescribable suffering, had returned to England. In the dream his family invited me to their house to meet him; I went, and found him changed be-yond recognition by cruel experience but unchanged towards myself, anxious to marry me and knowing nothing of G[ordon] in America. So sharp was the anguish of the decision to be made that I woke up quite suddenly.[52]

If this is interpreted as a wish-fulfilment dream, it might seem to suggest that Brittain would have preferred to marry Leighton instead of Catlin. In fact, in the same chapter of *Testament of Youth*, Brittain claims that '[t]he various men ... with whom [she] had come into contact since the War ... simply provided one proof after another that the best of their sex had disappeared from a whole genera-tion'.[53] Many years later, Brittain discovered that Catlin had always felt second-best to Leighton. After reading *Testament of Youth*, Catlin wrote, but did not send, a revealing letter to Brittain: '"It will not be, that which I have desired ... your book explains it. Sometimes I half hope that you may find your Lewis" (a reference to the lover in *The Fountain*). "But I do not think you will, for ... you have found him and lost him, and so keep him more than any living man can be kept"'.[35] When Brittain eventually found this letter, she admit-ted that, although '[f]or years he went on believing that Roland's passionate young ghost stood between us,' Catlin 'had in fact laid it [to rest] by his own loving-kindness'.[36]

It is possible to interpret Brittain's final dream of Leighton as indicative of her commitment to Catlin. Freud actually states that although most dreams depict 'the fulfilment of a wish', it is pos-sible for some to depict 'the realisation of an apprehension'.[55] Accordingly, Brittain's final dream of Leighton can be interpreted as a representation of her apprehension that some impediment might prevent her marrying Catlin – the man she truly wanted to marry. Indeed, I believe it is significant that Brittain describes Leighton as 'changed beyond recognition by cruel experience'. Soon after Leighton was posted to France, Brittain had begun to realise that 'the War would ... [put] a barrier of indescribable experience between men and the women whom they loved', thereby 'thrusting horror deeper and deeper inward' and 'linking the dread of spiritual death to the apprehension of physical disaster'. By 'spiritual death,' Brittain seems to mean a substantial erosion of subjectivity, serious enough to destroy an intimate relationship. Her diary entries express her concern that 'even if [Leighton] gets through, what he has experienced out there may change his ideas and tastes utterly'. She begins 'to look carefully through his letters for every vivid word-picture, every characteristic tenderness of phrase, which suggested that not merely the body but the spirit ... was still in process of survival'. Furthermore, her brother fuels her 'dread that [Leighton] could not help but come back changed' by telling her that '[t]hey're all changed ... after two or three months out there'. I would suggest that Brittain's final dream about Leighton can be interpreted as indicative of her recognition that their relationship probably would not have survived even if he had lived. As a nurse, Brittain would have understood that had he been physically injured or mutilated – as in her earlier dreams – they could have coped. In contrast, had he been spiritually damaged – as in her final dream, where he has been 'changed beyond recognition' – the man she had fallen in love with would have ceased to exist.[56]

But what of Brittain's dreams as evidence of shell shock or post-traumatic stress disorder? Soldiers suffering from war neuroses usually experience a combination of insomnia and dreams in which they relive their battle experiences. Although Brittain discusses her 'night terrors' and 'insomnia' in *Testament of Youth*, she is adamant that she 'endured none of those nightmare recapitulations of hospital sounds and sights of which other wartime nurses complained for two or three years'.[57] Although this revelation points to the fact that nurses were susceptible to shell shock (dreams of 'hospital sounds and sights' being the nurses' equivalent of the soldiers' dreams of battle), Brittain seems intent on distancing herself from this diagnosis. She fails to recognise that her dreams of a 'mutilated' Leighton and a shocked Edward Brittain were informed by her knowledge of the physical and psychological wounds of the patients she had nursed and, hence, that her dreams were 'recapitulations of hospital sounds and sights', albeit in a condensed form.

As I have already mentioned, Brittain is happy to describe her illness as a 'nervous breakdown' (which is, arguably, a condition akin to shell shock, differentiated only by its cause). Nevertheless, she seems reluctant to admit that her war service caused the 'over-fatigue and excessive strain' which, in turn, caused her nervous breakdown. I would suggest that Brittain's later reluctance to describe her condition as a form of war neurosis could be both a further symptom of her sense of alienation in post-war Oxford and a consequence of her feminist conviction. However, the way Brittain recounts her dreams in *Testament of Youth* problematises her claim to have suffered only a post-war breakdown on her return to Oxford.

Brittain connects the onset of her hallucinations with the disturbing dreams she was having about Leighton and Edward Brittain, and her insomnia; however, she neglects to connect these symptoms of neuroses with those she had experienced in France. Even before her brother's death, whilst serving at the 24 General Hospital in Étaples, Brittain 'had already begun to have uncomfortable, contending dreams of the future'. She recounts: 'Sometimes I had returned, conscience-stricken and restless, to civilian life while the War was still on, and, as in its first year, was vainly struggling to give my mind to learning. In other dreams I was still a V.A.D., at thirty, at forty, at fifty, running round the wards at the beck and call of others, and each year growing slower, more footsore, more weary'. The 24 General was under heavy bombardment for weeks. In April 1918, the German offensive became so severe that plans were made to issue the medical staff with steel helmets and to dig trenches for them to shelter in. I would suggest that the heavy bombardment of Étaples during the Ludendorff offensive actually triggered Brittain's shell shock. She writes:

> That night, dizzy from work ... I sat up in bed listening for an air-raid and gazing stupidly at the flickering shadows cast by the candle-lantern ... Through my brain ran perpetually a short sentence which – having become, like the men, liable to sudden light-headed intervals – I could not immediately identify ... 'The strain all along,' I repeated dully, 'is very great ... very great.' What exactly did those words describe? The enemy within shelling distance – refugee Sisters crowding in with nerves all awry – bright moonlight, and aeroplanes carrying

machine-guns – ambulance trains jolting noisily into the siding, all day, all night – gassed men on stretchers, clawing the air – dying men, reeking with mud and foul green-stained bandages, shrieking and writhing in a grotesque travesty of manhood – dead men with fixed, empty eyes and shiny, yellow faces ... Yes, perhaps the strain all along had been very great.[59]

This passage not only acknowledges that Brittain suffered from 'over-fatigue and excessive strain' as a direct result of her war service, but that she recognised her symptoms to be like those of her shell-shocked patients.

Back in England, and serving at Millbank, Brittain begins to express almost suicidal tendencies. She writes, 'I couldn't see that it mattered to myself or anyone else if I caught and even died from one of my patient's dire diseases'. Her subsequent return to Oxford seems to intensify her death-wish: '"Why couldn't I have died in the War with the others?" I lamented ... "Why couldn't a torpedo have finished me, or an aerial bomb, or one of those annoying illnesses? I'm nothing but a piece of wartime wreckage, living on ingloriously in a world that doesn't want me!"'[60] It is possible to measure quite how depressed Brittain had become by the end of the war by comparing this passage with the sentiments expressed in her diary on 27 April 1915. After hearing about a neighbour's attempted suicide, Brittain had written: 'What a world of misery must have been there! Suicide is so obviously the last resort of the utterly desperate; sorrowful as I often am now, I yet cannot realise such utter depths of despair'.[61] Nevertheless, I would argue that Brittain did not suffer a post-war breakdown between 1919 and 1921, as her account in *Testament of Youth* might suggest. Rather, she began to suffer from shell shock as a result of the bombing of Étaples in 1918, although, since Leighton's death in 1915, she had been struggling to cope with the process of mourning, melancholia and depression.

Several critics observe that Brittain's first three novels are, in many ways, idealised autobiographical narratives. Interestingly, none of Brittain's early novels makes reference to the psychological problems that encumbered her between 1915 and 1925, although they all contain a character who seems to be a self-portrait. Moreover, the conflicting opinions about war service put forward in her fictional accounts suggest, to reiterate Showalter, that a battle was still being fought in Brittain's psyche. In her first published prose account of this difficult time, *The Dark Tide*, Virginia Dennison serves as a nurse during the First World War, but does not suffer from any consequent psychological damage. Although support for those who chose to remain at Oxford is expressed by Patricia O'Neill and endorsed by Daphne Lethbridge, Virginia's service is upheld as a reasonable act because of her subsequent decision to pursue a nursing rather than an academic career. In contrast, in Brittain's next account, *Not without Honour*, she not only criticises Virginia's decision to nurse, but also promotes the idea that choosing to remain at Oxford can be seen as a superior statement of pacifism. In her third novel, *Honourable Estate*, Brittain reconciles these conflicting attitudes by making Ruth Alleyndene a little older, thereby allowing her to avoid post-war Oxford altogether. However, Ruth still serves as a nurse, but is motivated by humanitarian and internationalist ideals. Revealingly, Brittain later classified Oxford's female students of this period, thus:

> First, and most fortunate, were those who had finished their university courses, and could go straight into the various responsible posts ... which were being increasingly offered to college graduates.
>
> A second and much smaller class of women included students ... who found safety intolerable while their unfulfilled male contemporaries were dying. In ones and twos these left their work at Oxford temporarily or permanently unfinished, and went off to serve at home or overseas ...
>
> In the third category came the majority, most valuable to a university deprived of its men, who remained to finish their courses.[62]

I would suggest that Ruth can be seen as fitting the first of Brittain's categories; Virginia the second; and Christine the third.

It would seem that Brittain was unable to face the fact that her hallucinations, nightmares and insomnia were indicative of shell shock or post-traumatic stress disorder. Instead, she chose to describe her symptoms as those of 'nervous breakdown'. Although these two types of psychiatric disorder share similar symptoms, shell shock has tended to be viewed as a masculine disorder, and nervous breakdown as a feminine disorder. Indeed, by the end of the nineteenth century, Darwinian psychiatrists had advanced the theory that '[m]ental breakdown ... would come when women defied their "nature," attempted to compete with men instead of serving them, or sought alternatives or even additions to their maternal functions'.[63] During the First World War, 'English psychiatry,' which was '[b]uilt on an ideology of absolute and natural difference between women and men ... found its categories undermined by the evidence of male war neurosis'.[64] The First World War 'was the first and ... last time during the twentieth century that men ... occupied a central position in the history of madness'.[65]

Showalter observes that for Darwinian psychiatrists, '[f]emale intellectual inferiority could be understood as the result of reproductive specialization, and the "womanly" traits of self-sacrifice and service ... as essential for the survival and improvement of the race'.[66] As I have shown, the First World War demanded that these extant gender roles be redefined. Consequently, when Brittain made the transition from nurse back to student, she rejected these 'womanly traits' and began, once again, to 'compete with men' on an intellectual level at Oxford. This difficult process was made all the more problematic by the widespread misogyny of the very men she had been caring for during the war – the returning soldiers. Neither a combatant back from the front, nor a non-combatant who had remained at the home-front, Brittain found herself totally alienated. Although Showalter argues that '[w]omen understood the lesson of shell shock better than their male contemporaries', Brittain seems to be an exception to this rule, perhaps because her wartime experiences were, in many ways, masculine.[67] Showalter explains that 'in the decade after the war, male veterans were struggling to repress their war experience, to banish the most painful memories from their minds. For this reason ... there were very few men's war memoirs ... published during the 1920s; they did not begin to appear in substantial numbers until the 1930s, after the Depression had 'closed the gap between civilian and ex-soldier'.[68] Similarly, Brittain struggled with the symptoms of post-traumatic stress disorder until 1925, and only began work on *Testament of Youth* in 1926.

Although Brittain later came to acknowledge that female and male civilians could suffer from shell shock as well as male combatants, she never reappraised the situation of female and male medical staff working close to the front line. Brittain was accustomed to approaching her fiction as a kind of 'writing cure' through which she addressed her personal problems. However, when she finally came to write a novel about shell shock, Brittain's central protagonist was, for the first time, not a self-portrait. *Account Rendered*

(1945) is the story of Francis Halkin, an ex-soldier who, having been bombed during the First World War, suffers from shell shock but goes undiagnosed until the Second World War. When recovered, Halkin pledges to help the victims of war neuroses: 'Anything I can do to help them will be part of my life's work from now on.'[69] At first, he considers helping civilian bomb victims at an East End 'Settlement' run by his own psychiatrist, 'Dr. Flint'.[70] Ultimately, however, he leaves his pregnant wife to work at 'an advanced psychiatric centre' dedicated to helping shocked soldiers in Tunisia.[71] In conclusion, even at the close of the Second World War, Brittain still seems to have privileged the war neuroses of male combatants over those of predominantly female civilians, even though she had begun, in principle, to acknowledge that women, too, could suffer from shell shock. However, she remained incapable of recognising that she herself had suffered from shell shock, or post-traumatic stress disorder, as a result of coming under heavy bombardment during the First World War. In her final attempt to put her 'War Service in Perspective' (1968), Brittain acknowledges just one type of war neurosis. When considering the passive role of the female civilian, she notes that 'many women developed an anxiety neurosis which lasted until the end of their lives' because of '[t]he wearing anxiety of waiting for letters'.[72] Brittain ultimately failed to acknowledge the many soldiers, medical staff and civilians who, like herself, had suffered from shell shock as a result of aerial bombardment.

Notes

1   V. Brittain, *Testament of Youth* (London: Fontana, [1933] 1979), p. 12.
2   *Testament of Youth*, pp. 496, 497.
3   V. Brittain, 'War Service in Perspective', in G. A. Panichas (ed.), *Promise of Greatness: The War of 1914–1918* (London: Cassell, 1968), p. 375.
4   V. Brittain, *Lady into Woman* (London: Andrew Dakers, 1953), p. 187.
5   *Testament of Youth*, p. 482.
6   V. Brittain, *The Dark Tide* (London: Virago, [1923] 1999), p. 175.
7   V. Brittain, *The Women at Oxford: A Fragment of History* (London: Harrap, 1960), p. 143.
8   *Testament of Youth*, pp. 478, 484.
9   *Testament of Youth*, p. 496.
10 *Testament of Youth*, p. 496, emphasis added.
11 E. Showalter, *The Female Malady: Women, Madness and English Culture, 1830–1980* (London: Virago, [1985] 1987), p. 172.
12 Showalter, p. 197.
13 Showalter, p. 175.
14 Showalter, p. 175.

15 *Testament of Youth*, p. 582.
16 D. Healy, *Images of Trauma: From Hysteria to Post-Traumatic Stress Disorder* (London: Faber & Faber, 1993), p. 92.
17 *Testament of Youth*, p. 24, emphasis added.
18 *Testament of Youth*, p. 24.
19 *Testament of Youth*, pp. 422, 424.
20 *Testament of Youth*, p. 24.
21 P. Berry and M. Bostridge, *Vera Brittain: A Life* (London: Pimlico, [1995] 1996), p. 288.
22 E. L. Ash, *The Problem of Nervous Breakdown* (London: Mills & Boon, 1919), p. 277.
23 Ash, p. 277.
24 Ash, p. 273.
25 Ash, p. 240.
26 Ash, pp. 241–4.
27 *Testament of Youth*, pp. 32, 28, 29, 28, 24.
28 *Testament of Youth*, pp. 24, 437, 260.
29 E. Leed, *No Man's Land: Combat and Identity in World War I* (Cambridge: Cambridge University Press, 1979), p. 164.
30 Ash, pp. 275–6.
31 S. R. Grayzel, *Women's Identities at War: Gender, Motherhood, and Politics in Britain and France during the First World War* (Chapel Hill and London: University of North Carolina Press, 1999), p. 47.
32 Grayzel, p. 48.
33 V. Brittain, *Chronicle of Youth: Vera Brittain's War Diary 1913–1917*, ed. A. Bishop with T. Smart (London: Gollancz, 1981), p. 208.
34 *Testament of Youth*, pp. 427–8.
35 Showalter, p. 170.
36 *Testament of Youth*, p. 417.
37 Ash, p. 272.
38 Ash, p. 272.
39 *Testament of Youth*, pp. 353–4.
40 S. Hynes, *The Soldiers' Tale: Bearing Witness to Modern War* (London: Pimlico, [1997] 1998), p. 100.
41 Hynes, p. 100.
42 R. Graves, *Goodbye to All That* (London: Penguin, [1929] 1957), p. 228.
43 *Testament of Youth*, pp. 460–2.
44 S. Ouditt, *Fighting Forces, Writing Women: Identity and Ideology in the First World War* (London: Routledge, 1994), p. 38.
45 E. A. Waites, *Trauma and Survival: Post-Traumatic and Dissociative Disorders in Women* (New York: W. W. Norton, 1993), p. 125.
46 Waites, *Trauma*, p. 124.
47 *Testament of Youth*, p. 496.
48 S. Freud, *The Interpretation of Dreams*, trans. A. A. Brill (Ware: Wordsworth, 1997), p. 34.
49 Freud, p. 38.
50 Freud, p. 46.
51 Freud, p. 46.
52 *Testament of Youth*, pp 650, 648, 650.
53 *Testament of Youth*, p. 608.
54 V. Brittain, *Testament of Experience* (London: Virago, [1957] 1979), p. 92.
55 Freud, p. 35.
56 *Testament of Youth*, pp. 650, 143, 158, 650.

57 *Testament of Youth*, pp. 536, 496.
58 *Testament of Youth*, p. 496.
59 *Testament of Youth*, pp. 400, 423 (stress added, with the exception of 'had').
60 *Testament of Youth*, pp. 458, 490.
61 Brittain, Chronicle, p. 186.
62 Brittain, Oxford, pp. 137–8.
63 Showalter, p. 123.
64 Showalter, pp. 167–8.
65 Showalter, p. 194.
66 Showalter, p. 122.
67 Showalter, p. 190.
68 Showalter, pp. 190–1.
69 V. Brittain, *Account Rendered* (London: Macmillan, 1945), p. 309.
70 Brittain, *Account Rendered*, p. 316.
71 Brittain, *Account Rendered*, p. 320.
72 Brittain, 'War Service', pp. 374, 373.

3

Gender, war and writing in Aldous Huxley's 'Farcical History of Richard Greenow'

Erik Svarny

In the past decade there has been a tendency to interrogate the criteria by which 'war writing' is defined and to extend the parameters of the term beyond an exclusive concentration on the experience of (male) military combatants to include the experience of non-combatants, whether nurses, workers or ordinary civilians, caught up in the extremity of war experience. Particularly in the twentieth century, when the concept and practice of 'total war' became a reality which affected all levels of society, it is clear that a gendered conception of 'war writing' does not merely reinforce an assumed binary divide, but also leaves both 'male' and 'female' terms effectively unexamined, since neither is tested or scrutinised in relation to alternative forms of experience. This is especially striking in relation to the literature of the First World War, where the myth and experience of trench warfare on the Western Front – as expressed most memorably by the combatant war poets – left an impression on public consciousness that both formed and affected the public conception of warfare during the following century. In this chapter I will discuss Aldous Huxley's early novella 'Farcical History of Richard Greenow'[1] as an example of non-combatant war fiction, and offer a reading and critique of this text which examine discourses of gender during the war period. My reading of Huxley's novella is also a critique of Gilbert and Gubar's reading in No Man's Land,[2] where the text, designated a 'farcical Kunstlerroman'[3] is given an unnuanced feminist reading by which it is seen as merely evincing an early twentieth- century male fear of women's writing. I will argue that the crucial element omitted from Gilbert and Gubar's reading is the First World War itself. 'Farcical History' is, *pace* Gilbert and Gubar, more accurately seen as a parodic *Bildungsroman* of Huxley's early development, and when sited in its historical, cultural and biographical context is a much subtler and more suggestive text than they make it seem. Indeed, it is something of an unrecognised (minor) masterpiece.

Huxley's status as a non-combatant in the First World War was the consequence of the second of three tragedies that affected his early life: the sudden blindness that afflicted him while at Eton in the winter of 1911. The first tragedy almost certainly underwrote the second, in that the death of his mother Julia, aged forty-five, in 1908, had removed the emotional centre of his family. At her funeral, Julian Huxley writes in *Memories*, 'Trev and I were on the verge of tears, and Aldous, then at the critical age of fourteen, stood in stony misery.' Julian comments, 'I am sure that this meaningless catastrophe was the main cause of the protective cynical skin in which he clothed himself and his novels in the twenties.'[4] It seems reasonable to assume that, subsequently, Aldous and his two elder brothers, Julian and Trevenen, none of whom was particularly close to their father, Leonard, suffered from emotional neglect. Julia's sister Mary, the formidable Mrs Humphrey Ward, at this date one of the most famous authors in the world, attempted to fill the gap, and the brothers spent many holidays at her luxuriously appointed country house, Stocks. The third tragedy, the suicide of his brother Trevenen, following an unhappy love affair with a servant girl whom he had made pregnant, occurred some few weeks after the declaration of war in August 1914. While Huxley always expressed his affection for Mary Ward, as John Sutherland points out there is some (fictional) evidence that he held Mrs Ward's possessive emotional 'vampirism' and militant moral rectitude at least partly responsible for Trevenen's death. His novel *Eyeless in Gaza* (1936), in which the figures of Mrs Foxe and her son Brian offer very close portraits of Mrs Humphrey Ward and Trevenen, even down to replicating their speech patterns, suggests this reading, which in turn could explain the hint of animus that might inspire his satiric parody of Mrs Ward in 'Farcical History'.[5] Aldous, who had recovered partial, though severely impaired, sight, had followed Trevenen to Balliol College, Oxford, in the previous year. As his fellow students enlisted, Huxley was left in an almost deserted Oxford attending lectures on Anglo-

Saxon with the women undergraduates. Huxley's biographer, Sybille
Bedford, questioned Sir George Clark, Huxley's tutor, 'who had seen
the gay, intelligent schoolboy, as it were before the fall', as to the
effect of the events of those six years on Aldous. He replied, 'He
was – impaired.'[6]

While it is not my purpose to offer retrospective psychological
speculation as to the nature of this impairment, it seems reasonable
to agree with Julian Huxley that the extreme emotional disengage-
ment that earned Huxley's fiction its reputation for 'cynicism' has
its roots in the formative effect of extreme and tragic emotion
on a sensitive nature. However, the glib critical label of 'cynicism'
– 'scepticism' is a more accurate term – fails to perceive that there
is a good deal of often painful emotion in Huxley's fiction; it
is just not integrated within its discursive economy. Henceforth,
Huxley defended himself against emotion with ratiocination and
was never able easily to integrate or align the two. While this defines the terms of a personal and intellectual dilemma with which
Huxley struggled throughout much of his early adult life, it also
underwrites the distinctive quality of his earlier fiction: the disori-
entating juxtaposition of disparate points of view of the same event
or occurrence (scientific, metaphysical, physical, emotional, etc.)
which are allowed to exist simultaneously without the synthesis of
an overriding 'truth'. In Huxley's first novel, Crome Yellow (1921), the
philosopher Scogan (a satiric portrayal of Bertrand Russell) articulates
a distinctively Huxleyan observation in its disjunctive alignment of
the scientific and the affective:

> 'At this very moment,' he went on, 'the most frightful horrors are
> taking place in every corner of the world. People are being crushed,
> slashed, disembowelled, mangled; their dead bodies rot and their eyes
> decay with the rest. Screams of pain and fear go pulsing through the
> air at the rate of eleven hundred feet per second. After travelling for
> three seconds they are perfectly inaudible. These are distressing facts;
> but do we enjoy life any the less because of them? Most certainly
> we do not.[7]

Crome Yellow, a satiric country-house novel in the mode of Thomas
Love Peacock, was Huxley's representation of Lady Ottoline Morrell's
household at Garsington, which he had first visited in December 1915
during his final year at Oxford. Introduced as Thomas Henry Huxley's
grandson, he had an immediate entrée into this distinguished – or

soon to be distinguished – coterie of literary and artistic figures, which included most of the Bloomsbury Group as well as such rising talents as D. H. Lawrence and T. S. Eliot. During the war years, Philip Morrell was to become a leading parliamentary spokesman for the opposition to the war, which from its early years was composed of a disparate collection of 'socialists, Bloomsbury aesthetes, radical women, trade unionists, Quakers, Christians [and] a few Cambridge dons'.[8] As a representative of the last, Bertrand Russell, Ottoline Morrell's lover, was to be particularly prominent in the peace movement; his militancy led to prosecution under the Defence of the Realm Act in 1916, and he was eventually imprisoned for six months in 1918. It was to Garsington that Siegfried Sassoon travelled while convalescing from injury in June 1917, a visit that resulted in the famous statement of protest against the war that he published that year. Since the institution of conscription in 1916, Garsington had become 'a gathering place for conscientious objectors. Some – Clive Bell, Aldous Huxley and David Garnett among them – came to do alternative service as farm labourers; others came to discuss pacifist policy – Bertrand Russell, Miles Malleson and Clifford Allen of the No-Conscription Fellowship, were all Garsington guests.'[9]

While there is no evidence that Huxley was declaredly a conscientious objector, he didn't need to be; his partial sightedness ensured that he was rejected by various medical boards throughout the course of the war. Towards the end of the war, he took up a post as a schoolmaster at Eton, during which time he revisited Garsington in the holidays. Thus Huxley was, during the war years, involved with the most prominent and culturally powerful centre of intellectual opposition to the war, and this can be seen as underlying his long-term intellectual and political development: that is, his commitment to the pacifist Peace Pledge Union in the later 1930s. Garsington, however, offered the complete cultural antithesis to Stocks, where in the latter years of the war Mrs Humphrey Ward threw herself into writing war propaganda for C. F. G. Masterman's War Propaganda Bureau, secretly based in Wellington House. The intellectual antinomies of 'Farcical History of Richard Greenow' are in this context geographically, biographically and intellectually located in the contrast between Stocks and Garsington. While throughout these years Huxley seems to have been ostensibly more concerned with the uncertainty of his own personal prospects than wider political issues, the experience of Garsington was formative on both his life and fiction. At the time of the armistice of November 1918 Huxley was working on 'his dual personality story'[10] while working as a schoolmaster at Eton. He finished it in the early part of 1919, in which year he took up a post on the editorial board of The Athenaeum, then edited by Middleton Murry, and married, in July, Maria Nys, a Belgian refugee whom he had met at Garsington. While Huxley had published two volumes of poetry previously, his first volume of short stories, dominated by the novella 'Farcical History of Richard Greenow', was published as Limbo in January 1920. Sybille Bedford writes, 'The actual sales were only about 1600 copies but the book was pounced upon by the high-brows and the literate young who were carried away by the cool bugle call of that new astringent voice expressing so essentially the coming post-war mood.[11] Seen in context, the title of the volume, Limbo, seems expressive both of Huxley's position during the war years and of the dominant tenor of his collection of stories.

'Farcical History' itself is in part a parodic Kunstlerroman (a novel on the development of an artist) and in part a tale of gender dualism. However, the artist is not Richard Greenow but his alter ego, the romantic novelist Pearl Bellairs, and Pearl Bellairs is, as John Sutherland suggests, a 'hilarious (and transparent) spoof of Mrs Humphrey Ward, who gave up writing fiction of ideas for romance after 1900'.[12] There are obvious similarities between Huxley's experience and that of Richard Greenow as he passes from Aesop College (Eton) to Cantaloupe College, Oxford (Balliol); and, while the text does not require immediate biographical reference, there exists an additional ironic resonance if one knows something of the circumstances of Huxley's early life. Thus, the text begins with the intellectually precocious Dick developing an incongruous passion for his sister Millicent's doll's house – the first intimation of the 'feminine' in his nature:

> When he wasn't playing with the doll's house, Dick spent his holiday time in reading, largely, devouringly. No length or incomprehensibility could put him off; he had swallowed down Robert Elsmere in the three-volume edition at the age of eight. When he wasn't reading he used to think about Things in General and Nothing in Particular; in fact, as Millicent reproachfully put it, he just mooned about.[13]

The author of the (in its day) heretical novel Robert Elsmere (1888) was, of course, Mrs Humphrey Ward, who in the Edwardian period had became both a bestselling novelist and the living embodiment of Victorian respectability. While Aldous resembles the intellectually precocious Dick, he was crucially more mischievous. In 1912, while staying at Stocks, an Eton contemporary reports that 'Mrs Humphrey Ward's complete works – a set of them – were in every spare bedroom in the house. Aldous went about muddling them up, managing to put three *Robert Elsmere's* in a row and so on. He loved mischief.'[14]

The gender divisions in the text are organised through a contrast between the austerely masculine 'intellectual' pursuits of algebra and mathematics, at which Dick excels at Aesop, and the feminine 'aesthetic' pursuits of the arts and poetry. The masculine predominates in Dick's personality until he falls precipitately in love with his schoolfellow, the incongruously named Lord Francis Quarles (once a metaphysical poet), 'a superb creature, with the curly forehead of a bull and the face and limbs of a Graeco-Roman statue' and with a lack of intelligence and sensibility to match. The experience propels the bewildered Dick into 'reading novels and the poetry of Mrs. Browning, and at intervals writing something rather ecstatic of his own'. Poetry and emotionalism go together, and when Quarles refuses an invitation to tea 'he actually burst into tears. He had not cried like that since he was a child.' This unrestrained emotionalism is brought to a close when a schoolfriend's ironic remark, 'But I always find Pater's style so *coarse*', restores him to his sceptical, rational self. The 'feminine' in Dick's psyche doesn't resurface until after he enters Cantaloupe College, where he becomes a leading light of the college Fabian Society, and discusses such cerebral topics as 'Art in a Socialist State'. One night, after suffering a relapse into the aesthetic, perhaps brought on by the mention of Lord Francis Quarles, Dick pens, as a species of automatic writing, the beginning of a sickly sentimental novel entitled *Heartsease Fitzroy: The Story of a Young Girl*. The sleep-writing continues, but Dick is reassured to find he is not affected during the day. On the completion of the manuscript he sends it to a literary agent and receives an enthusiastic offer to serialise his work from *Hildebrand's Home Weekly*, a mass-circulation woman's journal. The editor presumes Dick is a Madame, which leads him to the realisation that 'He was a hermaphrodite … A hermaphrodite, not in the gross obvious sense, of course, but spiritually. Two persons in one, male and female. Dr. Jekyll and Mr. Hyde: or rather a new William Sharp and Fiona MacLeod – a more intelligent William, a vulgarer Fiona.'[15]

The solution to the puzzle of his identity seems satisfactory to Dick. His female literary alter ego is named Pearl Bellairs, and goes on to have a runaway success as a sentimental woman's writer, penning such immortal works as *La Belle Dame sans Morality* and *Daisy's Voyage to Cythera* as well as 'weekly articles 'For the Girls of Britain' ... in the pages of *Hildebrand's Sabbath*, that prince of Sunday papers', while Dick devotes himself to philosophy and socialist politics. On going down, 'He started work on his new Synthetic Philosophy, and at the same time joined the staff of the *Weekly International*, to which he contributed both money and articles. The weeks slipped happily and profitably along.' All is well, until while on a holiday with his sister Millicent in Scotland, he is thrown into crisis as he learns of the declaration of war. The European war ends the fragile psychic truce between Dick and Pearl Bellairs. While, in the unreality of the first months of the war, he throws himself into his work for the *Weekly Internationalist*, he also suffers from bouts of amnesia in which Pearl gets the upper hand and pens such inspiring patriotic articles as 'To the Women of the Empire. Thoughts in War-Time. By Pearl Bellairs.' Dick is horrified, 'Her bank balance was the only thing about her that interested him. But now she was invading the sanctities of his private life. She was trampling on his dearest convictions, denying his faith. She was a public danger. It was all too frightful.'[16]

Dick finds that the cultural insanity of the war is internalised in his fissured psyche, and that Pearl represents the dominant, jingoistic discourse. He seeks treatment from Rogers (a version of Sassoon's psychotherapist at Craiglockhart, W. H. R. Rivers), who was versed in the then novel psychoanalytic ideas of 'Freud, Jung, Morton, Prince, and people like that'. Rogers subjects him to a word association test, in which Dick's responses cannot but recall aspects of Huxley's personal development. Seeking to investigate Dick's childhood, Rogers begins with 'Mother'. Dick responds 'Dead'. 'Father' elicits the response 'Dull'. 'Sister' evokes 'Fabian Society' in relation to the coolly rationalistic Millicent, while 'Aunt' evokes in Dick a vision of himself as 'a perfect Bubbles boy, kneeling on Auntie Loo's lap' (a photograph of Aldous in such a guise with Mrs. Humphrey Ward is extant) and elicits the more promising response 'Bosom'. Soon Rogers tries 'a frontal assault on the fortress of sex itself': 'Women'. This elicits the disappointing response 'Novelist'; while 'Breast' evokes 'Chicken'. 'Christ' evokes 'Amen' and 'God' evokes a schoolboy called Godfrey Wilkinson, or God for short, hence 'Wilkinson'. Dick dismisses Roger's hypothesis of 'a Freudian passion for his aunt' followed by a religious fervour 'for someone called Wilkinson'.[17] Unimpressed, Dick decides not to continue his psychotherapy.

Dick's isolation is accentuated when his sister, the practical, rational Millicent, throws herself into voluntary war work, moving from organising a hospital supply depot to working in the Ministry of Munitions 'controlling three thousand clerks with unsurpassed efficiency'.[18] Thus, both representatives of the 'feminine' in Dick's life – the pragmatic Millicent, his sister, and the gushily sentimental Pearl, his literary alter ego – combine in opposition to his opposition to the war. Here, it is pertinent to note that, rather than uniting the women's suffrage movement in opposition to a patriarchal war, its leading lights, Mrs Pankhurst and her daughter Christabel, threw their patriotic weight behind the British war effort, believing that it was an opportunity to demonstrate the capacities of women. While there was a splinter movement of women opposed to the war, the Women's International League, this was marginal, and suffragist activity effectively ceased in August 1914. The Pankhursts' patriotic offer was gratefully accepted,

> The Suffrage societies had accustomed women to organizing and being organized, and provided already functioning structures and trained officers for the planning and administration of women in war work and in the military services. Suffragist volunteers staffed the first women's war service, the Women's Emergency Corps, and had it functioning on the second day of the war, finding war work for women. Such organizations multiplied and expanded as the war went on.[19]

Millicent can be taken as representative of the 'emancipated' middle-class woman who staffed such voluntary (unpaid) organisations, while it was working-class women (some 800,000) many transferred from jobs in domestic service, who came into industry and munitions factories. It is clear that the granting of women's suffrage, at least for women over the age of thirty, in 1918, was in part a reward for wartime loyalty.[20]

If Millicent represents the response of the potentially radical middle-class woman in the war period, Pearl is a parodic, but not entirely parodic, representation of the conservative woman. Here, the immediate comparison is with the career of Huxley's aunt, Mrs Humphrey Ward, who, as 'the first president of the Anti-Suffrage

League from 1908, suggested in her novels that self-realisation and rebellion against motherhood would "un-sex" women.'[21] A prominent supporter of the Victorian ideology of 'separate spheres' for men and women, she threw herself into the work of Masterman's Bureau of Propaganda, which had recruited the talents of most of the established writers of the Edwardian period, and, as it were, never looked back; 'she was given tours of war industries, the Western Front, and Royal Naval vessels. She writes sentimentally of an England in which workers are happy putting in long shifts in the factories, of women doing men's work making munitions, and of cheerful troops going up the line to give battle.'[23] After the sinking of the Lusitania Mrs Humphrey Ward directed her efforts towards bringing the USA into the war, and wrote two propaganda books in the form of letters (directed implicitly, then explicitly, to Roosevelt) entitled England's Effort and Towards the Goal. She never deviated from the official demonisation of the Germans as those who have 'fouled civilization with deeds of lust and blood',[23] and concludes Towards the Goal with the statement that 'We feel we are terribly right in speaking of the Germans as barbarians: that, for all their science and their organization, they have nothing in common with the Graeco-Latin and Christian civilization on which Europe is based.'[24] From this perspective, Pearl Bellairs is merely a sentimental extrapolation of the existing hegemonic discourse, which endorsed the doctrines of Empire and motherhood, and demonised the Germans as 'The Aggressor'.

At the same time the government, through such engines of ideological control as the Bureau of Propaganda, and such direct legal instruments of state repression as the Defence of the Realm Act (DORA), waged a ceaseless and ruthless campaign against any form of dissent. After opposition to the war grew after the introduction of conscription in 1916, the atmosphere became increasingly authoritarian and hysterical; such manifestations of 'decadence' as homosexuality were prosecuted as a threat to the moral health of the army. As Hynes writes, 'Sexual deviance was a crime against the army. It could also be seen as a crime against a civilian society at war. Deviants could be attacked on patriotic grounds, and were.' It is only a short step from this to the persecution of any form of cultural nonconformity. From late 1916, the independent MP Noel Pemberton Billing 'edited his own weekly journal, the Imperialist, which ... attacked Jews, German music, Pacifism, Fabianism, Aliens, Financiers, Internationalism, and the Brotherhood of Man'.[25] The

argument that opponents of the war mounted, that a war that
purported to be in defence of 'freedom' had effectively eradicated
civil liberties, was unanswerable; but this did not prevent the state
directing its most virulent ire against pacifists. 'Pacifists were regarded
with such repugnance and mistrust by patriotic Englishmen that in
the same year as women got the vote, that in June 1918 Parliament
voted to exclude them altogether from post-war political life; the
Representation of the People Act disqualified conscientious objectors
from voting for a period of five years after the end of the war – the
only legislative act of modern times to reduce the British electorate.'[26]
It is pertinent to the discourse of 'Farcical History' that in the same
year as women got the vote, conscientious objectors lost theirs.

Since I will discuss these issues subsequently, we can return to the
progress, or rather decline, of Richard Greenow, who, clinging to
his pacifist principles, finds himself more and more socially isolated.
The psychic split between Dick and Pearl Bellairs, and the growing
power of the latter, is a literary and psychological representation of
the degree to which the individual is unable to resist the internalisation of the values of the dominant culture, especially in wartime.
The price of resistance to the dominant ideology (in Althusserian
terms: an imaginary representation of real social relations) is guilt,
anxiety and fear; not merely fear of persecution, but fear that the
prevalent social condemnation might be correct and the individual
deluded. Dick experiences the 'unreality' felt by soldiers returning
from the front, without a compensating, if disillusioning, sense of
'the real'. His isolation is compounded by his realisation that he
has no particular affection or respect for his fellow conscientious
objectors; 'neither morality nor reason would ever bring him to take
pleasure in the company of democrats or revolutionaries, or make
him find the oppressed, individually, any less antipathetic.' There is
little in the text to suggest that Richard Greenow would dissent,
or even exempt himself, from Beatrice Webb's negative response to
a meeting of the No Conscription Fellowship in 1917: 'The intellectual pietist, slender in figure, delicate in feature and complexion,
benevolent in expression, was the dominant type. These youths are
saliently conscious of their own righteousness.'[28]

The point of crisis is reached when Dick is summoned to appear
before a military tribunal. In consultation with his mentor, Hyman,
he intends to stand by his principles and go to prison, but as the
court proceedings develop he lapses into a disorientated, disgusted

lassitude and then amnesia. When he returns to consciousness, he is doing land work at Crome (Huxley's pseudonym for Garsington) and on discovering a rough copy of Pearl's, on the delights of being a land girl, he realises that 'Pearl was being a land-girl; but he could hardly explain the fact to Hyman.'[29] Dick experiences no Tolstoyan joy from his contact with the land and becomes an object of derision and persecution to the village children. His psychic destruction is completed when the pacifist Hyman and the pro-war Millicent unite in condemning his cowardice in not going to prison and decide to marry. At this point, in the summer of 1918, Dick's psychic dualism manifests itself as schizophrenia. He enters Wibley Town Hall and (as Pearl Bellairs), a woman of thirty, claims his right to be registered for the vote. He is promptly incarcerated in the local lunatic asylum.

He awakes in the Belbury County Asylum, which he had previously regarded 'as one of those mysterious, unapproachable places, like Lhassa or a Ladies' Lavatory, into which he would never penetrate.' On being addressed by the doctor as Miss Bellairs, Dick breaks into uncontrollable sobbing and is defined by the doctor as 'A bad case'. Protesting his sanity and unlawful detention, he goes on hunger strike, and is violently force-fed. As Gilbert and Gubar point out, this was a treatment meted out to protesting suffragettes – but Dick/Pearl's behaviour and its treatment also recollects a case of 'shell shock' (amnesia was one of the possible symptoms of shell shock) as well as the cruel treatment applied to conscientious objectors. The torture inflicted on him elicits a horrified vision of the war, which qualifies any sense of the text's 'cynicism':

> He thought of the millions who had been and were still being slaugh-tered in the war; he thought of their pain, all the countless separate pains of them; pain incommunicable, individual, beyond the reach of sympathy; infinities of pain pent within frail finite bodies; pain without sense or object, bringing with it no hope and no redemp-tion, futile, unnecessary, stupid. In one supreme apocalyptic moment he saw, he felt the universe in all its horror.

As pneumonia sets in, Dick asks for a paper and pencil to formulate his 'testament':

> They are killing me for my opins. I regard this war and all wars as utter bad. Capitalists' war. The devils will be smashed sooner later.

Wish I could help. But it won't make any difference,' he added on a
new line and as though by an afterthought. 'World will always be hell.
Cap. or Lab., Engl. or Germ. – all beasts. One in a mill. is GOOD. I
wasn't. Selfish intellect. Perhaps Pearl Bellairs better. If die, send corp.
to hosp. for anatomy. Useful for once in my life!'

As he lapses into delirium, Pearl wrests control of the pencil, and
having scratched out what Dick has written, begins to write her
own, considerably more florid statement: 'We are fighting for honour and the defence of small nationalities. Plucky little Belgium! We
went into the war with clean hands.'[30]

Dick/Pearl's response to this is, like Lady Macbeth, to try compul-
sively to clean his hands. She continues in xenophobic vein, echoing
the popular fiction of a German 'fifth column' of spies in England:
'Self-respecting Britons will refuse to shake a Hunnish hand for may
a long year after the war. No more German waiters. Intern the Forty-
seven Thousand Hidden Hands in High Places!' Turning to a fresh
topic, she addresses 'The Girls of England' to warn them about the
sinister implications of fraternisation with 'Hun prisoners': 'Imagine!
Clean, healthy British girls allowing themselves to be kissed by the
swinish and bloodstained lips of the unspeakable Hun!....Will she
repeat the offence if she realizes, as she must realize if she will only
think, that this thoughtless fun, this mawkish and hysterical pity,
is nothing less than Treason?' Finally, noting Dick's request that his
body be sent to a hospital for an anatomy, she reacts with disgust
and tries to arrange her burial 'in a little country churchyard, with
lovely marble angels like the ones in St. George's at Windsor, over
Princess Charlotte's tomb.'[31] She then falls into the coma which has
blotted out Dick's mind, and two hours later both are dead.

While the fantastic form of 'Farcical History' is distinctive in
Huxley's early writing, its central themes of division and self-division
are anticipatory of his subsequent development up to and including
Brave New World (1932). In the 1920s Huxley employed the genre of
the novel of ideas to examine the disparate modes of intellectual,
cultural and political division that were evident in the post-war period
and the related modes of self-division that affected the individual.
Point Counter Point (1927) was to be Huxley's most extensive treatment
of these themes; here the title, indicative of disharmony (a 'point'
against the harmony of contrapuntal music), suggests the manner
in which the novel juxtaposes various disparate and antagonistic

viewpoints without the reconciliation of an overriding 'synthesis'. The novel is prefaced by an epigraph from the metaphysical poet Fulke Greville, which is helpful in considering Huxley's treatment of these themes in 'Farcical History':

> Oh, wearisome condition of humanity
> Born under one law, to another bound,
> Vainly begot and yet forbidden vanity,
> Created sick, commanded to be sound.
> What meaneth nature by these diverse laws,
> Passion and reason, self-division's cause?

The final two lines are clearly apposite to, but also crucially different from, 'Farcical History'. While Pearl represents 'passion' in the guise of 'female' emotion, and Dick 'reason' in the guise of 'male' rationality, what is most striking and historically symptomatic is that Greville's 'traditional' antinomies have become antagonistically *gendered* and lack any real sense of their original metaphysical paradigm. In the Renaissance 'reason' and 'passion' would be implicitly related to the Christian division between 'body' and 'soul', but in Huxley's text the soul is indiscernible. If one compares, as historically a median term, Blake's 'Contraries', such as 'Reason' and 'Energy', Huxley's antinomies lack Blake's sense of dialectical interdependence, whereby 'Without Contraries is no progression'.[32] As the grandson of Thomas Henry Huxley, who coined the term 'agnostic' and was known as 'Darwin's bulldog', Huxley is representative of a post-Darwinist world-view, itself a crucial paradigm shift from the theocentric to the secular. Clearly, Huxley's treatment is an ironic and parodic inversion of gender expectations in that it is Pearl Bellairs who is active and bellicose, and Dick the opposite, but this can be historically contextualised by considering a subsidiary binary opposition that leads back to the division between male and female, which was crucially operable during the war period: the division between combatants (male) and non-combatants (female). Dick Greenow is already metaphorically 'feminised' by his pacifism, and the text explores the blurring of gender identity that follows from such rigid divisions. In the post-Darwinist ideological turmoil that characterised the early twentieth century, gender (and in this historical context, patriarchal discourse) has become the *primary term* in the sequence of binary cultural oppositions and differences and semiotically deploys and informs the following sequence of subsidiary terms.

In *No Man's Land*, Gilbert and Gubar offer a vigorous, if univalent,
reading of Huxley's text in terms of its representation of the male
writer's anxiety about woman's writing. While, clearly, this is an
element in the text's dynamic, its emphasis leads to tendentious
reading and involves a number of crucial distortions. For example,
while Pearl might register for the vote in 1918, and, as Dick Greenow,
be force-fed, like a suffragette, her ultra-conservative discourse
precludes, as much as that of Mrs Humphrey Ward, any possibility
of a feminist identity. In general, it leads to false contextualisation.
Thus, 'as Dick gradually loses his intellectual potency and becomes
little Dick, Pearl (with her fanciful belle airs) increasingly manifests
herself as the belle-heir, a twentieth-century inheritor of the wom-
en's tradition founded by such precursors as *Jane Eyre*. Worse still,
as his writing becomes increasingly elitist and occult, her work,
inspired by his readings of George Sand, Elizabeth Barrett Browning
and Mrs Humphrey Ward, becomes ever more popular.' Arguing
from within the context of 'the battle of the sexes', Gilbert and
Gubar align Huxley's novella with Max Beerbohm's contemporary
short story 'The Crime'; but the central difference is that while
Beerbohm's male narrator admires his literary woman's 'creative
work immensely – but only in a bemused and miserable manner'[33]
– Dick Greenow, and the narrator, find Pearl's work deplorable. The
problem with Gilbert and Gubar's reading here, and elsewhere,
seems to be a gender essentialism by which any manifestation of
female literary effort is judged intrinsically 'good' in divorce of
its contents (which may be, as Pearl's are, reactionary, xenophobic
and racist) – a stance which leaves the larger issues of gender and
writing unexamined.

Gilbert and Gubar's idealist conception of literary production
would seem to contradict their overall project. Arguably, the lack of
innovative women's writing in the early years of the twentieth century
was a result of the claustrophobic constraints that informed socially
acceptable versions of 'feminine' behaviour, and the emergence of a
new generation of ground-breaking 'modernist' women during and
immediately after the Great War was in part a consequence of the
erosion of patriarchal assumptions that war inadvertently accelerated.
Literature should not be isolated from wider cultural discourses, and
when the cultural space existed for a more challenging exploration
of female experience, writers such as West, Richardson, Woolf and
Mansfield swiftly occupied it. Returning to Gilbert and Gubar's read-

ing of Huxley's text, at the risk of being critically punctilious, it is worth pointing out that Dick Greenow is only a 'literary man' in a limited sense; his interests lie in philosophy and political science. Like Huxley himself, he is deeply fearful of emotion ('From childhood upwards Dick had suffered from the intensity of his visceral reactions to emotion.'[34]) and Pearl, as his alter ego, functions as a suppressed repository of conformist, sickly sentimental 'feminine' emotion. It is pointless aligning her hilariously mindless work with what, from the point of view of masculinist discourse, is the genuinely threatening Jane Eyre, because in larger terms Huxley's target, as that of many male modernists, is the fear of a sentimental, 'feminised' and commercialised mass culture, which both marginalises and eradicates 'male' intellectual and literary discrimination. The spirit of Huxley's work is thus close to that of Joyce's parody of Maria Cummins's The Lamplighter in the 'Nausicaa' chapter of Joyce's Ulysses (1922), where, as Gilbert and Gubar write, 'this parody indicts the banality and bathos inculcated in young girls by the pulpy fictions of literary women'.[35] While Mrs Humphrey Ward's war writings receive respectful critical attention in Raitt and Tate's Women's Fiction and the Great War,[36] already, long before the war, she had become a figure of derision to the rising generation of male and female literary moderns, and her war writings did not enhance her reputation. John Sutherland informs us that, 'As Enid Huws Jones records, a copy of Richard Greenow was found at Mary Ward's bedside in 1920 and that "it was probably one of the last books she read". It cannot have given her any pleasure'.[37]

The place of 'Farcical History of Richard Greenow' within the gothic tradition of psychic dualism should be taken seriously. Pearl functions as a kind of vampire or succubus, gradually taking over Dick's rational faculties; but the dynamic of their interaction is complex. While Dick's opposition to the First World War is both justifiable and sophisticated – he has stripped away contemporary ideology to write in his 'testament' that it is a 'Capitalists' war', thus implying a modern (or, at least, Leninist) understanding of the First World War as a 'trade war' to decide the issue as to which nation would be the top-dog imperial power – this realisation has led to nothing except social isolation, misanthropy and self-condemnation: 'One in a mill. is GOOD. I wasn't. Selfish intellect. Perhaps Pearl Bellairs better.'[38] On one level, Dick's self-condemnation is a representation of the internalisation and erosive effect of war propaganda on the isolated individuals who oppose it; but it also suggests that his pacifist 'male' rationality – modelled, perhaps, on that of Bertrand Russell – is emotionally desiccated and culturally sterile. In this context, it is significant that it is only in the lunatic asylum, when he is addressed as Miss Bellairs, that he is able to return to his childhood and express emotion by sobbing uncontrollably. Finally, though, I suspect that the real fear that motivates the dualism of the text is not that of women's writing per se, but something perhaps more subversive, the fear that 'creative' literary activity, with its deployment of sensibility and emotion, might be intrinsically 'female'. One can trace a discourse leading from responses to aestheticism and the Wilde trial, through to the Bloomsbury Group, and beyond, to, for example, *Lucky Jim*, which questions whether 'artistic' activity is entirely compatible with heterosexual masculine identity. Huxley, trying to reconcile his scientific, rationalist and 'creative' identities in the war and post-war period, would have been aware of and motivated more by this than by any envy of female literary prowess. In this context, homophobic discourse is more relevant than misogyny. Huxley's text should, I think, lead us to consider the construction of masculinity within the larger context of combatant war writing and cultural practice.

Here, the most pertinent comparison is with the externalised and satiric stance Robert Graves adopts in *Goodbye to All That* (1929),[39] which could well be subtitled 'The Farcical History of Robert Graves'. The after-effects of war experience had proved disabling for Graves as well as for many other veterans (in 1929 more pensions were granted for psychotic illness than had been granted in the four years immediately after the war)[40] and Graves had written his biographical memoir with declaredly mercenary intent: as a means to achieve the goal posited in his title by raising sufficient cash to leave England for good. Thus, the work itself is in part an 'entertainment', a stagy, cynical potboiler, which includes obviously fictional information, in part a reliving of the most traumatic events of Graves's life. In *Goodbye to All That*, Graves (a 'neurasthenic farceur' according to Fussell)[41] adopts a narrative tone of cool, parodic detachment which is almost the ethos of the 'stiff upper lip', with its suppression of masculine emotion, extended into a dislocated and dislocating narrative stance. This retrospective detachment is also self-detachment. Graves focuses his narrative through 'those caricature scenes that now seem to sum up the various stages of my life' and consistently represents his experience as a sequence of ridiculous external cameos. Even his impending nervous breakdown is represented in disturbingly cold, external terms:

> My breaking point was near now, unless something happened to stave it off. Not that I felt frightened. I had never yet lost my head and turned tail through fright, and knew that I never would. Nor would the breakdown come as insanity; I did not have it in me. It would be a general nervous collapse, with tears and twitchings and dirtied trousers. I had seen cases like that.[42]

Here, the masculine officer ethos of the 'stiff upper lip' is revealed as a means of controlling such turbulent emotions as may afflict the individual when faced by traumatic experience and the possibility of death in battle; but it also serves, at least in literary retrospect, as a technique to posit and ironise such self-alienation and underline the absurdity and unreality of such a depersonalised stance.

In Goodbye to All That, one of the key incidents, in historical as well as literary terms, concerns Siegfried Sassoon's article 'Finished with the War: A Soldier's Declaration', which was published in the Bradford Pioneer in 1917. In it Sassoon, Graves's close friend, had stated 'I believe this war, upon which I entered as a war of defence and liberation, has now become a war of aggression and conquest.' Graves found himself 'most bitter with the pacifists who had encouraged him to make this gesture', which he regarded as 'magnificently courageous' but also as politically 'inadequate'. While Sassoon was clearly reluctant to present his principled protest as a psychological disorder, the military authorities were as reluctant to give his letter publicity through a court martial; 'At last, unable to deny how ill he was, Siegfried consented to appear before the medical board.' Graves, at the time almost as ill as Sassoon, had managed to rig up this board before which he himself testified histrionically, bursting 'into tears three times during my statement' to incur the comment 'Young man, you ought to be before this board yourself.' As Graves commented, 'The irony of having to argue to these mad old men that Siegfried was not sane!' Sassoon was diagnosed as suffering from neurasthenia and sent to a convalescent home, Craiglockhart, or 'Dottyville' as Graves and Sassoon referred to it, near Edinburgh, where he was treated by W. H. R. Rivers. However, the issues raised by Sassoon's 'Soldier's Declaration' were not easily resolved, for, as Graves was uneasily aware, the 'Soldier's Declaration' was not quite 'gentlemanly' conduct, and was liable to be misunderstood by the troops. Graves, in conversation with Sassoon before the medical board, posited the 'correct' course of conduct: 'We discussed the political situation; I took the line that everyone was mad except ourselves and one or two others and that no good could come of offering common sense to the insane. Our only possible course would be to keep on going out until we got killed.'[43] Thus, in wholesale inversion of rational values, Sassoon's sanity has led to his being declared insane; while the 'honourable' response to the carnage of the Western Front, understood as that which revalidates masculine self-control, was, effectively, suicide.

Graves's advice supplemented rather than contradicted the treatment he received from W. H. R. Rivers, Sassoon's military psychiatrist at Craiglockhart War Hospital. Rivers was an important psychologist, one of the first in Britain to appreciate and understand Freud's work, though he disagreed with Freud in important respects, particularly as regards the latter's belief in the centrality of sexuality to the psyche. In the preface to *Conflict and Dream*, Elliot Smith commended Rivers' attempt to 'prune from the method of the psychoanalytic school most of the repulsive excrescences that have brought upon it so much odium',[44] but one might well argue that a sanitised Freudian unconscious is no longer a Freudian unconscious. At Craiglockhart, Sassoon, as an officer who was suffering from an 'anxiety neurosis', was offered psychotherapy. Diagnosing Sassoon as suffering from a 'very strong anti-war complex', Rivers' treatment encouraged him to accept his revulsion at the horrors he had experienced but also sought to break down his rational opposition to the war. As Elaine Showalter details,

> In lengthy conversation three times a week, Rivers and Sassoon talked not only about Sassoon's life and war experiences but also about European politics, German military history, and the dangers of a premature peace. The talking cure was intended to make Sassoon feel uneasy about the gaps in his information and to emphasise the contrast between his emotional, and thus feminine, attitude to the war and Rivers' rational, masculine, Cambridge don's view of it.[45]

The 'cure' was successful. Sassoon began to feel guilty about abandoning his men and being confined with the other 'nervous wrecks' at Craiglockhart, and renouncing his 'anti-war complex' retrieved his status as 'an officer and a gentleman' by returning to the front.

Rivers had thus succeeded in reinscribing a gendered notion of 'rationality' onto the psyche of his grateful patient, which allowed Sassoon to control his anxieties and return to combat.

Thus, Rivers functioned as an ideal 'father figure' to Sassoon, encouraging him to accept his 'feminine' emotional revulsion at the cost of the war, and express it through poetry, but also returning him to a 'masculine' political discourse, which contained and neutralised it. He has received a good press, largely because of Sassoon's consistently expressed gratitude to him. Had Sassoon, like Wilfred Owen, his poetic protégé at Craiglockhart, died in combat, one might suppose it would have been a different story. However, reviewing the history of their relationship, it is clear that Rivers' dismissal of the role of sexuality and gender in the war neuroses, and his separation of them from the anxieties of civilian life, were contradicted by his own therapeutic practice. If gender was overtly erased from the therapeutic discourse, one can presume that the same was true for sexuality; and here it is clear that Sassoon's homosexuality had accentuated his gender anxieties. Homosexuality had been criminalised by Labouchere's Amendment in 1885, and in the inflamed atmosphere of the later years of the Great War, as previously indicated, sexual deviance as a manifestation of 'decadence' was integrated with degenerationist discourses and openly regarded as a direct attack upon the 'health' of the state, while it was actively prosecuted as a military offence. (During the war 22 officers and 270 other ranks were court-martialled for indecency.[46]) Undoubtedly, Sassoon's acts of extreme, almost suicidal, bravery at the front, which earned him the nickname 'Mad Jack', were a sublimated response to such homophobic sentiment, and to the insulting insinuation of 'cowardice' and 'effeminacy' they contained. What better answer to homophobia than heroism? Within this context, the fact that Dick's Greenow's first 'feminine' passion is for Francis Quarles is indicative of the tensions generated by such restrictive and hypocritical sexual and gender ideologies. As attested to in Robert Graves's *Goodbye to All That*, homosexuality and homoeroticism were endemic in the single-sex English public school system; indeed, given the lack of alternatives, they were norms rather than deviations; and it is no accident that many of the most gifted First World War poets were homosexual (Sassoon, Owen, Ivor Gurney et al.). It is precisely their sexuality that lends their poetry its sense of complete emotional commitment.

My argument in this chapter has sought not to assimilate the various literary, cultural and political discourses I have examined, but rather to discuss their structural organisation and logical contradictions. Thus, in Huxley's 'Farcical History of Richard Greenow', Dick's masculine, rational anti-war convictions are set against Pearl's irrational, feminine pro-war propaganda; in Rivers' treatment of Sassoon, the masculine and rational is deployed to convince Sassoon to return to the front; while, in Goodbye to All That, Graves posits that in an insane world a concept of implicitly suicidal masculine decorum is all there is to hold on to. However, in structural terms what is striking is the consistency of the strict gendered divisions of male/female, reason/emotion, rationality/irrationality, active/passive, strength/weakness, which were supplemented by the division combatant/non-combatant, the privileging of the former according to patriarchal assumptions, and the suppression of the modes of internal incoherence noted above. In Britain, as was not the case in, for example, Russia, the binary structure replicates the overt division between men and women as combatants and non-combatants in British First World War society, but works to conceal the experiential blurring of these roles in social practice. Intellectually what is clearly lacking in all these gendered binary discourses is a concept of rationality that is neither, or is both, male and female. It is this constitutive absence that underlies the absurd and satiric dichotomies and antinomies of Huxley's and Graves's texts. With hindsight it is easy to appreciate how these restrictive and repressive discourses of gender could be manipulated to serve the needs of the imperialist state; but even those who served those discourses most assiduously, such as Rudyard Kipling, whose only son was killed in battle, became their victim. It is within this context that Huxley's allegory of gender dualism is far more than the 'deliciously sardonic diversion' that Gilbert and Gubar regard it as intended to be.

A more integrated concept of intelligence and rationality, which accepts emotion, transcends the sexual divide and attempts to destabilise restrictive notions of gender, had to await the arrival of a new culture and a new literary generation. While the leading Edwardian novelists were tainted by their association with Masterman's Bureau of Propaganda, the swift emergence of the Bloomsbury Group in the post-war period was in part a function of their opposition to the war, which already, by the time of the Versailles Treaty ('The peace that passeth understanding', according to Vera Brittain's Testament of

Youth) could be seen as having bled Europe white without having resolved any major political issue. The leading literary voices of the 1920s were to be Huxley and Virginia Woolf, and her anonymous review of *Limbo* in the *TLS* is interesting reading. Commenting on the volume as a whole, she advises Huxley to steer clear of satirising the English upper middle classes, for 'They lie, apparently, so open to attack, they are undoubtedly ... an obstacle to vision.' Having satirised upper-middle-class modes and conventions, 'they suddenly turn the tables on him. Now they seem to say, talk about something that you do believe in – and behold, Mr. Huxley can only stammer. Love and death, like damp fireworks, refuse to flare up in such an atmosphere, and as usual the upper middle class escape unhurt.'[47] I agree with the analysis, but not the conclusion. Huxley (like Graves) is undoubtedly trapped, in that in attacking the repressive culture that has formed him, he doesn't escape its constrictions. However, his scepticism acted as a dissolvent on the political ideologies of the age, and if his ironism became a keynote of the 1920s it was as a salutary rejoinder to the patriarchal convictions of the previous decade. Perhaps unsurprisingly, it was in the 1930s, when political realities pushed him into making an explicit pacifist commitment, that his career as an important novelist effectively terminated. Conviction was not Huxley's natural mode. Towards the close of *Eyeless in Gaza* (1936) Anthony Beavis, Huxley's persona, listens to a disagreement between his mentor, the benign, pacifist philanthropist, Dr Miller, and his cynical, misanthropic friend, Mark Staithes, which concludes with Staithes suggesting to Beavis that they 'Huddle together among the cow-pats and watch the doctor trying his best anthropological beside manner on General Goering. There'll be some hearty laughs.' Beavis responds, '"In spite of which," said Anthony, "I think I shall go and make myself ridiculous with Miller."'[48] This time history was to ironise Huxley rather than vice versa.

Notes

1 Aldous Huxley, 'Farcical History of Richard Greenow', in *Limbo* (London: Chatto & Windus, [1920] 1946), pp. 1–146.

2 Sandra M. Gilbert and Susan Gubar, *No Man's Land: The Place of the Woman Writer in the Twentieth Century*, Volume 1: *The War of the Words* (New Haven: Yale University Press, 1988), pp. 131–6.

3 Gilbert and Gubar, p. 131.

4 Julian Huxley, *Memories* 1 (Harmondsworth: Penguin, 1978), p. 65.

5 See, *Eyeless in Gaza* (Harmondsworth: Penguin, 1955), p. 362; also John Sutherland,

Mrs Humphrey Ward: Eminent Victorian, Pre-eminent Edwardian (Oxford: Clarendon Press, 1990), p. 339.

6　Sybille Bedford, *Aldous Huxley: A Biography*, Volume 1: *The Apparent Stability* (London: Paladin, 1987), p. 49.

7　Aldous Huxley, *Crome Yellow* (Harmondsworth: Penguin, 1967), p. 89.

8　Samuel Hynes, *A War Imagined: The First World War and English Culture* (London: Pimlico, 1992), p. 86.

9　Hynes, p. 174.

10　Bedford, p. 100.

11　Bedford, p. 108.

12　Sutherland, p. 201.

13　'Farcical History', pp. 3–4.

14　Bedford, p. 36.

15　'Farcical History', pp. 8, 12, 37.

16　'Farcical History', pp. 49, 44, 61, 62.

17　'Farcical History', pp. 65–8.

18　'Farcical History', p. 95.

19　Hynes, pp. 88–9.

20　See Claire M. Tylee, *The Great War and Women's Consciousness* (London: Macmillan, 1990), p. 37.

21　Tylee, p. 67.

22　Peter Buitenhuis, *The Great War of Words: Literature as Propaganda 1914–18 and After* (London: Batsford, 1989), pp. 58–9.

23　Quoted in Buitenhuis, p. 59.

24　Quoted in Buitenhuis, p. 59.

25　Hynes, p. 226.

26　Hynes, p. 217.

27　'Farcical History', p. 81.

28　Angela K. Smith, *Women's Writing of the First World War: An Anthology* (Manchester: Manchester University Press, 2000), p. 118.

29　'Farcical History', p. 89.

30　'Farcical History', pp. 104, 109, 110–11, 112.

31　'Farcical History', pp. 113, 113–14, 112–15.

32　William Blake, *The Marriage of Heaven and Hell*, ed. G. Keynes (Oxford: Oxford University Press, 1975), p. xvi.

33　Gilbert and Gubar, pp. 132, 128.

34　'Farcical History', p. 78.

35　Gilbert and Gubar, p. 146.

36　Helen Small, 'Mrs Humphrey Ward and the First Casualty of War', in Suzanne Raitt and Trudi Tate, eds, *Women's Fiction and the Great War* (Oxford: Clarendon Press, 1997), pp. 18–47.

37　Sutherland, p. 202.

38　'Farcical History', pp. 110–11.

39　Robert Graves, *Goodbye to All That* (Harmondsworth: Penguin, 1960).

40　Eric J. Leed, *No Man's Land: Combat and Identity in World War I* (Cambridge: Cambridge University Press, 1979), p. 189.

41　Paul Fussell, *The Great War and Modern Memory* (Oxford: Oxford University Press), p. 206.

42　Graves, pp. 150, 164.

43　Graves, pp. 213, 214, 216, 215.

44　W. H. R. Rivers, *Conflict and Dream* (London: Kegan Paul, Trench, Trubner, 1923), p. vii.

45 Elaine Showalter, 'Rivers and Sassoon: The Inscription of Male Gender Anxieties', *Behind the Lines, Gender and the Two World Wars*, ed. M. L. Higonnet et al. (New Haven: Yale University Press, 1987), p. 66.

46 Hynes, p. 225.

47 Donald Watt (ed.), *Aldous Huxley: The Critical Heritage* (London: Routledge & Kegan Paul, 1975), p. 42.

48 Huxley, *Eyeless in Gaza*, pp. 359–60.

4

How gender serves Trotskyism:
the Spanish Civil War in Ken Loach's
Land and Freedom

Alan Munton

I

At the climax of *Land and Freedom*, Ken Loach's film about the Spanish Civil War, Blanca is shot dead by soldiers of the People's Army. She is hit in the back twice as she runs towards another member of the militia group to which she belongs, the POUM. She is wearing a Red Cross armband. The People's Army and the POUM are both fighting against Franco, yet the POUM is about to be forcibly elimi-nated, and Blanca's violent death is the film's dramatic, and moving, exemplification of this political turn. *Land and Freedom* explained the complex politics of this war for a new generation when it was released in 1995, and its audience included young people in Spain itself, where post-Franco liberalisation had not yet told either the full story of the rebel generals' success or of the dissension among the parties of the left that contributed to it. This is, however, a film with a politics of its own, a politics that I shall argue is Trotskyist. Two complexities consequently require interpretation: the war itself, and the film's reading of that war. What Loach has to say about the war is inseparable from the death of Blanca. It is upon her body, both when she is alive and at the moment of her death, that he concentrates a Trotskyist reading of the politics of the Spanish Civil War.

Land and Freedom has two prominent women characters, Blanca and Maite. Both are shown fighting, not in the problematic circumstances of a state army, but as fully-participating volunteers in a revolutionary militia. The defeat of that militia is prefigured by Blanca's demotion to medical worker, whilst Maite is reduced to being a cook. Women take an active part in the film's most important political scene, the debate about collectivisation that follows the capture of a village by the militia. This projection of women as active participants in war and politics serves a double function. That women fought for the Republic is authentic history; but in this Trotskyist reading the emphasis upon women also projects specific ideas about political leadership in revolutionary situations. The film's welcome attention to the possibilities of war for women conceals, or encodes, a political position whose full implications are never made clear.

This coding can be approached through Loach's own remarks about those scenes in the film that are performed in Spanish and Catalan, as well as in English. 'The language is very important for the sense of internationalism', Loach told an interviewer.[1] The angry response throughout the world to the generals' rebellion in Spain in July 1936 was striking. From all over Europe and North America, volunteers came to fight; according to Communist Party statistics, the largest numbers were from France, Poland, Italy, the United States, Germany, the Balkans, England, Belgium, Czechoslovakia, Austria and the Baltic states.[2] Most fought with the International Brigades, which were organised by the Communists. This is not the internationalism to which Loach refers. From a Trotskyist position the word means a belief in the necessity of worldwide Marxist revolution. In the film, the astonishing range of nationalities among the POUM militia – as well as Spanish, there are English, Scottish, Irish, French, German, Italian, American – is intended as a model for this conception of international revolution.

The same coding occurs when Loach speaks of the Spanish Civil War as being 'one of those enduring stories of the struggle for the leadership of the working-class movement or the revolutionary movement or whatever you like to call it'.[3] The question of who leads a political movement or a revolution is obviously important. But in the Trotskyist context, 'leadership' has a specialised meaning. Trotskyist parties believe themselves to be the vanguard of the working-class movement, for it is they who possess the correct analysis of capitalism and they who know how to build a revolutionary party. This theory of leadership derives from Lenin's success in the Russian revolution of 1917, and it is essentially authoritarian. Where the Bolshevik-Leninist parties lead, others must follow. The fact that this analysis has not led to success anywhere in Europe or elsewhere is the consequence of a betrayal of the working class by other parties on the left. Trotsky's belief that betrayal was inherent in all reformist movements established 'the revolution betrayed' as Trotskyism's explanatory narrative. Loach tells this story in relation to Spain when he speaks of 'the great energy and power that was released then and how it was diverted and subverted. That has perhaps been the tragedy of the 20th century.'[4] The agent of betrayal in Spain was the Communist Party, which stifled the revolutionary energy of the anarchists and the POUM. Loach presents the central issue as one of people taking over control of their own lives, an evidently desirable outcome. It is less certain that this need be attached to Trotskyist dreams of world revolution.

Trotsky himself was a prodigious letter writer who encouraged revolutionaries in Britain during the 1930s, beginning with the Balham Group, which was expelled from the Communist Party in 1932. In 1934 Trotsky urged members of The Marxist Group to infiltrate the Independent Labour Party (ILP) to persuade it to adopt a Marxist programme, a tactic known as 'entryism'; when they were expelled, the Revolutionary Socialist League was formed in 1938. One of the League's members was C. L. R. James, the great Trinidadian intellectual – and cricket correspondent of the *Manchester Guardian* – whose book *World Revolution* (1937) influenced Orwell's understanding of Soviet policy in Spain.[5] James was an adviser to the publishers Secker & Warburg, which became known as publishers of Trotskyist books such as Mary Low and Juan Breá's *Red Spanish Notebook*, discussed below. Secker published *Homage to Catalonia* in 1938, but the political influence here came from the ILP, which encouraged Secker to publish books – Orwell's among them – that would counter the influence exercised by the Communist Party through the Left Book Club.[6]

The story of *Land and Freedom* is essentially that told by George Orwell in *Homage to Catalonia* (1938), of his experiences fighting with the POUM militia in early 1937, and of the party's suppression after the 'May Days' disturbances of that year in Barcelona. In the film, the middle-class Orwell (who is nowhere mentioned in the film's credits) is replaced by David Carr, a young working-class Communist Party member from Liverpool, whose political education this is to be: he will abandon communism for the POUM and Trotskyism. In a significant addition, Loach and his screenwriter, Jim Allen, faced the difficulty of constructing a narrative that would tell the story of the Spanish Civil War and at the same time make the Trotskyist case against communism. 'The story just kept breaking down', Loach told an interviewer.[7] Consequently, the argument for Trotskyism is carried by Blanca and Maite. The theory of revolutionary internationalism is displaced upon two female Spanish nationals.

Many scenes in Land and Freedom can be read doubly, as both 'true' and Trotskyist. For any revolutionary party, Leninist discipline is a necessity, so that in the early scene at the Communist Party meeting in Liverpool, when David decides to go to Spain, there is attached to the wall a poster reading '¡CON DISCIPLINA SE DEFIENDE LA REPUBLICA! ('With discipline we can defend the Republic!') Two scenes involving Maite insist upon necessary discipline, but they carry a Trotskyist second meaning. During drill at the Lenin Barracks in Barcelona, Maite drops out of the line when the training officer asks the recruits to march by the left, and then by the right. To her 'Hey dickhead, make up your mind!' the officer replies 'Where are you going, love?' When she objects to being called 'love' ('bonita'), the officer hurries after her calling 'Camarada! Camarada!' He persuades her back into the line by saying, 'This is vital for the revolution – for both men and women. We've got to have discipline.' Later, at the Aragón front, Maite herself prevents a young POUMist, Pigat, from deserting when he learns that his wife has left him. She pushes him to the ground and tells him that 'If we don't win this war there will be no future for anyone.' Maite has first learned discipline, and subsequently exercises it. The overt meaning of these scenes is that if you have volunteered to fight, you should find the personal discipline to do so properly. The concealed Trotskyist meaning is that strict internal discipline is necessary for the success of a vanguard revolutionary party.

II

Land and Freedom appeared in 1995 and has become a reference point in the historiography of the war. In the 'Epilogue' to Britain and the Spanish Civil War (1997), Tom Buchanan writes that since the 1960s 'the revival of Trotskyism and anarchism and the withering of Stalinism has given new life to the Orwellian interpretation of the Spanish Civil War' – and Loach's film is 'openly Orwellian'.[8] On the political right, the editors of a collection of documents from the Moscow archives, Spain Betrayed: The Soviet Union and the Spanish Civil War (2001),

argue that the Communists provoked the civil war within the civil
war that led to the suppression of the POUM and the exclusion of
the anarchists from government because they 'feared a coup led by
anarchist troops against the regime of the Popular Front'. Orwell
and Loach are both invoked to justify this interpretation of the
Communists' motives in provoking the Barcelona 'May Days'.[9]

I argue here that *Land and Freedom* is part of the Trotskyist revival
to which Buchanan refers, and that Loach, together with his screenwriter Jim Allen, produce this politics by means of a gendered
narrative that appropriates 'strong woman' feminism for a particular
political purpose. It is rare for Trotskyism to be debated in Britain,
as distinct from being pursued by marginal political groups such
as the Socialist Workers' Party and the Workers' Revolutionary Party.
Nevertheless, there exists within British culture an influential group
of writers, academics and filmmakers who are, or who have been
(turnover is considerable) Trotskyists. Allen's work for television, for
example, in such plays as *The Lump* (1967) and the series *Days of Hope*
(1975), are among the most important achievements of a medium
which has now turned its back on such seriousness. Allen's work,
it has been said, 'fuse[s] lived experience with Marxist, specifically
Trotskyist, beliefs',[10] but the specific content and consequences of
such beliefs are rarely if ever examined.

Trotskyism is better understood in Europe, so when Loach went
to Madrid to promote *Land and Freedom* in April 1995 he was obliged
to be more explicit than in his British interviews. *El País* described
him as 'a former Trotskyist activist' (*antiguo activista trotskista*), and he
is quoted as saying

> I think it is very difficult to understand the politics of the twentieth
> century without understanding what Trotsky's contribution has been.
> Our Spanish comrades in the POUM wanted to detach themselves
> from Trotsky. I think it would have been impossible to complete this
> film without recognising the influence of Trotsky, but there are other
> influences, such as the anarchists and libertarian communists.[11]

The politics of the film are eclectic, therefore, but the Trotskyist element is fundamental. A vigorous anti-Stalinism is inseparable from
Trotskyism, but Allen's remarks on Stalin and Spain in the production notes to *Land and Freedom* go beyond what is plausible. He says
that the Communist Parties knew 'that if a democratic revolution
had succeeded in Spain then Stalin's days were numbered. It was

the last thing he wanted because then the dictatorship in Russia would not have been tolerated.'[12] Trotskyists believe that a successful revolution in Spain would have so enthused the Soviet masses that a workers' democracy would have arisen to overthrow Stalin. Equally implausible is a remark in Loach's obituary notice for Allen, who died in 1999. The Spanish revolution was betrayed by Stalin and by the social democrats because 'they preferred Franco to the possibility of a workers' state'.[13] To speak of an active *preference* for Franco anywhere on the Republican side shows a willingness to be dominated by theory, and masks a perverse refusal to recognise the strength of the external forces that determined the outcome.

The Spanish Civil War began as a revolution and became the most important small war of the twentieth century. In the areas not taken by the generals in July 1936, mass popular revolts thrust aside established government in favour of new institutions of local or regional control. The POUM were powerful in Lérida, and the anarchists dominated in Catalonia. Farming, industry and commerce was collectivised, and in places a system of dual power developed, with the republican government obliged to work alongside the new decentralised organisations. The excitement and hope for the future generated by these events was immense, and difficult now to recapture. The early part of *Land and Freedom* goes a considerable way towards doing so.

This was a war of personal involvement for which individuals could volunteer to fight, and so make their political commitment dangerously actual. Later, it became a preparation for the Second World War when Nazi Germany and Fascist Italy supported Franco, and the Soviet Union supported the Republic. Missing from this proleptic schema are the major European democracies, Britain and France, whose refusal to supply arms to the Republic was a substantial cause of its defeat. In August 1937 Orwell wrote to a correspondent: 'I doubt indeed whether the war can now be won unless France intervenes.'[14] The Soviet Union gave less support than it could have done because Stalin did not want to offend (by supporting 'Red Revolution') the two countries with which he expected to form an alliance against Germany and Italy. However, France and Britain regarded communism, not fascism, as the problem, and intended no such alliance. Instead they pursued the policy of non-intervention, and Spain was lost to Franco as a result. Money and *matériel*, guns and equipment, were required, and they were not made available.

Revolutionary energy, of the kind invoked by Ken Loach, was never going to be enough. It is a weakness of *Land and Freedom*, or of the ideas behind it, that these wider political realities are never acknowledged.[15]

When George Orwell arrived in Spain in December 1936 he was exasperated by 'the kaleidoscope of political parties and trade unions, with their tiresome names – PSUC, POUM, FAI, CNT, UGT, JCI, JSU, AIT'.[16] By May 1937 he had learned that it was a matter of life and death as to which party one belonged. When Orwell – whose real name was Eric Blair – with his wife Eileen, and two POUM members, John McNair and Stafford Cottman, fled Spain on 23 June, the situation was more dangerous than they knew. On 13 July there was typed out in Barcelona a report on the Blairs which would have led to their imprisonment (and perhaps their deaths) had they been caught. Eric and Eileen Blair were *trotzquistas pronunciados*, that is, pronounced or confirmed Trotskyists.[17] The peculiar spelling here – the Spanish for Trotskyist is *trotskista* – and the misspelling of Blair's name as 'Enric' (the Catalan form of Enrico), together with other errors, suggests that this document was not produced by a native Spanish or Catalan speaker. There can be no doubt that this report, prepared for the Tribunal for Espionage and High Treason in Valencia, was the work of Barcelona agents working for the Soviet NKVD. The statement that 'ERIC B. took part in the events of May' would have been profoundly damaging to Orwell, had he been arrested. The conclusion – which stands at the head of the report – is fatal: 'Their correspondence reveals that they are confirmed Trotskyists.' This sinister document, which was unknown to Orwell, represents an incursion of totalitarianism into British political life, and offers ample evidence for the anti-Communist case made by *Land and Freedom*.[18]

The POUM was the Partido Obrero de Unificación Marxista, usually translated as the Workers' Party of Marxist Unification. ('It's Spanish Workers' Party. Revolutionary', a puzzled David is told in *Land and Freedom*.) The party was the result of an alliance made in 1935 between the Bloque Obrero y Campesino (BOC; Workers' and Peasants' Bloc) and the Izquierda Comunista (IC; Communist Left). The BOC provided the mass element, whilst the tiny IC provided the intellectual or Trotskyist element. Of the latter, there were only about two hundred, for actual Trotskyists have always been thin on the ground, even during a revolution. The POUM consisted of a majority of libertarian revolutionaries with a thin top layer of Trotskyist intellectuals. Orwell said that it 'was not a Trotskyist body, though for a while it had Trotskyists working for it'.[19] A Soviet agent calling himself 'Cid' reported to Moscow that in Catalonia the POUM division had 4,000 men under arms.[20] Within the Spanish political structure the POUM threatened both the Communists and the Republicans. It was independent of Moscow, and so could never work with the Partido Comunista de España (PCE; Spanish Communist Party), yet it stood for insurrectionary revolution and the dictatorship of the proletariat. Andrés Nin, its leader, broke with Trotsky in 1934 when the latter, out of touch and interpreting Spain as if it were Russia in 1905 and 1917, ordered the Communist Left to practice 'entryism' – that is, join the Socialist Party (PSOE), set up a faction and try to move it towards revolution. This was an absurd proposal, as Nin could readily see, though some Trotskyists regard it as an example of betrayal.[21] The POUM leadership was Trotskyism without Trotsky, the membership libertarian socialists largely indifferent to such technicalities. The Communist denunciation of Nin and the POUM as Trotskyists was therefore not descriptive but opportunistic.

The POUM's most important doctrine, as it affects an understanding of both Orwell's autobiography and Loach's story of David Carr, was that the most effective way to defeat fascism was to continue the revolution whilst fighting the war at the same time. The Communists argued that the war had to be won first, and the POUM believed, with good reason, that this was a way of abandoning the revolutionary gains of July 1936. The Anarchist newspaper *Solidaridad Obrera* gave a vivid account of this position:

> The scolding refrain [of the communists'] 'first win the war' pains us. That is a desiccated slogan, without substance, nerve or fruit. First win the war and make the revolution at the same time, for the war and the revolution are cosubstantial, like sun and light.[22]

This was the policy difference that led to the fabricated accusations that POUM and its leaders were 'Trotsky-fascists'. In 1995 Loach himself used the Spanish press to confront Santiago Carrillo, the former leader of the Spanish Communist Party, on this issue. He reminded Carrillo that at the time he had 'called his [Trotskyist] companions fascists', and in a weak defence Carrillo referred to the context of the times. *Land and Freedom* exists to correct this libel.[23] Ken Loach's remarks on this occasion confirm that *Land and Freedom* occupies a

double position, at once an historical film and an intervention in
contemporary politics: 'It is important that history should be written
by us, because whoever writes history controls the present.'[24]

III

It is possible to discern differing attitudes towards gender and
gender issues among the parties of the Spanish left. The Anarchists,
for example, had a policy, of sorts, on prostitution, whilst Andrés
Nin began a reform of the divorce laws when he was appointed
minister of justice in Catalonia in 1936. Despite this, the left had
by no means thought through such questions. The Spanish feminist
Margarita Nelken (1894–1968), whose ground-breaking examination
of the social conditions of Spanish women had been published as
early as 1919, suffered throughout the war a misrepresentation of
her views and a salacious interest in her sexual life, often from
men politically on the left. In his biographical account of Nelken,
Paul Preston writes that 'The attitude to sex of both the Socialist
and Communist Parties, to which she belonged at different times,
ranged, behind a rhetoric of liberality, from harsh puritanism to
lubricious prurience'.[25]

The experience of Nan Green, who worked at the front as a nurse
and a medical administrator, shows how accusations of Trotskyism
could be used to threaten women. Her story is told by Preston in *Doves
of War* (2002), where she is described as 'a staunch and uncomplicated
Communist'.[26] Green, who was English and married – her husband
George was in Spain, and died in the fighting – worked for an
authoritarian German communist surgeon, Dr Herbert Kretzschmar,
and turned down sexual approaches from him. In her unpublished
autobiography she wrote that at Valdeganga in March 1938 'I had
fallen victim to an ephemeral affair with a patient', probably William
Day, an International Brigader from Canterbury. Unfortunately Day
deserted, perhaps worried for his pregnant wife at home (there
are parallels and contrasts here with Maite's controlling of Pigat),
and this gave Kretzschmar the opportunity to go to William Rust,
the representative of the Communist Party of Great Britain (CPGB)
in Spain, to make false allegations against her. These made their
way to Moscow, where they have been recently discovered in the
archives. Rust, as chief political commissar, made a separate report
in which he accused her of being an 'adventurer', which Preston

explains was code for sexually promiscuous. In a third report, this time to the CPGB on Day, Rust not only wrote that Day was 'either a fascist or a Trotskyist', but reported Kretzschmar's entirely false allegation that 'a letter full of criticisms of the Soviet Union from a Trotskyist point of view had been found in Nan Green's room'. Finally, Rust's reports reached André Marty at the International Brigades' headquarters at Albacete, with the consequence that she was described as 'politiquement très suspecte'. This could have been extremely dangerous for her, given Marty's disciplinary, not to say murderous, attitude towards dissidence.[27]

The story of Nan Green is an instance of the conversion of sexual desire into bureaucratic texts by which a brutal authoritarianism seeks to make real an alleged but fantastic Trotskyism. The argument of *Land and Freedom* moves in the opposite direction: the love that arises between Blanca and David is converted by means of a persuasive naturalistic text (the film itself) into an equally unreal Trotskyist story of betrayal. The practical authoritarianism of communism is opposed by a virtual alternative which foregrounds desire. In both cases the purpose is political. Between 1937 and 1939, the Communists invoked Trotskyism to deflect attention from their failure to win the war. In the 1990s a Trotskyist interpretation of that defeat must validate the only permitted explanation, that the revolution in Spain was betrayed by other forces on the left.

Land and Freedom attempts to validate the Trotskyist point of view by means of a narrative in which political processes and a love story are skilfully related. The love affair between Blanca and David develops gently and gradually, and has attached to it none of the aggression that the Communist Party machine imposed upon Nan Green's experience. Yet the relationship is framed by a narrative that invokes, and then repudiates, prostitution. Prostitution, as act and concept, is a form of aggressivity. When David first sees Blanca at the front – she is embracing her lover, Coogan – he shares the assumption of other newly arrived militiamen that she is a prostitute:

> MAX: Hey, David … look. [Long shot from above: Blanca and Coogan embracing under a tree.] The whores are also at the front.
>
> DAVID: They're better looking than the ones back home.

A little later, he is tricked by his companions (including Maite) into approaching Blanca as a client. (José: 'She is good, and cheap!').

Blanca explains, with a combination of exasperation and controlled politeness:

BLANCA: Coogan is my man. Mi compañero.

DAVID: Oh ...

BLANCA: Since the war we live together. We joined the militia together. We fight together.

Blanca and Coogan are a revolutionary couple. David returns, abashed, to much laughter. The scene lasts two and a half minutes, but has attracted no comment in the longer published discussions of the film. Much later, when David and Blanca break up in Barcelona after a political argument, David decides to rejoin the POUM after a dispute with People's Army soldiers who assert that the women who fight at the front are having sex with the enemy. In the film, prostitution is first a comedy of misunderstanding, and later a motive for David's political journey to the far left.

The women who fought with the non-communist militias were indeed denounced as prostitutes. Rosario Sánchez ('Rosie the Dynamiter') told Shirley Mangini that 'They called the milicianas prostitutes and the milicianos thieves.' Sánchez later 'admitted that it was likely that there were some prostitutes at the front lines',[28] which suggests that the story of Blanca as the fighter misread as a prostitute derives from a complex actuality. Among the books that Loach and Allen draw upon is *Red Spanish Notebook* by Mary Low and Juan Breá, two enthusiastic Trotskyists who were with the POUM at the height of the revolutionary period in Barcelona between August and December 1936.[29] Mary Low's forthright accounts of gender politics, public and private, may have suggested that Blanca could be situated at once within the male imaginary as an object of desire, and beyond it as a woman who fights.[30] Blanca is shown both firing at the enemy and, in an exchange of abuse, shouting 'Castradas fascistas' ('Fascists – you've got no balls').

In a chapter entitled 'Women...', Low recalls the response of young Anarchist militiamen to the Anarchists' poster against prostitution:

'Finish with prostitution', read one of them. 'What do you think of that?'

They stood around uneasily, obviously annoyed, and awkward at finding themselves annoyed ...

'Well, what's a man going to do if they really start suppressing it? It's not as though they were so oncoming themselves that we could do without it.'

Conversation ensues amongst Low's friends:

'So they [prostitutes] did go to the front at first. But being hardened by prostitution doesn't necessarily make one cool under fire. A lot of them were in the way, and then the men were always being sent home with venereal [sic] because there was no control.'
    'I don't care. Something ought to be done for them.'
    'The militias would growl, and they deserve a lot of indulgence for the fight they're putting up ... And above all you have to change the mentality of the women in this country first.'

Eventually, Low reports, the Barcelona prostitutes organised themselves and joined the anarchist CNT.[31]

Such exchanges provide an uncommon insight into the discussions actually taking place among people engaged in a revolution of attitudes within a revolutionary war. Juan Breá's attitudes were less examined, as when he describes a mixed bathing expedition near the front, the women's 'naked bodies glowing an ardent amber colour in the sunlight', with a chauffeur remarking 'Ha, ha, comrade, there's the revolution for you.' When a Swiss woman bather says the men are harmless, but 'of course sometimes one or other of them does a little masturbation', we realise how far the change in attitudes and behaviour had to go.[32] This in turn is a reminder that many of the foreign arrivals in Spain brought a degree of urbanity and sophistication that could not be matched even by the Catalans. Mary Low acknowledges that foreigners were 'inclined unwisely to stress their intellectualism and to show off a boasted education', so that the Catalans 'reacted with a wounded dignity mixed with a peck of chauvinism'.[33] Revolutionary internationalism was not easy to sustain.

Breá provides an equally uncommon record of a *miliciana* at the front. At Tierz a captured fascist officer is to be executed, but the political commissar hesitates because the officer is wounded. When 'the little militia-girl' in the unit says she is sorry for him, the commissar reminds her that 'this morning you were insulting the man and wanting to tear his eyes out':

'This morning he was a Fascist. Now he's only a poor sick thing ...
But I don't want them to kill him.'

   There was nothing the commissar could say. So he tweaked her
nose affectionately, and we went away. ...

   [At the dawn shooting the officer is unsteady.] The little militia-
girl ran forward to him with one of the wicker chairs, and pushed it
behind his knees. This was how it happened that he died seated.[34]

Breá seems not to realise that his story of the *miliciana*'s act of
sympathy can be interpreted as a criticism of the execution.

Land and Freedom is far from patronising the *milicianas* in this way,
for Loach and Allen bring forward Blanca and Maite as exemplary
and uncomplicated revolutionaries. During the militia unit's debate
on whether to integrate into the People's Army, Gene Lawrence (the
American communist) says 'We're not going to win this war with
a bunch of amateurs', and Blanca replies sharply: 'You may be an
amateur. I'm not.' We should remember that they are represented in
this way in order to be betrayed by Stalinism. When David at last
realises what the Communist Party is, the film is cut to his voice-
over to show that he is integrated at last into the militia community.
The men appear in long- or medium-shot (LS, MS), but Blanca
and Maite, who have always known the revolutionary truth, appear
repeatedly in close-up (CU).

   [Liverpool. CU KIM reading letter intently. DAVID (voice over):] The
   Party stinks, kid, and I never thought the day would come when I had
   to say that. It's evil and corrupt. In Barcelona I saw good comrades
   snatched off the street and executed. Others disappeared into torture
   chambers, and it's still going on.
   [Spain. MS DAVID under a tree rereading this letter. Gesture of dis-
   may.] Stalin's just using the working class like pieces on a chessboard.
   Being bartered, used and sacrificed. [LS of the militia group, BLANCA
   at centre in doorway under a large red cross (her symbol), the men
   grouped around.] Things have changed while I've been away. [DAVID
   enters shot from behind camera.] Some of the old faces are missing
   because they couldn't stomach all the infighting. And all in all we've
   taken a bit of a battering. It's rumoured we're going to make a big
   attack soon. Still no weapons, no support. [Sits among group.] But
   this one we're going to win. [CU BLANCA at door. Hold and brief
   pause.] Despite everything our spirits are high. [Singing begins. Shot
   slides away from BLANCA to militiamen. MAITE approaches group,
   follow her into CU. Two-shot of militiamen and she enters from left,

sits, CU of MAITE. Two-shot DAVID and MAITE, friendly greetings just audible. CU BLANCA rolling a cigarette and slide away to militiamen still singing. Cut to fighting in the final battle.]

The women are repeatedly seen in close-up, but the men are generalised. The anti-Stalinist speech and the images of a community gathered around its women members conclude David's political education. He understands that he has been betrayed.

IV

The almost idyllic aspect of this scene, in which the lost recognise their defeat but will not submit, makes the battle scene that follows all the more moving and all the more dismaying. The two scenes remind us that the Spanish Civil War was a necessary war, fought (on the Republican side) for the best of reasons. But not all the narrative strategies of *Land and Freedom* so persuasively combine politics and feeling. Why is David, a Communist Party member, not directed into the International Brigades? Because the Trotskyist narrative of betrayal requires a Communist who goes over to the POUM. During the May Days, David is shown on a rooftop, armed, but now in a Communist unit facing a group of Anarchists. He appears to have done what Orwell considered doing, but was well advised not to do: to pass from the 'Trotskyist' POUM to the 'Stalinist' People's Army. How this happens the film does not explain. These gaps indicate that, while Loach and Allen have a strong case against communism, on the limited grounds they have chosen they cannot find the narrative means to make their criticism stick. Consequently they pursue a double strategy. There is the political story of an American communist, Gene Lawrence, who belongs at first to POUM but improbably moves over to be an officer in the People's Army, and there is the gendered story of Blanca and Maite.

Both narrative strategies have their roots in what is by general acclaim the most successful scene in the film, the debate on whether to collectivise the land that follows upon the capture of a village by the POUM. The debate is an inspired invention by Loach and Allen, who involved non-professional actors, some of whom actually held the beliefs that they express. The scene, which lasts for thirteen minutes, has been praised for its spontaneity, which is certainly apparent, but some speeches are scripted, notably those of Gene Lawrence, who puts the 'Stalinist' case, and loses. It is difficult to anticipate that Gene will turn out to be the film's villain, though as Ian Christie remarks, 'we are clearly meant to smell a rat in Lawrence's fluent reasonableness'.[35] During his crucial speech he is in shadow, placed in the right-hand side of the frame. A window on the left casts no light.

> LAWRENCE: I want you to think beyond this village. Okay, at a much bigger picture. [Translation into Spanish.] Okay. I have no doubt that the Spanish people on their own could have licked Franco. [Translation.] But you are not fighting just Franco. You now have Mussolini and Hitler on your back. [Translation.] Okay. With the exception of Russia and Mexico [interruption] the rest of the world has turned its back on you. Okay. They refuse to sell the Republic arms. [Translation.] Okay. These are capitalist countries ... and if you want their help you have to moderate your slogans because you're scaring them away. [Confused shouting and discussion.]

This speech puts the Communist Party case so well that Loach and Allen are hard put to find the narrative strategies to escape its implications. They turn to Blanca.

David and Blanca meet, just after the May Days, in a Barcelona pension where she has deliberately arrived first. It is a love scene drenched in politics.

> BLANCA: Women aren't allowed to fight any more....[ironically] I must know my place as a woman ...Today I want to forget it all. Bullets, trenches, politics, killing, betrayal. I want to feel human for a change ... (They drink. Pause) Take off your shirt. Come on.

Next morning, Blanca is furious when she discovers the International Brigade uniform in David's knapsack. As she makes the case against the Communists, she is lit from behind by a window that throws light directly upon her.

> BLANCA: [Getting dressed. Angry.] Our leaders have been expelled from the government ...They are trying to ban us. We are a social[ist] party. You know this. Our papers are banned. Journalists arrested ...Why you didn't tell me yesterday? [sic] [Finishes dressing, leaves.]

Loach makes his case partly by technical means – the lighting – and partly through the convincing anger of a partly dressed woman who is also the hero's lover. Immediately after this comes the second 'prostitution' scene. It is this that at last changes David's mind. He sits eating in the café when three uniformed People's Army soldiers enter.

SOLDIER 1: The militias are a disaster. When it's decision time, every-one is the boss. ...

SOLDIER 3: They say the militia women aren't killing fascists, they are fucking them instead. [Arm gesture.]

[DAVID, eating. Over this shot:] They fuck them.

SOLDIER 2: They do nothing. They're crap. They're a disaster....

DAVID [in Spanish]: That's a lie!

The contrast between the post-coital erotic force of Blanca's political convictions and the soldiers' coarse remarks changes David's politics. He returns to his room and tears up his Communist Party card.

This scene completes the film's 'prostitution' theme, whose pur-pose has been to show that Blanca is *not* one. The early client scene with David is a British comedy of embarrassment which avoids the actual problems of prostitution at the front. Later, the fevered imag-inings and male aggressivity aroused by the thought of prostitutes at war are dissolved by David's recognition that Blanca has told him the truth about revolution. In a strategy out of melodrama, the pure woman must now die. When the People's Army arrive to disperse and arrest the POUM, Blanca and Maite assist (despairingly) in dis-arming their own people because they recognise the danger from the men's angry and excitable resistance. When Blanca runs to stop a militiaman who is firing into the air, she is shot in the back.

This final scene was suggested to Loach by the experience of Joan Rocabert, a POUM member in 1937 whose unit was arrested in this way.[36] Despite his influence on the film, Rocabert did not, as Loach describes it, tell the story of the killing of a woman medical worker. At this point, the film simultaneously climaxes, and unravels politically. Gene Lawrence is there, dressed as a captain, and, more improbably still, the Nationalist, or fascist, officer captured earlier in the film is present as the colonel in charge. (He kicks David back after Blanca is shot.) Martha Gellhorn, who as a journalist had unrivalled experience of the war, drew attention to the implications of Gene Lawrence's boots, at which Blanca hits out ineffectually moments before she turns away: 'Lawrence even wears highly polished boots, unheard-of in Spain, an over-the-top Gestapo touch.'[37] The image

betrays – to turn that word back upon the film's authors – the difficult position they choose to occupy: the People's Army was not just
Communist-dominated and therefore 'Stalinist', it was potentially, if
not actually, fascist. And it shot unarmed women nurses in the back.
These narrative choices are motivated by the same divisive political
interpretation that allowed Allen to believe that the Communists
preferred Franco's victory to their own. As the Trotskyist analysis
unravels, so does the coherence of the film.

V

Land and Freedom is significant because it exemplifies the cultural work
of the political left in a difficult period. It is not structured as 'the
individual against authority', but concerns a *group* attempting to
function in an intensely politicised context where it is eventually
overwhelmed by superior forces. This is one of socialism's primary
concerns, the relation that the preterite has with power. Here, both
'sides' are on the left, but the film nevertheless explores a relationship that may be generalised, one where a small, internally coherent
group has to endure a subaltern relationship towards a more powerful
force. Any individual member of such a group is a subject-in-rela-
tion who lives as part of a network susceptible to violation from
without. The Blanca who loves David is also the subject who must
defer, who is prevented from fighting because 'I must know my
place as a woman'. Rejected by Blanca, David suffers the ineffectual
pathos of the subject not yet fully in relation with the group, until
he recognises the reasons for the POUM's subaltern relationship
to the Communists. To counter the inevitable defeat and betrayal
imposed by reformist communism, he will return to Liverpool a
Trotskyist and a revolutionary.

There is a converse argument. The Trotskyist parties in Britain are
a negligible political force, but Trotskyism has considerable cultural
influence. 'World revolution' and 'the vanguard party' belong to fantasy, but 'cultural Trotskyism' does not.[38] When in a successful film
the POUM is projected as a vanguard party by means of the erotic
and killed body of Blanca, who is pure because not a prostitute,
and a pure revolutionary, then a significant intervention in culture
occurs. The POUM's defeat by the communists evokes sympathy,
but can also be read as an encouragement of division on the left,
which is consistent with Trotskyism's impatient dismissal of other

left alternatives. (Loach did not choose to tell the story of the defence of Madrid, where the left parties, including a small POUM element, worked together far more successfully than in Catalonia.) In Trotskyism there is a distinct authoritarianism in political structure, and a certain Puritanism of outlook. To attract support despite these dismaying attitudes, Trotskyist intellectuals seek to align their own doctrines with separate but more vital movements. So it is that today Trotskyists opportunistically attach their anti-capitalism and internationalism to the worldwide protests against globalisation. *Land and Freedom* attempts a related strategy, one that might be named gender appropriation.

Notes

This chapter is part of a research project supported by the Spanish Ministry of Science and Technology (BFF 2002-02842), the Comunidad Autónoma of La Rioja (ANGI-2002/05), and the University of La Rioja, Logroño, Spain (API-02-35). Earlier versions were given at the University of La Rioja in April 2003, and at the conference entitled 'George Orwell in Spain: A Centenary Celebration', held in Jaca (Aragón), by the University of Zaragoza, 22–24 May 2003.

1 John Hill, 'Interview with Ken Loach', in George McKnight (ed.), *Agent of Challenge and Defiance: The Films of Ken Loach* (Trowbridge: Flicks Books, 1997), pp. 173–4.
2 'Document 73' in Ronald Radosh, Mary R. Habeck and Grigory Sevostianov (eds.), *Spain Betrayed: The Soviet Union and the Spanish Civil War* (New Haven and London: Yale University Press, 2001), p. 468. Listed in descending order of numerical participation, as at 30 April 1938; seventeen countries in all, with 1,072 'Others', a total of 31,369. This document was prepared by Soviet intelligence working in Spain.
3 Hill, 'Interview', p. 175.
4 Hill, 'Interview', p. 175. The demanding and unrealistic concept of 'permanent revolution' is also central to Trotskyism. See Tony Cliff, *Lenin, Volume 1: Building the Party* (London, Pluto, 1975), pp. 201–4, for the origins of this concept in Marx, as argued by the foremost British Trotskyist theorist.
5 John Newsinger, 'The American Connection: George Orwell, "Literary Trotskyism" and the New York Intellectuals', *Labour History Review*, 64:1 (1999), 24. Noting Orwell's rejection of Trotsky and Trotskyism ('The essential act is the rejection of democracy', *New English Weekly*, 12 January 1939), Newsinger argues that in the 1940s 'he was nevertheless influenced by Trotskyist ideas' to an extent that it is meaningful to describe him as 'a "literary Trotskyist"' rather than as 'a *Tribune* socialist' (p. 40). See Ted Grant, *History of British Trotskyism* (London: Wellred Publications, 2002), Part One, *passim*.
6 Fenner Brockway, 'Minutes of the I.L.P. N[ational] A[dministrative] C[ouncil]' in *The Complete Works of George Orwell*, Volume 11: *Facing Unpleasant Facts 1937–1939*, ed. Peter Davison (London: Secker & Warburg, 1998), pp. 39–40.
7 Richard Porton, 'The Revolution Betrayed: An Interview with Ken Loach', *Cinéaste* 22:1 (April 1996), 30.
8 Tom Buchanan, *Britain and the Spanish Civil War* (Cambridge: Cambridge University

Press, 1997), p. 201. See also Jackson, *British Women and the Spanish Civil War* (London and New York: Routledge, 2002), p. 289 n.77, for a further reference.

9 Radosh et al., pp. 171–2. It is not certain that the Communists feared a coup; they may have intended to suppress POUM and the anarchists anyway, or provoke a confrontation to test the outcome. Radosh speaks of the 'May Days' as the 'revolution within the revolution', which is not the usual terminology. As these examples indicate, Radosh's anti-Soviet commentary must be treated with extreme caution.

10 Julian Petley, 'Factual Fictions and Fictional Fallacies: Ken Loach's Documentary Dramas', in McKnight, p. 35. The words quoted are from Paul Madden's entry for Jim Allen in George W. Brandt (ed.), *British Television Drama* (Cambridge: Cambridge University Press, 1981).

11 Rocío García, 'Ken Loach describe en "Tierra y libertad" la división del bando republicano en la guerra civil', *El País*, 6 April 1995, p. 32. Loach: 'Pienso que es muy difícil entender lo que ha sido la política del siglo XX sin comprender lo que ha sido la aportación de Trotski. Nuestros camaradas españoles del POUM querían separarse de Trotski. Creo que sería imposible haber hecho esta película sin reconocer la influencia de Trotski, pero hay otras influencias, como la de los anarquistas o comunistas libertarios'. I am grateful to Eva Cruz for finding and translating the material from *El País*.

12 Jim Allen, quoted by Patrick MacFadden, 'Saturn's Feast, Loach's Spain: *Land and Freedom* as filmed history', in McKnight, p. 144.

13 Ken Loach, 'Jim Allen' [obituary], *Guardian*, 25 June 1999, p. 20. Loach continues: 'This was at the heart of Jim's writing and belief', leaving it unclear whether he endorses Allen's position.

14 *Facing Unpleasant Facts*, p. 77. No. 393, 'To Amy Charlesworth'.

15 This case has been most eloquently and persuasively made by the foremost British historian of the war, Paul Preston. See *A Concise History of the Spanish Civil War* (London, Fontana, 1996), pp. 171–9. Paul Preston, 'Partisan', *New Times* 88 (30 September 1995), 9, and 'Viva la revolucíon [sic]', *New Statesman and Society*, 9:390 (16 February 1996), 18–21, discuss *Land and Freedom* in this context; I am grateful to Paul Preston for letting me see revised versions.

16 George Orwell, *Homage to Catalonia*, ed. Peter Davison, introd. Julian Symons (London: Penguin, [1986] 1989), p. 188; *Orwell in Spain*, ed. Peter Davison (London: Penguin, 2001), p. 169.

17 *Facing Unpleasant Facts*, p. 30, No. 374A, 'Escape from Spain, 23 June 1937'. Davison here translates 'pronunciados' overemphatically as 'rabid', and this is changed to 'confirmed' in *Orwell in Spain*, p. 26.

18 This document was discovered in a Madrid archive by Karen Hatherley in the 1980s. Her comments on the errors are incorporated into Davison's lengthy and important commentary. See *Facing Unpleasant Facts*, pp. 30–7. Davison's judgement is that 'genuine Terror haunted Albacete and Barcelona in and after May 1937' (p. 35).

19 *Facing Unpleasant Facts*, p. 87, No. 401, 'Review of *Red Spanish Notebook*'.

20 Radosh, p. 179. The report is undated.

21 The PSOE was and is the Partido Socialista Obrero Español, the Socialist Workers' Party of Spain. For the POUM's formal position in 1936, see Víctor Alba and Stephen Schwartz, *Spanish Marxism versus Soviet Communism: A History of the P.O.U.M.* (New Brunswick, NJ and Oxford: Transaction Books, 1988), pp. 94–5.

22 Quoted in Hugh Thomas, *The Spanish Civil War*, 3rd edn. (Harmondsworth: Penguin Books, 1977), pp. 525–6.

23 'Ken Loach recuerda que Carrillo llamó fascistas a sus compañeros trotskistas', *El*

País, 7 April 1995, p. 32. Loach was responding to Carrillo, 'El fascismo, olvidado' ['Fascism Forgotten'], *El País*, 6 April 1995, p. 32. POUM leader Wilebaldo Solana contributed '¿El estalinismo olvidado?' *El País*, 14–15 April, 20. Santiago Carrillo (b. 1915), exiled 1939–76, was secretary-general of the PCE 1960–82; expelled (by his own account) in 1985.

24 Loach: 'Es importante que la historia sea escrita por nosotros, porque quien escribe la historia controla el presente'.

25 Paul Preston, *Doves of War: Four Women of Spain* (London: HarperCollins, 2002), p. 300.

26 Preston, *Doves of War*, p. 156.

27 Preston, *Doves of War*, pp. 156–60 and 164–5. The efforts of Winifred Bates of Spanish Medical Aid ensured that Nan Green resumed her work in safety. For details, see Jackson, *British Women*, pp. 106, 114, 273 n. 133.

28 Shirley Mangini, *Memories of Resistance: Women's Voices from the Spanish Civil War* (New Haven and London: Yale University Press, 1995), p. 84. Interview conducted in 1986. There may have been fewer than 1,000 women fighting with the militias (p. 80).

29 For Allen and Loach's reading, see Richard Porton, 'The Revolution Betrayed: An Interview with Ken Loach', *Cinéaste* 22:1 (April 1996), p. 30, and Jacob Leigh, *The Cinema of Ken Loach: Art in the Service of the People* (London and New York: Wallflower Press, 2002), p. 173. Trotskyist and anti-communist texts predominate, and nothing by Paul Preston appears. My thanks go to Roger Scott for assistance with these and other sources.

30 Two scenes, drafted but dropped, probably derive from Low and Breá: a speech by Nin (pp. 50–2), and the funeral of the anarchist Durrutti (pp. 215–16). See Leigh, p. 168.

31 Mary Low and Juan Breá, *Red Spanish Notebook: The First Six Months of the Revolution and the Civil War* (London: Secker & Warburg, 1937), pp. 196–7, 198. Mary Stanley-Low (b. 1912 in England) was a classical scholar and poet. She has travelled widely and remained a revolutionary. She met the Cuban writer Juan Breá Landestoy (1905–1941) in Paris in 1933. A 'revolutionary couple', they were associated with the French surrealist poet Benjamin Péret, who was with them in Spain. See Agustín Guillamón, 'Perfiles revolucionarios: Mary Low y Juan Breá', the Introduction to the Spanish translation, *Cuaderno Rojo de Barcelona* (Barcelona: Alikornio, 2001), available at www.inisoc.org/marylow.htm.

32 Breá, 'Tierz', *Red Spanish Notebook*, pp. 98, 99.

33 Low, 'A Full Day', *Red Spanish Notebook*, pp. 64, 65.

34 Breá, 'Tierz', pp. 106–7.

35 Ian Christie, 'Film for a Spanish Republic', *Sight and Sound* (NS), 5:10 (October 1995), 37.

36 Jonathan Steele, 'Betrayed from within', *Guardian* G2, 29 September 1995, p. 4; Porton, 'Interview', p. 31

37 Martha Gellhorn, 'This Is Not the War that I Knew', *Evening Standard* (London), 5 October 1995, p. 27.

38 'Cultural Trotskyism' is adapted from John Newsinger, 'The American Connection'.

5

Clothes and uniform in the theatre of fascism: Clemence Dane and Virginia Woolf

Jenny Hartley

In his autobiography Leonard Woolf describes 'the last years of peace before war broke upon us in 1939' as 'the most horrible period of my life'.[1] War seemed inevitable, and many people were relieved when it was finally declared in September 1939. 'Appeasement' comes down to us as a dirty word, but to do justice to the climate of the time we should remember how recent were the devastations of the Great War. And far from the war fading away, a series of powerful memoirs by ex-soldiers such as Siegfried Sassoon and Robert Graves were appearing during the late 1920s and on into the 1930s. The growth of fascism in Europe prompted many to search for some explanation for war, some antidote or cure. The two greatest thinkers of the day, Freud and Einstein, corresponded in a series of letters called *Why War?*[2] They were joined by a host of other writers, all trying to answer such questions as why people make war, and what war does to people. Gender and warfare are firmly linked in feminist analyses of the time, which often deplore the male will to power and aggression, on the one hand, and forced or voluntary female subservience, on the other.[3] By the late 1930s Clemence Dane and Virginia Woolf were both well-established women writers (though Clemence Dane is little known today), and well known as feminists. Dane was a vice-president of the Six Point Group,[4] and Virginia Woolf's *A Room of One's Own* (1928) had established her profile as a feminist polemicist. Woolf's *Three Guineas* (1938) and Dane's *The Arrogant History of White Ben* (1939) address the issues of gender politics and war from a feminist perspective, and do so by foregrounding the trope of clothes and uniform. While Woolf's logic works with the connections between clothes and ideology, Dane links clothes to performance and theatre.

The Arrogant History of White Ben is one of a number of dystopias which were written by women novelists during this time (other examples include Storm Jameson's In the Second Year from 1936 and Murray Constantine's Swastika Night from 1937), which imagine the future under fascism. Dane's dystopia follows the birth and growth of a mass movement, and analyses the psychological phenomenon of dictatorship. The novel dramatises and deconstructs dictatorship as charisma and performance, the totalitarian state as brutal theatre. Clemence Dane was herself at various times actress, set designer, artist, sculptor, playwright and screenwriter as well as novelist; she was well-placed to appreciate the performative aspects of the burgeoning fascist movements in Europe.

The Arrogant History of White Ben is set twenty years on, at the end of 'the disastrous war of the 1950s',[5] a period which ominously resembles the 1920s and 1930s. Many men have been killed in the war, bands of the unemployed tramp the country. There is a sense of chronic unrest and the time is ripe for revolution. In Dane's fantasy logic the dictator is null and initially inanimate, brought to life only through the agency and transference of others: her White Ben starts as a scarecrow on a hillock of couch-grass.[6] He is dressed in white by the old gardener because white is supposed to be the best colour for scaring crows – crows being, of course, black. The woman of the house gives the gardener the clothes of dead men: her brother's surplice, her husband's white surgeon's operating coat, an old-fashioned pale grey top hat. In these dead men's clothes Dane's about-to-be dictator is literally constructed out of the trappings of male authority. The clothes make the man: 'He had been garmented with religion, diplomacy, the art of war, the art of healing'.[7] White Ben is a 'man of straw', to use Dane's phrase, and his clothes are a composite of the different institutions of patriarchy. But being only their clothes, he acts as a palpable illustration of Virginia Woolf's suggestion in Orlando that 'it is clothes that wear us and not we them; we may make them take the mould of arm or breast, but they mould our hearts, our brains, our tongues to their liking'.[8] Our clothes wear us: Dane demonstrates this neatly in her fantasy of the dictator who is only clothes.

White Ben's clothes not only wear him, they speak him. 'Men's memories were buttoned about him, ... every garment he wore had to have its say.' Ben absorbs and gives back a repertoire of clichés and stock phrases, the scripts of his clothes. His thinking is also constructed by what he sees around him (for instance the sign 'Trespassers will be Prosecuted') and by the voices of the dead in the village churchyard, with their grudges against foreign invaders going back to the Vikings and Normans. Most of all, White Ben naturally nurses his own particular grudge against crows. Get rid of the crows: this is Ben's great slogan, his rallying cry, his mission of hatred and persecution. Of course he means it literally, as a scarecrow would, but his followers immediately translate his slogan into allegory. 'By "crows" you mean the exploiters, the destructive, the hangers-on, the war-mongers, the middle-men, don't you? All the birds of prey. Oh yes, yes, I know exactly what you mean.'[9]

Dane's preparation for writing her dystopia included reading Hitler's autobiographical *Mein Kampf*,[10] which was to give her the insights she needed into the power and workings of propaganda and demagoguery. As Hitler's biographer, Alan Bullock, comments, 'the pages in *Mein Kampf* in which he discusses the techniques of mass propaganda and political leadership stand out in brilliant contrast to the turgid attempts to explain his entirely unoriginal political ideas.'[11] *Mein Kampf* shows Hitler's grasp of how propaganda must work by being 'addressed always and exclusively to the masses', and by taking the psychology of the masses into account. According to Hitler,

> The receptivity of the great masses is very limited, their intelligence is small, but their power of forgetting is enormous. In consequence of these facts, all effective propaganda must be limited to a very few points and must harp on these in slogans until the last member of the public understands what you want him to understand by your slogan. As soon as you sacrifice this slogan and try to be many-sided, the effect will piddle away, for the crowd can neither digest nor retain the material offered. In this way the result is weakened and in the end entirely cancelled out.[12]

Dane dramatises Hitler's doctrine of the single slogan in her turnip-faced demagogue with his single target. For Hitler the Jews, for White Ben the crows. The propaganda weapon of colour coding falls easily into Dane's lap. Black is crow colour so White Ben wears only white. Soon all his followers do; people who show hints of black are beaten up and hounded off the street. Crows or suspected crows are thrown off buildings, witch-hunts are orchestrated, 'rook-eries' (large houses belonging to crows) burnt down. The country is infected by crow fever. The definition of a crow is, one of Ben's subordinates explains, 'enlarged':

> At first we limited it to those of alien blood or descent within three generations, to those of no known occupation, and to those whose income was derived from usury or slum rents. But it has recently been decided that any man or woman under forty-five who has been proved to live on the earnings of any other person save her husband is to be regarded as a bird of prey.[13]

Crows and suspect crows are denied exit visas, rounded up in concentration camps in Richmond Park and killed. The parallels and prophecies are clear: this book was written in the aftermath of Munich, with all the foreboding of that period.

Dane's analysis also accurately reproduces the role of women in the fascist movements of the time. The scarecrow is brought to life by a little girl, and throughout the novel women serve as the handmaids of male dictatorship. 'I like to look up at people', says the woman who first seizes on Ben's potential. As we now know, women were well represented in the membership of German and British fascist parties; and Dane's brisk Lady Pont, who has 'never been so strongly drawn to any creature',[14] could stand in for some of the aristocratic ex-suffragettes active in British fascism between the wars.[15] In both Dane's and Hitler's gender analysis women or the feminine predominate in the relation between a demagogue and his audience. Dane's women display a fatal propensity for hero worship, being 'the inflammable element in any crowd'. But while she characterises the relation between the demagogue and the crowd in terms Hitler would recognise − 'they loved each other'[16] − she does not see the emotionality of the crowd in feminine terms, as Hitler had: 'The people in their overwhelming majority are so feminine by nature and attitude that sober reasoning determines their thoughts and actions far less than emotion and feeling.'[17] Dane prefers to explain women's devotion as driven by economic neces-sity: 'The women had lost their patriotism when they lost their men and homes' and had to fall back upon gleaning.[18]

With her charismatic dictator and his colour-coded clothing, and her presentation of politics in action, Dane draws her readers' attention to what she sees as the three related and determining factors of clothes, uniforms and performance. In Dane's analysis the dictator's exploitation of these properties helped to define and explain the success of European fascist movements in the late 1930s, and here her analysis has much in common with Virginia Woolf's. Clothes dominate *Three Guineas*, Woolf's elegant, savage critique of militarism, nationalism and patriarchy. (The performance of a pageant is the mainspring of her last novel, *Between the Acts*, which she started in April 1938 and finished at the end of November 1940.) In *Three Guineas*, as in *The Arrogant History of White Ben*, male clothing becomes trope and target, symbol and evidence for the prosecution. The three scrapbooks of sources, cuttings, quotations and pictures which Woolf compiled in the course of her composition show how central clothes were to her thinking about the book. Clemence Dane's man of straw, the scareman of clothes, is easily dismantled at the end of the novel by the little girl who made him – she wants the broomstick holding him together for her game of rounders – but Woolf's clothing is more resistant.

To start with, Woolf takes the line of the *faux-naïf*, the child who looks at the emperor's new clothes, or in this case the clothes of all the emperor's men. This is what Woolf calls looking 'sidelong from an upper window';[19] she needed to conceal her anger in this book, knowing how controversial it was going to be. 'If I say what I mean in 3 Guineas', she wrote in her diary in April 1937, 'I must expect considerable hostility. Yet I so slaver and silver my tongue that its sharpness takes considerable time to be felt.'[20] So the attack starts slyly, with the tweak of defamiliarisation. 'Your clothes', she observes, 'make us gape with astonishment. How many, how splendid, how extremely ornate they are – the clothes worn by the educated man in his public capacity! Now you dress in violet; a jewelled crucifix swings on your breast; now your shoulders are covered with lace; now furred with ermine'.[21] She illustrates her comedy with photographs of pompous-looking old men in wigs and gold braid – and not any old men. She has selected but not identified the most prominent men in the establishment of her day:

> The general with his dress uniform and honours was the hero of Mafeking and the founder of the Boy Scouts, the academic profession was headed by a former prime minister in his capacity as Chancellor of Cambridge University, the judge was the Lord Chancellor, and the cleric was the current Archbishop of Canterbury.[22]

She makes us laugh with her, and then she waits until the great closing passage of the book. Here she turns her attention to the photograph of a man in military uniform. 'His hand is upon a sword ... his body which is braced in an unnatural position, is tightly cased in uniform ... And behind him lie ruined houses and dead bodies – men, women and children'.[23] Woolf is looking at a photograph from the Spanish Civil War; her three scrapbooks come to a logical and tragic end with cuttings detailing the bombing of Madrid. She argues that the tyrant in uniform is a 'human figure', with whom we as fellow human beings are 'inseparably connected'. Not just connected, Woolf insists. 'We cannot dissociate ourselves from that figure' in the photograph but indeed 'are ourselves that figure'. This is the step of genius, which Dane does not take, the step which connects not just the blinkered and chauvinist ideology of Woolf's bedecked patriarchs, but our own straitjacketed thinking with that of the tightly uniformed dictator.

Woolf's logic is pessimistic, but less so than some of her contemporaries. Her analogic argument links clothes and education, the British education system which, in her analysis, excels at instilling militaristic values. Clothes and education are for Woolf two straitjackets, both of them removable. Clothes can be taken off, and the centuries of tradition and education that are leading us towards war can be brought to an end. Other writers in the 1930s saw aggression as less easy to discard, because they saw it as a fundamental element of the human psyche. The psychoanalyst Joan Riviere, for example, argued in 1937 that we need an external enemy as a 'conduit for aggression and hate'; aggression was, for Riviere, in us and inescapable.[24] Woolf, by contrast, characterises militarism and aggression as taught, learned behaviour. She therefore urges women to create a Society of Outsiders, to reject all the 'medals, ribbons, badges, hoods, gowns', clothes which constrict, stereotype and destroy. We must, says Woolf, 'refuse all such distinctions and all such uniforms for ourselves'.[25] In her scrapbooks she had monitored the ways in which women were being mobilised by fascist movements in Europe. A cutting from the Sunday Times dating from 1936 begins: 'Praise for Women, Their Part in the "Nazi Triumph". Herr Hitler praised the women's part in enabling the Nazi movement to triumph when he addressed the Nazi Women's League.'[26] Woolf seems to have been particularly incensed by the subservice of women to the pomp of male power, as we can see from her lengthy account of a service at St Paul's Cathedral in March 1937. Among the congregation she notes 'old woman in tweed coat with spectacle case sticking out of her pocket. Horrible expression of servility; superstition in its most visible form. A beaten dog crouching under its masters whip. Crying for comfort, for some emotional gratification. She crossed herself. Also laid her finger on her lips. Like a drug fiend.' Typing even more erratically than usual, she concludes her long description of the sermon and procession: 'Mere fulsome and filthy playacting feeble rhetoric.'[27]

Woolf pasted pictures of fascists into her scrapbook, and she would have had many to choose from in the British press in the 1930s. She juxtaposes a picture of Mussolini's son-in-law, the dashing 'Count Ciano in Flying Kit', with a newspaper cutting from 1935 headed 'Outspoken Essex Woman Arrested'. The woman had recommended a chocolate shop run by a Jew because she did not carry the brand in her own shop, and is quoted as saying 'The thorn of hatred has been driven deep enough into the people by the religious conflicts and it is high time that the men of today disappeared.'[28] With the third scrapbook the cuttings, pictures and quotations about uniforms increase, in pace with the tenor of the times. A Gaumont newsreel in 1938 refers to Germany as 'the land of uniforms', and they fill the papers and newsreels of the time. A young man in Woolf's 1937 novel *The Years* rejects the heady mix of uniform and performance which he sees all round him on his return from Africa: 'black shirts, green shirts, red shirts – always posing in the public eye; that's all poppycock'.[29]

Uniforms can bind in many ways. As Nathan Joseph observes, they 'exert control over their wearers and signal commitment'.[30] They can bind the wearer to duty and honour: this is the *Ehrenkleid* or garment of honour, token of Hitler's promise to return honour to the German labourer. Observing the popularity of uniform in Nazi Germany in 1937, Alfred Vagts, writing at the same time as Dane, commented: 'The assumption of uniforms by fascists made use of the widespread longing for distinction; to the homeless and jobless, and those who saw the future as dark and inglorious, the resumption of khaki and medals seemed like admission to a band of heroes and a splendid past.'[31] J. C. Flugel's classic *Psychology of Clothes*, which was published by the Woolfs' Hogarth Press in 1930, differentiated character types in terms of their attitudes to clothes. He identified:

The duty type in which certain features of costume (for the most part either those actually associated with uniforms or other working clothes, or those that are distinguished by a certain stiffness, tightness or severity of line) have become symbols or work and duty ... outward and visible signs of a strict and strongly developed Super-Ego or moral principle.

Flugel closely associated conventional stiff men's clothing with repression and inhibition; in his gendered analysis men were too trapped in 'fixedness', and women too addicted to 'modishness'.[32] For some girls and women, however, the desire for uniform could take priority over fashion, as Katrin Fitzherbert recalls when looking back to her childhood years in Nazi Germany. She was born in 1936, and both her mother and her grandmother were English. This seems to have made her all the keener to enrol:

I loved all the Nazi paraphernalia, and though still several years too young, longed to join the BDM, Bund Deutsche Madchen, the girls' Hitlerjugend equivalent. The minute I was six, the youngest age possible, I joined the Kindergruppe. We had a sort of semi, better-than-nothing uniform: a white blouse, navy skirt with shoulder straps and a beautiful stainless steel swastika badge to pin onto the crosspiece in front.[33]

Uniform for the young Katrin signified 'belonging', something particularly desirable for a young girl of dubiously mixed parentage. And 'Belonging' is, indeed, the title she gives to the chapter covering this episode in her life.

Fascists always wore uniforms, but not always black, as John Harvey points out in his stimulating book *Men in Black*: 'In Spain, the Falangists wore blue shirts (theirs was the "Era Azul", the Azure Age), Hitler's SA in Germany wore brown (the party having inherited a large consignment of ex-army shirts).'[34] However, in 1932, Hitler's elite Storm Troops, the newly formed SS, 'now run by Himmler and expanded in numbers from hundreds to tens of thousands, adopted the famous all-black uniform ... Himmler remarked, chillingly enough, "I know there are some people who get ill when they see the black tunic. We understand that and do not expect to be loved by too many people."'[35] In that same year, 1932, Oswald Mosley was designing a uniform for his British Union of Fascists. He also chose the all-black look, and told would-be followers what the clothes signified: 'If you should join us, we will promise you this:

when you have put on the Black Shirt, you will become a Knight
of Fascism, of a political and spiritual Order. You will be born anew.
The Black Shirt is the emblem of new faith that has come to our
land.'[36] Mosley said that the uniform would break down class barriers, but his own black shirt was made of silk – 'Savile Row Fascism'
according to the Evening Standard in 1933, while Trotsky dismissed
him as 'the perfumed popinjay of scented boudoirs'.[37] The uniform
was banned in a Public Order Act of 1936; nevertheless Mosley had
shown that he well understood some of its uses.

> Below the senior echelons, the full uniform could be worn only by
> those willing to give the movement two nights a week. Those mak-
> ing a lesser contribution wore differing fractions of it – but could
> obtain additional garments, by, for instance, selling more copies of
> *The Blackshirt*.[38]

Mosley's Blackshirts: people as clothes – this is the point Clemence
Dane is making in her novel with her clothes-only man of straw.
Her white supremacists could be seen to reverse the fascist black,
although of course white could also be a racist colour, in the robes
of the Ku Klux Klan. Her novel also illustrates Hannah Arendt's dic-
tum that if uniform binds and controls, it also releases: 'Somehow
these uniforms eased considerably the consciences of the murder-
ers.'[39] White Ben mouths the inflated bombast of Mosley, Mussolini
and Hitler; his white-clad followers gladly surrender themselves to
'mob logic', to the simple oppression of 'Strength is in the right',
to violence, looting, and an orgy of hatred.[40]

Clothes and uniform, the stock-in-trade of performance, are
central to the theatre of fascism, and Dane's insight into the dressing rooms of 1930s' fascism is confirmed by subsequent historians.
It was no accident that the birthplace of twentieth-century fascism
was in the land of opera. Fascist black made its first appearance on
the glamorous backs of the Arditi, a volunteer force of elite shock
troops in the Italian Army during the Great War. This is the black
of the courageous warrior boldly facing and even announcing his
own death; John Harvey calls it 'kamikaze black'.[41] In the early
years of Italian Fascism many idealists and artists were attracted
to the cause: Puccini, Toscanini, D'Annunzio and Marinetti. The
Futurists saw in the Arditi the Man of the Future, and Marinetti
explained the significance of clothes to the new movement: 'one
thinks and acts according to how one dresses'. In his 1914 'Manifesto

of Anti-Neutral Clothing' Marinetti advocated bright and 'cheerfully bellicose clothing'.[42] But by the late 1930s Italy was under the influence of Achille Starace, the secretary of the Fascist Party, who was determined to mould Italians into obedient conformists, and who had a passion for uniforms and medals. By his decree the national tennis team were supposed to wear black shirts and refuse to shake hands. The raised arm Roman Salute was an Italian contribution to fascism. German fascists stole the Roman Salute for themselves, and the Italians returned the compliment by stealing the goose-step.[43]

These dramatic gestures are the body language of fascism: the body as well as the clothes must behave in an ostentatiously uniform manner. As early as 1929, according to Hannah Arendt, Hitler recognised what he saw as the '"great thing" of the movement in the fact that sixty thousand men "have outwardly become almost a unit, that actually these members are uniform not only in ideas, but that even the facial expression is almost the same. Look at these laughing eyes, this fanatical enthusiasm and you will discover ... how a hundred thousand men in a unit become a single type".'[44] The body thus performs totalitarianism, is totalitarianism on display, and is itself subsumed into a wider performance. The historian Norbert Frei has remarked on the way in which the Third Reich transformed the whole of Germany into a vast theatre, staging itself. This was done quite literally and deliberately in countless parades and pageants. The Berlin Spectacle in the summer of 1937, for instance, was entitled 'Two Thousand Years of German Culture', a huge procession with elaborate floats and costumes. [45]

The master designer of the theatre of fascism was Hitler's architect, Albert Speer. The need to put power on display was the mother of his stunning inventions. In his autobiography he recalls livening up a parade of minor party functionaries – middle-aged men with paunches who could not march in time – through the 'saving idea' of making them march up in darkness, flanked by hundreds of the new anti-aircraft searchlights blazing straight up into the sky, a 'cathedral of ice' according to the watching British Ambassador Nevile Henderson. Speer had a keen eye for what he called 'scenic drama': 'I arranged for veritable orgies of flags in the narrow streets of Goslar and Nuremberg, with banners stretched from house to house, so that the sky was almost blotted out.'[46] His designs for the Nuremberg rallies were filmed to great effect by

Leni Riefenstahl, another creative artist who imaginatively grasped the visual drama of politics.

The starring role in the theatre of fascism is, of course, played by the dictator himself. Both Hitler and Mussolini were keen theatre-goers in their youth (both favoured opera), and both have been described by their biographers as great actors.[47] A chilling sequence of photographs in John Keegan's *The Mask of Command* shows Hitler rehearsing his speeches.[48] They were taken by his private photographer so that Hitler could work on his oratorical technique as he deliberately controls the apparently uncontrollable frenzy. Unity Mitford was particularly impressed by Hitler's talent as an imitator:

> She claimed that if he were not the Führer of Germany, he would make a hundred thousand dollars a year on the vaudeville stage. He often did imitations of his colleagues – Goering, Goebbels and Himmler – but, best of all, he liked to imitate Mussolini. This always provoked roars of laughter. 'And sometimes,' added Unity, 'he even imitates himself'.[49]

Both Hitler and Mussolini became adept at the language and drama of clothes. When they first met, in 1934, they were both in civilian clothes, Hitler in yellow mackintosh and striped trousers, awkwardly holding a grey felt hat. Mussolini had also arrived in civilian clothes but quickly changed into a splendid uniform complete with dagger, high black boots and spurs. Power dressing indeed. When Mussolini was invited to Germany he only accepted on condition that he would not have to bring formal clothes with him. He knew he looked insignificant in civilian clothes, and had a lavish uniform designed for the occasion.[50] On the other side of the battlefield dressing down was the order of the day. General Douglas MacArthur wore flamboyant uniforms during the first part of the war until he was informed of the modest dress of General Eisenhower, whereupon MacArthur also adopted a simple uniform.[51]

The distinction that the clothes historian Anne Hollander draws between theatrical and dramatic costume illuminates some of the work done by uniform:

> Essentially, a theatrical costume is an expansion of the performer's own self, whereas a dramatic costume transforms him completely into a character. The dramatic costume may consist of a mere scarf, hat, or a few patches of make-up, or it can be a completely masked disguise,

like the Greek tragic costume; but while the actor wears it he must be acting the part it indicates or the costume will be meaningless or ridiculous. His real self will be mocked by it, and vice versa. In contrast, the theatrical costume does not transform the actor into his character but, rather, it amplifies him and shows him as something else without eliminating him; it may also quite simply embellish him and focus visual attention on him, and have no symbolic significance.[52]

She cites Charles I and Louis XIV as wearers of theatrical costume in masques and ballets, clearly recognisable as themselves, and refers to Cher and Mick Jagger dressed for stardom. The point is that the person of the star (king, leader, singer) must be recognisable, their self must be enhanced and amplified by what they wear, whereas the wearer of the dramatic costume takes on the meaning of that costume and acts the part it suggests. The military dictator must wear military uniform, but in ways which distinguish him from his followers, as we can see from contemporary photographs. John Harvey's comments on a photograph of Hitler and Himmler inspecting an SS guard of honour are apposite:

> Hitler, as Führer, wears not the black uniform of his elite guard, but the brown uniform of his SA and of the whole Nazi movement: he is the leader of all of them, and this difference in colour between him and Himmler does then give Himmler's black the aspect of the black worn earlier by king's ministers, whether or not the prince wore black (as for instance Thomas Cromwell wore black, though Henry VIII did not). That is, the black of the man devoted to being an implement of the will of his leader: and to being, vested with the leader's authority, an especially ruthless executant of that will on those under this command and surveillance.[53]

Clemence Dane's dictator knows how to exploit the principles of theatrical dress and behaviour. As a scarecrow he 'had always stood alone, elevated above weeds, expecting to hold the eye', and he subsequently uses his odd, inhuman physical presence to powerful effect. Dressed and coached by his own theatrically trained angel of darkness, the appropriately named actress Angela Darkness, White Ben is often described as an actor. Characters in the book liken his effects to Henry Irving's; they fall for his glamour, his spellbinding powers. This is the charismatic aspect of the mass leader, and Dane attributes White Ben's ascendancy to the alchemy of the mass meeting. The crowd are 'in the grip of religion';[54] grown men weep. Those under his spell talk about the effect of his eyes, much as they did about Hitler's. And Dane's manifestation of the demagogue as performance fittingly enjoys an afterlife, once he himself has disappeared from the scene, as a secondary spectacle in popular plays and films.

Dane's prescient appreciation of the theatre of fascism may have been assisted by the interpenetration of theatre and reality in her own life. Born Winfred Ashton, she had an early career as an actress under the stage name of Diane Cortis. She started writing under the pseudonym Clemence Dane, the name a miniature performance in itself with its reminders of both church and nursery rhyme. A flamboyant figure, she had what her obituary called 'an abiding interest in the theatre and theatrical history',[55] but for her theatre was not something which happened only on the other side of the footlights. She lived in the heart of Covent Garden, where she said, life was one big theatre and she had the best seat in it. What particularly fascinated her was theatre as process; the best chapters in her reminiscences are the two about rehearsals.[56] From her first novel, *Regiment of Women* (1917), Dane showed an interest in the workings of charisma. In her view it was a two-edged sword, something which could work for good as well as evil. In a war a nation needs strong leaders, and this became the hallmark of Dane's wartime output. She wrote plays about Queen Elizabeth and Nelson, and a series of radio plays called *The Saviours* dramatising legends of heroes such as Arthur, Alfred and Robin Hood, who help their people in times of need. During the blitz her poem 'Trafalgar Day' was a bestseller, and in 1942 her pageant *Cathedral Steps* was performed at St Paul's and later at Coventry, a huge and successful affair.[57] It involved a large choir, an orchestra conducted by Sir Henry Wood, and stars such as Edith Evans and Lesley Howard. This was an exuberant pageant of virtue to counter the dark pageants of Nazi Germany.

In the last year of the war Dane wrote the script and screenplay for Alexander Korda's film *Perfect Strangers*.[58] What she understood about the uses of uniform in wartime seems to have struck a chord with many cinema-goers. In the film a dowdy married couple get out of their civvies and into uniform to fight the war; in the process they become exciting and sexually attractive. This is uniform as glamour and allure, and many women remember the film affectionately as one of their favourites from the time. Clemence Dane won an Oscar for 'Best Original Story'.

Notes

1   L. Woolf, *The Journey Not the Arrival Matters, An Autobiography of the Years* 1939 to 1969 (London: Hogarth Press, 1973), p. 10.

2   A. Einstein and S. Freud, *Why War?*, trans. Stuart Gilbert (Paris: International Institute of Intellectual Co-operation, League of Nations, 1933).

3   See, for example, M. Ulrich (ed.), *Man, Proud Man* (London: Hamish Hamilton, 1932).

4   See M. Whately, *Dorothy Evans and the Six Point Group* (London: Six Point Group, 1945).

5   C. Dane, *The Arrogant History of White Ben* (London: Heinemann, 1939), p. 1. The book was written between 1938 and 1939, and published in September 1939. It was the 'first choice' of 'Novels of the Week' in the *Times Literary Supplement* for 23 September 1939; the reviewer described it as 'a highly topical book, topical in the sense that it gives substance and shape to the premonitions and searchings of heart that have accompanied us on the road to the war in which we are now engaged'.

6   Talking scarecrows had been made popular three years earlier with the debut of Barbara Euphan Todd's *Worzel Gummidge; or The Scarecrow of Scatterbrook* (London: Burns & Oates, 1936).

7   Dane, *The Arrogant History*, p. 20.

8   V. Woolf, *Orlando* (Harmondsworth: Penguin, [1928] 1993), p. 132.

9   Dane, *The Arrogant History*, pp. 19, 76.

10 See C. Dane, Preface to *The Nelson Touch, An Anthology of Lord Nelson's Letters*, compiled by Clemence Dane (London: Heinemann, 1942).

11 A. Bullock 'Deception and Calculation', in A. Mitchell (ed.), *The Nazi Revolution: Hitler's Dictatorship and the German Nation* (Toronto, D. C. Heath, 1990), p. 46.

12 A. Hitler, *Mein Kampf*, with an Introduction by D. C. Watt, trans. R. Manheim (London: Hutchinson, 1969), pp. 163, 165.

13 Dane, *The Arrogant History*, p. p. 362.

14 Dane, *The Arrogant History*, pp. 33, 315.

15 See R. Thurlow, *Fascism in Britain, A History* 1918–1985 (Oxford: Blackwell, 1987), p. 70; M. Durham, *Women and Fascism* (London: Routledge, 1998), pp. 20, 46–69.

16 Dane, *The Arrogant History*, pp. 246, 324.

17 Hitler, p. 167.

18 Dane, *The Arrogant History*, p. 246.

19 V. Woolf, *Three Guineas* (London: Hogarth Press, [1938] 1986), p. 71.

20 V. Woolf, *Diary, Volume V:* 1936–1941, ed. A. O. Bell (London: Hogarth Press, 1984), 30 April 1937, p. 84.

21 Woolf, *Three Guineas*, p. 23.

22 Introduction to the Shakespeare Head Edition of V. Woolf, *Three Guineas* ed. Naomi Black (Oxford: Blackwell, 2001), p. lxii.

23 Woolf, *Three Guineas*, p. 162.

24 J. Riviere and M. Klein, *Love, Hate and Reparation* (London: Hogarth Press and the Institute of Psycho-Analysis, 1937), quoted in D. Pick, *War Machine: The Rationalisation of Slaughter in the Modern Age* (New Haven: Yale University Press, 1993), p. 231.

25 Woolf, *Three Guineas*, p. 26.

26 Monk's House Papers/*Three Guineas* Scrapbook, University of Sussex, Second Scrapbook.

27 Second Scrapbook.

28 Second Scrapbook.

29 V. Woolf, *The Years* (London: Hogarth Press, 1937), p. 329.

30 N. Joseph, Uniforms and Nonuniforms, Communication through Clothing (New York: Greenwood Press, 1986), p. 66.

31 A. Vagts, A History of Militarism, Romance and Realities of a Profession (London: George Allen & Unwin, 1937), p. 481.

32 J. C. Flugel, The Psychology of Clothes (London: Hogarth Press, 1930), pp. 97, 213.

33 K. FitzHerbert, True to Both My Selves: A Family Memoir of Germany and England in Two World Wars (London: Virago, 1997), p. 58.

34 J. Harvey, Men in Black (London: Reaktion Books, 1995), p. 233.

35 Harvey, p. 234.

36 The Blackshirt, 4 May 1934, quoted in Harvey, p. 240.

37 R. Skidelsky, Oswald Mosley (London: Macmillan, 1975), pp. 293–5; B. Pimlott, 'A Very British Fascist', The Guardian, 12 February 1998.

38 Harvey, p. 241.

39 Hannah Arendt, The Origins of Totalitarianism (London: Andre Deutsch, [1951] 1986), p. 370.

40 Dane, The Arrogant History, pp. 331, 350.

41 Harvey, p. 232.

42 G. Berghaus, Futurism and Politics, Between Anarchist Rebellion and Fascist Reaction, 1909–1944 (Providence and Oxford: Berghahn Books, 1996), p. 76.

43 C. Hibbert, Benito Mussolini, The Rise and Fall of Il Duce (Harmondsworth: Penguin, [1962] 1965), pp. 81–2.

44 Arendt, p 418.

45 N. Frei, National Socialist Rule in Germany: The Führer State 1933–45, trans. S. B. Steyne (Oxford: Blackwell, 1993), pp. 83, 96.

46 A. Speer, Inside the Third Reich, Memoirs, trans. R. and C. Winston (London: Macmillan, 1970), pp. 58–9.

47 See Bullock, p. 51; L. Fermi, Mussolini (Chicago: Phoenix Books, [1961] 1974), p. 73.

48 J. Keegan, The Mask of Command (London: Jonathan Cape, 1987), illustrations between pp. 260–1.

49 V. Cowles, Looking for Trouble (London: Hamish Hamilton, 1941), p. 159.

50 See Hibbert, pp. 99, 106.

51 Nathan Joseph offers this as an example of the 'abstract rubric of showmanship which includes both over and understatements'. Uniforms and Nonuniforms, p. 27.

52 A. Hollander, Seeing through Clothes (Berkeley: University of California Press, [1978] 1993), p. 250.

53 Harvey, pp. 234–6.

54 Dane, The Arrogant History, pp. 174, 343.

55 The Times, Obituary, 29 March 1965.

56 C. Dane, London Has a Garden (London: Michael Joseph, 1964), pp. 120 ff. Noel Coward was a good friend and appreciated her hospitality. His autobiography of his wartime years is dedicated to Dane, whom he describes as 'large in every way'; Future Indefinite (London: Heinemann, 1954), pp. 90–1, and photograph facing p. 312.

57 See D. W. Smithers, 'Therefore, imagine...' The Works of Clemence Dane (Tunbridge Wells: Dragonfly Press, 1988), pp. 15, 49.

58 For an extended discussion of the film, see A. Lant, Blackout (Princeton, NJ: Princeton University Press, 1991), pp. 117–27.

6

Women and the battle of the Atlantic 1939–45: contemporary texts, propaganda, and life writing

G. H. Bennett

The purpose of this chapter is to demonstrate the extent of women's involvement in a theatre of the Second World War, the Battle of the Atlantic, which in the popular memory is an entirely masculine affair. It also aims to show the diversity of contemporary and life-writing texts produced for women, about women and by women in relation to their involvement in this particular theatre. The simplest text is often the most revealing, and the following list of female nurses killed when the British merchant vessel SS *Khedive Ismail* was sunk in February 1944 tells the reader a very great deal. It serves as a reminder that even though the war at sea was a predominantly male enterprise, several hundred women were killed as a result of naval action between 1939 and 1945. An even larger number survived shipwreck and less successful enemy attacks against British merchant vessels.

Quite apart from those women who served as crew or sailed as passengers on merchant vessels during the war, through family ties and the home front every women was ultimately involved with the 'Battle of the Atlantic'. That term is itself problematic, a label given to a campaign by Churchill and others who had seen the Battle for France and the Battle of Britain before the British war effort became dependent on her sea lines of communication in a Battle of the Atlantic. In reality the Battle of the Atlantic spread across every ocean. A ship that was in the Indian Ocean one week could be in the Atlantic the next. The *Khedive Ismail* was in the Indian Ocean when she was torpedoed and sank within forty seconds. She was sunk not

Gender and warfare

Casualty List for SS *Khedive Ismail*, sunk 12 February 1944
East African Military Nursing Service

Airey Freda	Sister/*260226	Arnott Constance	Sister/Edcc/359
Atkin Joyce Kathleen	Sister/*270574	Barwell G.M.	Sister/Edcc/360
Bateman Edith Mary	Sister/*257776	Beecher Grace	Sister/Edcc/359
Brown Amy	Sister/*274633	Burrows Isabella	Sister/*266663
Cashmore Patricia	Sister/Edcc/371	Clark-Wilson J.M.	Sister/Edcc/362
Dalgarno Elsie Alice	Sister/*208105	Dann Elizabeth D.	Sister/*250095
Davies Margaret E.	Sister/*238669	Dervan Gertrude	Sister/*266750
Dewar Alice W.	Sister/*270637	Dowling Beatrice O.	Sister/*266662
Dryden Clara Martha	Sister/——	Farrelly Mary	Sister/*274735
Fitzgerald Catherine	Sister/*274636	Harvey Grace W.	Sister/*274658
Hastings Valerie F.	Sister/*263805	Humphrey Muriel C.	Sister/*274079
Ievers Eileen Mary E.	Matron/*206235	Jarman Marie	Sister/*274755
Johnston Maud F.	Sister/*274737	Kells Maggie Jane	Sister/*274727
Kells Winifred E.	Sister/*274733	Leckey Muriel Emily	Sister/*208615
Leech Barbara E.	Sister/*266730	Littleton Mary J.	Sister/*236448
Maclaren Jean Noel	Sister/*238130	Mcmillan Marion L.	Sister/*266937
Moore Isabella	Sister/*215107	Morgan Sarah	Sister/*274164
Nuttall Phyllis	Sister/*274639	Pirie Barbara	Sister/*274846
Richardson Sybil G.	Sister/*206418	Robertson Helen M.	Sister/*274402
Senior Doris Ena	Sister/*260544	Smith Marjorie	Sister/*260546
Spence Isobel	Sister/*274753	Taylor Katherine M.	Sister/*266464
Thomas Jane Mair G.	Sister/*270493	Urquhart Mary A.	Sister/*274611
Walker Kathleen H.	Sister/*266754	Warwick Roberta	Sister/*266463
Whitaker Mafalda S.	Sister/*274344	White Gwendoline M.	Sister/*274074
Willis Annie Amelia	Sister/*209648	Wolseley-Lewis A.	Sister/Eddc/363
Young Eleanor Jane	Sister/*274629		

* denotes Queen Alexandra's Imperial Military Nursing Service.

by a German U-boat, the grey wolf of the Battle of the Atlantic, but by a Japanese submarine. If 'Battle of the Atlantic' represented the failure of language to convey the full enormity and horror of the war against British merchant shipping, then it would not be the last. This chapter will also show how concerns about national morale, a desire to secure the fullest level of female involvement in the war effort, and a willingness to utilise existing stereotypes about gender led to the production of strikingly similar narratives to explain the involvement of women in the war at sea. It will argue that the tendency in narratives to represent the experience of women survivors of shipwreck as being virtually the same as men led to a lack of medical and psychological understanding about the survival problems faced by women.

On 1 October 1941 *Lloyd's List and Shipping Gazette* announced the award of an MBE and Lloyds War Medal to Miss Victoria Alexandrina Drummond, Second Engineer on the motor vessel *Bonita*:

> When 400 miles from land [on 25 August 1940] the ship was attacked for 35 minutes by an enemy aircraft, but skilful handling saved her from many hits. Miss Drummond went below and took charge when the alarm sounded. She was flung against the levers and nearly stunned when the first bombs exploded. When everything had been done to increase speed, she gave orders for the engine-room and stokehold staffs to leave. Scalding steam ran out from a joint in the main injection pipe over her head, but she tended this essential pipe as each salvo exploded, easing down when the sound of the enemy told her that bombs were likely to fall, and then increasing steam. Her devotion to duty saved the ship from more serious damage, and her disregard of danger inspired all on board.[1]

Beyond the reference to Drummond as 'Miss' there was little to differentiate her story, and her gallantry, from that of hundreds of other ships' engineers whose vessels came under enemy attack between 1939 and 1945. Her medal citation appeared alongside others and no special attention was drawn to it. However, Drummond's case was special, so much so that when the ship eventually reached Norfolk Virginia she was fêted in the American press and locals quickly raised £500 to purchase the Victoria Drummond mobile canteen for use in London during the ongoing blitz. Drummond was special because she was the only female engineer in the merchant navy, and one of a small number of women serving as crew on British merchant ships during wartime. This was an aspect of the Battle of the Atlantic that the majority of the British public did not appreciate. Drummond became the first woman to receive a Lloyd's medal for bravery. It was perhaps unsurprising that, with the need to involve women fully in every aspect of the war effort, propaganda writers should seize on the case of Drummond. In Leonard R. Gribble's *Heroes of the Merchant Navy*, published in 1944, alongside chapters stirringly entitled 'The Convoys Strike Back', 'Across the

Arctic Circle' and 'Through E. Boat Alley', was a chapter headed 'Women of the Red Duster'.[2] 'War is no longer a masculine prerogative' it asserted before encouraging every woman to involve herself in the war effort whether it be through supporting war production, serving in the forces or by some other means. The cases of Victoria Drummond and other women who served in the merchant navy were used as a means to demonstrate that even in the most unfamiliar fields women were making a contribution to winning the war. A woman serving in the merchant navy was atypical, but in Gribble's book that atypicality was used to show the extent to which women could do 'a man's job'.

Drummond's experiences formed the centrepiece of the chapter, but her story threatened to prove problematic. A ship's engine room, with its dirt, grease, steam and heat, was about as masculine an environment as it was possible to imagine in 1944. Engineers were expected to have strength as well as considerable technical ability to maintain the engines. The stokers, greasers and other seamen they worked alongside were not renowned for the strength of the feminine side of their characters, and the ports which tramp steamers like the *Bosnia* frequented were less than salubrious. Therefore Gribble constructed Drummond's narrative in a way designed to emphasise that she was as feminine as any other woman, and even offered the reader a photograph of her as final proof. To explain her interest in engineering it was mentioned that, although she had been born in London, her parents were Scottish, to suggest that her bloodline went back to James Watt, the inventor of the steam engine. But her technical skills were camouflaged beneath her femininity. Gribble was at pains to reveal that when asked about her skill with engines she meekly replied: 'I just talk to them nicely … You can coax or lead engines – but you mustn't ever drive them.'[3] He echoed this phrase in his description of the action in which Drummond won her award. Borrowing from the description of the action by another member of the crew, the images that he created were emotional and heroic, showing her capabilities and her feminine delicacy:

> In ten minutes she had 'talked' to those engines to such good purpose that our miserable speed of nine knots had risen to twelve and a half. As a result of the bombing our pipes were fractured, electric wires parted, and tubes were broken. The main engine stop-valve started a joint, and scalding steam whizzed past her head. With anyone less skilled down there that pipe must have burst under the extra pres-

sure, but she nursed it through each explosion ... I saw her once when I looked down the skylight to shout a few words of cheer to her. She was standing on the control platform, surrounded by spent machine-gun bullets, which had fallen through the skylight, one hand stretched straight above her head, holding down the throttle control as if trying by her touch to urge another pound of steam through the straining pipes. Her face as expressionless as the bulkhead behind her, was turned up to the sunlight, but she did not see me. From the top of her forehead down her face, completely closing one eye, trickled a wide black streak of fuel oil.[4]

Drummond was both feminine and angelic. She was also a competent woman in a 'man's job'. Attributing the description of the action to a male member of the crew established the respect of her shipmates for her. She was a paragon of feminine virtue and a role model for all other women who would be called to make sacrifices and work in strange jobs in unfamiliar surroundings. In propaganda terms the Victoria Drummond story was ideal. To it, during the course of the war, would be added the exploits of other female crew members. Their unadorned stories would appear in the pages of the press, using the same kind of language that was a feature of Drummond's and, indeed, all citations.

If the gallantry of Drummond and other women crew members was represented in ways designed to show that they were an equal part of the professional team that was the crew of a British merchant ship, then the same was not true in texts about women passengers. While the number of women serving as crew on British merchant ships was relatively small, a large number travelled on them as passengers. Again the casualty list for the *Khedive Ismail* is instructive. In addition to the 51 nurses who lost their lives, a further 8 fatalities served in the Women's Territorial Service and 17 in the Woman's Royal Naval Service. The final female fatality was a civilian passenger, Mrs Merrill, who died along with her five-month-old son. While the professional work of women crew members could be celebrated by the likes of Gribble, the primary focus in the texts on women passengers was their role as victims. This impulse to make women casualties of the Battle of the Atlantic was in uneasy juxtaposition to the image of heroines like Drummond, a woman at home in a man's world.

From the sinking of the 13,581 ton SS *Athenia* of the Donaldson Atlantic Line, on 3 September 1939, onwards, women passengers as victims was a rich topic for the press and the propagandists, just as it had been during the First World War. The 'murder' of innocent women passengers by German submariners elevated the moral righteousness of those who opposed Germany. Men were at pains to highlight their role in protecting the womenfolk, and contemporary diaries and other accounts went to great lengths to emphasise it. The law of the sea demanded the evacuation of women and children first, and male writers did their best to show themselves upholding it. The Chief Officer's report on the sinking of the *Athenia* gives a good example of this:

> On arrival aboard H.M.S. ELECTRA and on going through the list of survivors in my boat, I discovered that one woman was missing. Earlier in the day, she had fallen down a ladder and was suffering from concussion and I personally had taken her to the sick bay, unconscious ... I immediately went to the Captain of the Destroyer and informed him that there was a woman on board in the ATHENIA'S sick bay and asked to be put aboard at once. I was given a boat and we put off to the ATHENIA and went on board with the Bo'sun and the and one A.B. [able seaman] ... The Bo'sun and the A.B. immediately went to the sick bay. The door was burst open and the woman was found inside still unconscious ... We immediately got back into the boat and returned to H.M.S. ELECTRA with the woman. As soon as I got back on board the ATHENIA sank.[5]

Just as the Chief Officer was at pains to emphasise his own role in maintaining the custom of the sea, the German Admiralty was at pains to cover up its involvement in the attack which had cost 112 lives, including 69 women and 16 children. The press in the neutral nations were informed that German submarines were not involved in the sinking, and that the British had probably sunk their own vessel to create a 'new *Lusitania*'. The log of Oberleutnant Lemp's offending U-30 was doctored after a secret enquiry that revealed that Lemp's mis-identification of the vessel was responsible for an attack which was contrary to orders. Those orders, not to attack passenger vessels, were paraded like a holy text by the German Admiralty. However, this did not stop the press from treating the attack as an example of German barbarity. In particular they highlighted the presence of women from neutral America in the lists of survivors and casualties. The death of British women had propaganda value, but it was far behind the death of women from neutral nations in the Battle of the Atlantic.

The American newspaper the *Baltimore Evening Sun* took particular pains to interview and record the experiences of American women who had lived through the sinking:

> Mrs Dexter ... hated to talk of her experience. 'We felt just a jolt when the explosion came.. Oh it was terrible. I can't describe it.'
>
> 'We almost hit the submarine,' said Mary Katherine Underwood of Athens, Texas. 'We were in a boat with thirty-eight women and only three men.' ...
>
> Miss Caroline Stuart of Plainfield, N.J., said: 'I rowed for eight continuous hours. Look at these hands.' They were still covered with blisters.[6]

The pro-British *Baltimore Evening Sun* used the female victims of the *Athenia* to denounce the Nazi regime in the strongest terms:

> The passengers of the *Athenia* were non-combatants, trying to get away from the war ... A great many of the passengers were women and children, whom Herr Hitler said he did not want to fight. Americans will find the calm of their neutrality somewhat disrupted by three facts:
>
> 1. That a great many women and children were unnecessarily attacked.
> 2. That a considerable number of these were Americans.
> 3. That it took Herr Hitler less than three days to offer this latest example of his lack of respect for his own word.[7]

As victims of the Battle of the Atlantic, women had a particularly high value in the propaganda war. In the early part of the war British and American newspapers were very ready to feature stories involving women caught up in the war at sea, although by 1941 the need to maintain morale in Britain saw their decline, at least in the British press.

Those women who did survive the sinking of their ships often had to face the prospect of a long lifeboat passage and the embarrassment of the complete absence of privacy. In general women seem to have been able to cope with these privations. Some showed that they could quickly learn skills like rowing or steering the boat; some provided examples of leadership; and some by their example stiffened the resolve of male passengers. In a more traditional role, they often provided skilled and tender nursing for the sick and injured. There were many individual examples of women surviving long lifeboat passages with men dying around them in large numbers, such as Doris Hawkins, sunk on the *Laconia*; Margaret Gordon and Diana Jarman, both of whom were sunk on the *City of Cairo*; and Maria Ferguson, sunk on the *Avila Star*. However, in textual terms little remains with which to try and reconstruct the experiences of women facing long lifeboat journeys.

Again, the gallantry citations in *Lloyd's List and Shipping Gazette* provide only the merest glimpse of women's experiences. The *Avila Star* was torpedoed on 5 July 1942. Once in the boats a lengthy passage lay ahead:

> Miss Maria Ferguson behaved with conspicuous courage. Throughout the night she sat in the stern of a waterlogged boat and tended four badly injured men. At daylight she calmly dived overboard and swam to another boat which had arrived. She cheerfully endured the ordeals of the 20 days boat journey which followed, and her splendid example was an inspiration to the rest of her companions.[8]

Leonard Gribble included the story of Diana Jarman in his chapter on 'Women of the Red Duster'. The 21-year-old widow of a British officer killed in Singapore Jarman found herself, after the sinking of the *City of Cairo* on 6 November 1942, in lifeboat No. 1 containing fifty-four survivors, three of whom were women. She worked tirelessly to help everyone in the boat even as they died in large numbers. After thirty-six days in the boat, only she and two men remained. Again images were invoked which were angelic, patriotic and a little exploitative. She was feminine but also a hero. As one of the two male survivors told Gribble: 'I don't know much about Mrs Jarman ... She did not talk about herself, but I feel sure she came from London. She had been in India some years, and had been married only a few months. We called her Diana.'[9] As postwar accounts were to demonstrate, the two male survivors knew a great deal more about Jarman and remembered their experiences in the boat in rather less ethereal terms.[10] The image of her as a sole Florence Nightingale waiting on the needs of the dying in the boat would be corrected to that of a particularly determined leader working alongside the men on the boat. While Jarman may have taken a lead, the occupants of the lifeboat supported each other as a group. This was not, however, the image that Gribble wanted to advance. In his text Diana Jarman would appear as a mystery angel, or Greek Goddess, and to it he would add the patriotic. The

three survivors were eventually picked up by the German blockade
runner *Rhakotis*, only for Jarman to die on board. Gribble records:
'Gallant Mrs Jarman even won the admiration of her enemies. The
German's gave her a ceremonial funeral.'[11] The death of the gallant
Mrs Jarman could also be exploited in one further way. Not only
was she a patriotic embodiment of feminine virtue; she was also a
victim. As Gribble tells the reader *sotto voce* 'She had spent her life
out there in the drifting lifeboat.'[12] While Gribble's narrative of the
voyage and death of Diana Jarman conformed to 1940s notions of
how the feminine could be represented, striking also was his willingness to minimise the experience of the surviving men in the boat.
For them the horror continued after Jarman's death. The *Rhakotis* was
later sunk and they would experience a further boat journey before
one landed in Spain and the other was picked up by a German U-
boat. Gribble was content to record the sinking of the *Rhakotis* as a
reminder to his readers of the supremacy of the Royal Navy, but his
desire to promote the role of women in the Battle of the Atlantic
led him to largely ignore the men's experience in this case.

While male propagandists such as Gribble shaped their narrative
of women's survival experiences according to the need to depict
women as selfless, feminine patriots and role models for all British
women, the same was also true of female writers. Doris Hawkins
survived the sinking of the *Laconia* on 12 September 1942 and went
on to describe her experiences in *Atlantic Torpedo: The Record of 27 Days
in an Open Boat*, published in 1943.[13] At every turn of the narrative she minimises her gender. This is done to the extent that the
reader is left thinking that literary androgyny is a direct result of
the damage done to the personality of Doris Hawkins by the horror of what she witnessed. Hawkins was employed as a nurse to a
baby. Her description of the moment their lifeboat capsized and she
lost the baby is truly chilling in its detachment: 'Just as Sally was
passed over to me, the boat filled completely and capsized, flinging
us all into the water. I lost her. I did not hear her cry even then,
and I am sure that God took her immediately to Himself without
suffering. I never saw her again.'[14] Later Hawkins found herself in
another lifeboat; her narrative records how male survivors did all
they could for the women in the boat. She also records how she
and other survivors were taken on board a U-boat, before later
having to return to lifeboats: 'The Germans treated us with great
kindness and respect the whole time; they were really sorry for our

plight. One brought us eau-de-Cologne, another cold cream for our sunburn, which was really bad; others gave us lemons from their own lockers.'[15] Apart from recording the acts of kindness that she received because she was a woman, Hawkins did not play on her gender at any point, but continued to suppress it throughout her account. Some of the kindness – particularly being given masculine clothing by other survivors and the crew of the U-boat to clothe her semi-naked body – was symbolic of the psychological process apparently taking place to enable Hawkins to survive. She became both androgynous and detached from the horrors surrounding her. The foreword to her book gives her reason for producing an account of the sufferings she witnessed: '[To] spur on to yet greater efforts those in whose hands lies the production of those sea weapons which are the only answer to the Nazi unrestricted sinkings.' From the text there appears to be little of cathartic value to the writer in setting down her experiences. Her experiences are allowed to stand for themselves in their propaganda value, in contrast to the adorned accounts of Gribble and some newspaper accounts of sinkings involving women.

Few women survivors set down their experiences at any length like Doris Hawkins, and this had very practical significance during the war. From 1939 to 1945 the Casualty Section of the Admiralty Trade Division interviewed the senior surviving crew member from the vast majority of British vessels lost at sea due to war causes. The interview reports provide a fascinating insight into the problems of surviving shipwreck and often protracted boat journeys. However, all the interviewees of the Casualty Section were male and most were deck officers. The testimony of women survivors was not gathered – in the same way that testimony by ordinary seamen and engine room staff was not usually solicited. The Casualty Section considered that the senior surviving deck officer could tell the Admiralty more about the sinking of his ship and the resulting survival issues than the lower ranks or women passengers. Quite apart from any concerns on literary or historical grounds about the failure to gather texts from women, lascar and other ordinary seamen, there were perhaps very practical reasons to lament this omission. When the Admiralty and, later, the Medical Research Council began to investigate the problems of survival facing those in lifeboats and on open rafts, their starting point was the interviews carried out by the Casualty Section. Those reports were sometimes followed up by further interviews, and sometimes by experiments on volunteers, some of whom were conscientious objectors. In part the government was forced to act to improve the survival chances of shipwrecked mariners by the kind of horror stories that the press featured early in the war, often with the added horror that some of the victims were women. The government was also forced to act because of prodding in the House of Commons by MPs, such as Eleanor Rathbone, who campaigned hard to highlight the plight of shipwrecked mariners. It was ironic that, despite the campaign by Rathbone and others, the textual evidence that would be used to address survival concerns was skewed towards a narrow section of shipboard society. Efforts by the Medical Research Council and others to prolong life at sea, which culminated in changes in legislation, innovations in lifeboat design and the publication of *A Guide to the Preservation of Life at Sea after Shipwreck* in 1943, assumed that the survival problems facing the shipwrecked were the same irrespective of gender and race.[16] As later research was to demonstrate, the physiological differences between men and women play a significant role in determining survival. Women, with their greater reserves of subcutaneous fat and higher pain threshold are in some ways better equipped to survive than men, certainly in the circumstances of swimming in the North Atlantic. Psychological and cultural differences created a further series of issues that could not be probed owing to the skewed sample collected by the Casualty Section. And yet in some of the reports the need to investigate such areas is clearly revealed. Doris Hawkins's narrative of her experiences shows exceptional memory and reflection on the psychological and emotional aspects of survival – areas where men would perhaps be less useful. The presence of women in the boats did seem to act as a stabilising influence on the rest of the group. 'Looking after the women' gave the men a focus to the daily life of the lifeboat. Women's response to this role is hard to define. Some seem to have accepted their role as the weaker sex and were prepared to die quickly; others like Diana Jarman accepted what help was available while carrying significant burdens in their own right.

In addition to direct participation in the Battle of the Atlantic as potential survivors or victims, a large number of shore-based women were intimately involved with the actual conduct of maritime combat. These included members of the Women's Royal Naval Service (WRNS) and members of the Women's Royal Air Force (WRAF).

The former served at various maritime headquarters such as the Admiralty and at Western Approaches Head Quarters in Liverpool. They helped to maintain the fleet in port in Britain and overseas. Some members of the WRNS were to have direct experience of the war at sea. Margaret Gordon BEM, surviving a fifty-one day lifeboat journey in lifeboat No. 4 after the sinking of the *City of Cairo* and being widowed in the process, would later join the WRNS.[17] Other members of the service would lose their lives when the ships carrying them overseas were sunk. WRAFs worked as photographic interpreters for the Royal Air Force, packed parachutes for Coastal Command aircrews and armed their aircraft. Special mention must also be made of the women involved in various branches of intelligence gathering, especially in radio direction finding to establish the position of enemy submarines and in the ENIGMA code-breaking organisation of the Government Code and Cypher School at Bletchley Park. The lives of these women revolved around deciphering various texts. However, the absolute secrecy of ENIGMA was maintained for decades after the war, so that little attention was given to their work until comparatively recently. Those who worked on the ENIGMA texts were effectively hidden in the text of history.

For many women involved in the war at sea through membership of the armed services, retelling their part in it would have to wait until after the end of the Second World War. Such texts as were produced are usually marked by a continuing discretion and deference to the male on gender issues. In oral history accounts and letters women continually downplay the significance of their role in fighting the war at Sea. *The Wren*, the magazine of the Women's Royal Naval Service, has provided a valuable place of publication for women who might not otherwise have told their stories. Its letters column provides a rich source of wartime reminiscences that strikingly illustrate the gender limitations inherent in the old wartime recruiting slogan 'Join the WRNS and free a man for the fleet'. One wartime WREN recalled in a letter to the magazine in June 2002:

> We were a band of torpedo WRENS stationed at HMS *Caroline* in Belfast. The frigates came in their groups for repair from their Atlantic convoy escort duty ... We worked in the ships when they came in, doing electrical work, or rather helping the E[lectrical] A[rtificer] do the work by carrying the bag, handing him the appropriate tool, rolling his cigarettes and generally keeping his spirits up.[18]

Gender stereotyping, or evidence of actual discrimination, might be inherent in many of the letters, but through the magazine women have managed to record experiences which might otherwise have been prevented by commercial and other considerations. From this record an impression of the full scope of women's role in supporting and participating in the conflict at sea can be gained. The magazine has also served a valuable role in memorialising the dead of the *Khedive Ismail* and the *Aguila*, lost on 19 August 1941 with the loss of twenty-two WRENs. Many of the letters are also coded to the extent that only another WREN would truly be able to understand. Phrases like 'we had a tremendous time, as we were then 100 WRENs to 10,000 servicemen', contain a wealth of experience which does not need to be stated.[19] Her ex-WREN readers know precisely what is implied in a phrase constructed to conform to 1940s' notions of female modesty and chastity. More than fifty years after the conflict, the social imperatives conditioning women's behaviour in the 1940s continue to condition the production of autobiographical texts.

Conditioning was also a major factor in the lives of women on the home front. From the outset of the war it was apparent that the transatlantic carrying capacity of the British merchant marine would be seriously reduced by such factors as sinkings, ships damaged and awaiting repair, ships delayed in slow convoys or by evasive routing, and the reluctance of neutral nations to incur war risks. To offset reductions of that kind, it was necessary to reduce demand for imported items. Women had a key role in that process. Throughout the war, and especially after German victory in the west in June 1940, the government directed a sustained propaganda campaign by radio, newspaper advertisements, speeches and leaflets to persuade them to modify the way they fed and clothed themselves and their families. This campaign included such aspects as: rationing of food, clothing and petrol; avoidance of waste; recycling; make do and mend; use of home-grown foodstuffs instead of imports; advice on recipes to maximise nutritional value; keeping hens and rabbits for food in the back garden; encouragement of home jam-making, fruit bottling and preserving supported by organisations like the Women's Institutes.

While campaigns such as 'Dig for Victory' have been romanticised into the myth of a curious wartime idyll in which togetherness and equality have been the dominant features, what is frequently over-looked is the way in which women were advised of the significance of their actions on the home front. They did not make jam or dig potatoes purely for its own sake, or because of the necessities of rationing. Rather, through a variety of media, they were explicitly told that the Battle of the Atlantic and the everyday battle of the wartime kitchen were different features of the same imperative: the need to maintain Britain's importing capacity.

The campaign to convince women that they had a big role to play in winning the Battle of the Atlantic began well before the fall of France in 1940. As rationing was steadily extended from 1939 to 1942, advertisements were the primary textual weapon in the campaign for economy. An advert in the *Daily Telegraph* in January 1940 placed by the National Savings Committee showed its readers the silhouettes of three ships. In the style of the well-known children's rhyme 'This Little Pig Went to Market' the advert told the reader: 'This one is loaded with foodstuffs and necessaries; this one is loaded with munitions; this one is loaded with unnecessary goods.' Readers of the advert were told 'By limiting your purchases of the goods contained in Ship No. 3, you leave more cargo space for the goods we need to win the war.'[20] The style was intended to appeal to women, and to emphasise the maternal duty to do everything to bring the war to a successful conclusion. The advertisement perhaps also revealed a concern on the part of the authorities that, whilst men and women might be prepared to put up with hardships to maintain Britain's importing capacity, they did find it difficult to see their children suffer privation for the sake of 'tonnage space'. The advertisement also reflected a growing concern in 1940 about shortage-driven inflation of prices. By June 1940 the price of clothing had risen to 137 per cent above pre-war values.[21] As a textual persuader, to economise and 'make do and mend' the price ticket could be more effective than any government-sponsored advertisement.

For the middle-class women readers of the *Daily Telegraph* gentle encouragement and rising prices were perhaps sufficient to enlist their help in the tonnage war, but for working-class women a more direct approach was considered necessary. The Ministry of Food under Lord Woolton combined advertisements giving recipe hints with details about changes to the ration and explanations of the importance of making do. For example, an advertisement in the *Daily Herald* in November 1942 gave the information that in the run-up to Christmas a 'limited quantity' of canned chickens and turkeys would be available in one-pound tins at the rate of twenty ration points per tin. By this stage of the war rationing had reached its peak and food imports had fallen to 'less than half their pre-war level'.[22] The advertisement also sought to remind its readers of the importance of the ongoing struggle in the light of Allied success in the invasion of North Africa:

> You remember how we have preached ship-savers, day in and day out. Now you know why! Oran, Algiers, Egypt – ships that once carried food to us now carry guns to Africa … More and more ships are needed. Your part is to use the foods that fit into the war economy … Every scrap of bread saved releases ships and shortens the war'.[23]

If advertisements encouraged thrift and spelt out to women precisely what was at stake on the home front, then the government also produced texts which forcibly compelled women to play their part in the Battle of the Atlantic. Advertisement campaigns by the Ministry of Information and the Ministry of Food to prevent waste were backed by the letter of the law and where women were prosecuted for their failure to do the government's bidding newspapers were encouraged to carry details of their prosecutions:

> Miss Mary Bridget O'Sullivan, Normandy Avenue, Barnet, Herts, was fined a total of ten pounds, with two guineas costs, at Barnet today for permitting bread to be wasted. Her servant, Miss Domenica Rosa Persi, was fined five shillings for wasting the bread. It was stated that the servant was twice seen throwing bread to birds in the garden, and when Miss O'Sullivan was interviewed she admitted that bread was put out every day.[24]

In a patriarchal and, in the circumstances of war, authoritarian society wartime texts reveal the extent to which women's involvement in the Battle of the Atlantic was monitored and shaped by the authorities. Asking the shopkeeper when fruit might next be available seemed an innocuous question, but it invited suspicion about whether the questioner was really fishing for details of when the next convoy might be discharging its goods. By July 1940 the Ministry of Information was becoming seriously alarmed at the dangers of rumour and gossip. At the Ministry of Information Policy Committee on 5 July, General Ismay reported that he had been instructed by the prime minister to ask that a wide campaign should immediately be put in hand against the dangers of rumour.[25] With that, as Ian McLaine has observed, began 'the ill conceived and ill fated Silent Column campaign'.[26] The British public, and particularly women, were asked to join the Silent Column and keep dispiriting news to themselves. The public were also asked, 'If you know anybody who makes a habit of causing worry and anxiety by passing on rumour and who says things persistently that might help the enemy – tell the police, but only as a last resort.'[27] Despite posters and cartoons exhorting women to keep silent, some transgressed and were publicly punished both before the courts and before the wider public, thanks to newspaper reporting which was at pains to stress the seriousness of any violation of the need to keep silent. Within a few weeks of its initiation the Silent Column was quietly dropped. Accounts of court cases had served as salutary texts to the many, but they had also produced a reaction. Prosecutions for gossip smacked of the totalitarianism that the British public were asked to believe was a feature of the Nazi regime. New texts were required to get around the public disquiet and these came in the form of posters and adverts, usually with a humorous edge, reminding the British people of the need to maintain secrecy. Some of the advertisements explicitly targeted women. 'Keep Mum' warned one famous wartime poster showing two women next to each other on a bus, while behind them sat a fat caricature of Goering.

Perhaps the most spectacular case came about long after the silent campaign had been wound up. Dealing with individuals who refused the call to 'Keep Mum' remained a problem and the police sometimes fretted at their inability to deal effectively with such people. In 1944 a Scottish materialisation medium named Helen Duncan was prosecuted under the 1735 Witchcraft Act for pretending to exorcise a conjuration of spirits. She had come to the attention of the authorities for revealing the loss of two British battleships, HMS *Hood* and HMS *Barham*, in two separate seances in Portsmouth. It was after the sinking of HMS *Hood* in May 1941 that she first came to the attention of British military intelligence. Duncan informed her sitters of the sinking of the battleships before the news was made public. She was eventually jailed in May 1944 for nine months. Although half a century later her supporters in the spiritualist community would claim that she was jailed because she might reveal details about D-Day – and that she was a victim of her religious practice – what seems more likely is that the police who arrested her in Portsmouth had rather more mundane concerns. German propaganda radio had broadcast the loss of HMS *Hood* on the day of one of the seances, and news of the loss of HMS Barham circulated widely in the time between her sinking on 25 November 1941 and the official announcement of her loss on 27 January 1942.[28] To the police in Portsmouth, Helen Duncan was someone for whom the 'Keep Mum' campaign had failed and they were determined to silence this particular channel of gossip and rumour. They were also determined to settle accounts with someone who was making a substantial living out of what they saw as spreading gossip through fraudulent mediumship. What was particularly distressing to some was that she was exercising her mediumship in a city intimately involved in the Battle of the Atlantic, where naval families grieved in large numbers and the Blitz of 1940–41 had taken its own toll on citizens. As The Times noted in 1944:

> There were many people, especially in wartime, sorrowing for their loved ones, and there was a great danger of their susceptibilities being exploited, and out of this yearning for comfort and assurance were those, unfortunately, who were ready to profit. Many of the people who sought solace were trusting by nature and poor in circumstances. In this case Mrs. Duncan made £112 in six days, which was some indication of how willing some people were to dabble in the occult.[29]

The case revealed an all-round failure of texts aimed predominantly at women. The silent campaign had been dropped after adverse public reaction; some were patently not prepared to 'Keep Mum' and the police lacked suitable laws to deal with those who might spread dispiriting news about the Battle of the Atlantic or seek to profit from the relatives of the dead. Hence, someone who was seen as a public nuisance, rather than as a threat to public security, was prosecuted under an obsolete law, the Witchcraft Act of 1735, simply because the police in Portsmouth felt they could make a charge under it stick.

The Duncan case also has significance when it comes to examining texts about British women and the Battle of the Atlantic. Underlying the case, and yet somehow too unpleasant to be spelt out clearly in contemporary newspaper accounts, was the concern that the wives and mothers of dead Portsmouth seamen were being exploited by Helen Duncan and her circle. There was widespread concern about the morale of women, and that had particular relevance for merchant seamen. Propaganda that U-boat crews routinely machine-gunned survivors of sunken British ships, and the harsh realities of surviving a sinking, threatened the morale of the relatives and sweethearts of merchant seamen. It was realised that maintaining the morale of those at home would help to maintain the morale of those at sea. Likewise there was also a realisation that women could provide a good indication of the morale of the men serving at sea. Hence, in the pages of evidence gathered by Mass-Observation can be found the views of prostitutes in the sea ports, whose clients included seamen of the merchant and Royal navies. To maintain the morale of those women, whose interest in seamen was not entirely financial, in 1942 the Ministry of War Transport put on a travelling exhibition designed to show the latest in lifesaving equipment and the vital role of the merchant navy. The purpose of the exhibition, which toured major ports around Britain, was to reassure women that their menfolk were as well protected as possible, and that they stood every chance of reaching safety if their ships were sunk. The exhibits included the latest food developed for lifeboats and devices like portable lifeboat transmitters. The exhibition constituted a rather unusual text in the representation of the war at sea. Added to it in 1945 was the first colour film from the Crown Film Unit, *Western Approaches*. The narrative of the survival of a shipwrecked crew and the eventual destruction of a the U-boat which had sunk them was shaped by the same imperatives that had shaped the travelling exhibition. In both cases women needed reassurance about the Battle of the Atlantic: that torpedoing would not result in a slow agonising death; that the merchant navy was carrying out vital work and was helping to win the war. The references in *Western Approaches* to 'back home' and to female relatives served as a further reminder that the Battle of the Atlantic was a front in which women also fought.

Finally, it is worth reflecting that it was not just the women of Britain who were intimately involved in the war at sea, and contemporary texts reflect the fact. The American housewife 'Rosie the Riveter', who left domesticity for work in the shipyard, was immortalised in film and poster. German propaganda film of returning U-boat crews to ports such as Lorient and La Palice depicted tired, unshaven and victorious seamen being welcomed by female members of the German navy and by French women. Russian women were intimately involved in the Battle of the Oceans serving as crew on merchant ships and in a variety of other roles. In Britain and the United States the female contribution was the subject of a variety of propaganda texts. In Germany, highlighting the role of women in the struggle clashed with the underlying ideals of 'Children, Kitchen, Church'. In Russia it was expected that everyone would fight, but the extent to which some women were involved in the Battle of the Oceans came as a considerable shock to some of the combatants. Autobiographical accounts by male merchant seamen of encounters with women in the course of their mutual duties express genuine surprise. Robert Carse, an American merchant seamen on the North Russian convoys, was shocked to see women crew members and family on board some of the Russian ships as his convoy assembled off Iceland in 1942. He was even more astonished to see female Russian dockers and labourers when he reached Murmansk, but the sight led him to think deeply about the contrasts between the involvement of Russian and American women in the Battle of the Atlantic. As he recalled in an account of his visit to North Russia, published in New York in 1943,

> They were old women; fifty was probably the age of the youngest of them. They were carrying big baulks of pine timber, rigging telephone poles, and building the roof of an air raid shelter. The thought couldn't help but come to us: why the hell didn't we have the same thing at home? It was the same war, against the same enemy, and the Nazi bombs killed any and all whom stood in their way.[30]

Carse's thoughts serve as a reminder that the experience of those women who were involved in the Battle of the Atlantic varied greatly according to factors such as ideology and geography. In Russia women were expected to play a full role in the affairs of the country and their contribution was not romanticised for the purpose of propaganda. In Germany, which was to face critical shortages of personnel, the regime had misgivings about fully involving women in the war and so underplayed their contribution to the war at sea in wartime propaganda. In the United States and in Britain the contribution of women was accepted, albeit with some reluctance. Women would be encouraged to play their role in the Battle of the Atlantic, but not coerced to participate to the same extent as in Russia. A range of texts were produced to persuade women to involve themselves in the struggle at a variety of levels. Text was also used to shape women's involvement in other way,s from 'Keep Mum' to reports of the prosecution of Helen Duncan. The same forces that shaped the production of propaganda texts also fed through to how women would describe their experiences of the war at sea. Women wrote about and described themselves as being little different to their male counterparts. Perhaps this was, in some way fitting because, as Atle Thowsen, a Norwegian historian, reminds us, 'we still lack accurate data for the total loss of lives'.[31] We don't know how many women perished alongside men in the Battle of the Atlantic. Estimates of total casualties vary considerably and in their anonymity there is no gender difference.

Notes

1   Lloyd's List and Shipping Gazette, 1 October 1941, reproduced in R. J. Scarlett, Under Hazardous Circumstances: A Register of Awards of Lloyds War Medal for Bravery at Sea 1939–1945 (Uckfield: Naval and Military Press, 1992), p. 22.

2   Leonard R. Gribble, Heroes of the Merchant Navy (London, Harrap, 1944), pp. 158–74.

3   Gribble, p. 159.

4   Gribble, p. 160.

5   Chief Officer Copeland's Report to the Admiralty Trade Division on the loss of the S.S. Athenia, 23 November 1939, British Public Record Office, ADM 199/2130.

6   Baltimore Evening Sun, 14 September 1939, p. 20. For the sinking of the Athenia see Max Caulfield, A Night of Terror: The Story of the Athenia Affair (London: Frederick Muller, 1958).

7   Baltimore Evening Sun, 4 September 1939, p. 5.

8   Lloyd's List and Shipping Gazette, 16 December 1943, reproduced in Scarlett, p. 16.

9   Gribble, p. 166.

10 Ralph Barker, Goodnight – Sorry for Sinking You (London: Collins, 1984), pp. 186–211.

11 Gribble, p. 166.

12 Gribble, p. 167.

13 Doris Hawkins, Atlantic Torpedo: The Record of 27 Days in an Open Boat, Following a U-Boat Sinking (Bath: Cedric Chivers, [1943] 1969).

14 Hawkins, pp. 8–9.

15 Hawkins, p. 14.

16 G. H. and R. Bennett, Survivors: British Merchant Seamen in the Second World War (London: Hambledon Press, 1999), p. 185.

17 Barker, pp. 196–225.

18 Marion Smyllie, The Wren, 344 (June 2002), 19.

19 Marjorie Finlayson, The Wren, 343 (February 2002), 18.

20 Daily Telegraph, 5 January 1940, p. 5.

21 Angus Calder, The People's War (New York: Ace Books, 1969), p. 276.

22 Calder, p. 318.

23 Daily Herald, 17 November 1942, p. 2.

24 Reproduced in Calder, p. 320.

25 Ministry of Information Policy Committee Minutes, 5 July 1940, INF 1/849, Public Record Office.

26 Ian McLaine, Ministry of Morale: Home Front Morale and the Ministry of Information in World War II (London: George Allen & Unwin, 1979), p. 81.

27 McLaine, p. 82.

28 For rumours about the sinking of the Barham, see Home Intelligence Weekly

Reports for late 1941 to early 1942, in INF1/292, Public Record Office. See also G. Jones, *Battleship Barham* (London: William Kimber, 1979), pp. 251–2.

29 *The Times*, 4 April 1944, p. 2.
30 Robert Carse, *There Go the Ships* (New York: Garden City Publishing, 1943), pp. 152–3.
31 Atle Thowsen, 'The Norwegian Merchant Navy in Allied War Transport', in Stephen Howarth and Derek Law, *The Battle of the Atlantic, 1939–1945* (London: Greenhill Books, 1994), p. 61.

7

'The best disguise':
performing femininities for clandestine purposes
during the Second World War

Juliette Pattinson

> All the girls would have found it difficult to carry out their missions
> unless they had been consummate actresses, studying each new
> person that they were to become and slipping into it like a character
> on the stage.
>
> Beryl Escott, historian[1]

> Women performed dangerous missions in gender-integrated combat
> groups, short of combat itself, because it was commonly recognized
> that of all resisters, they had the best disguise: they were women!
>
> Paula Schwartz, historian[2]

War is a revealing site for a discussion of femininity. Ideologically,
the waging of war is premised on the underlying principle of
combatant males fighting to protect non-combatant females. Yet the
role of women in the Special Operations Executive (SOE), a Second
World War organisation, undermines this rationale since involvement
in paramilitary work provided opportunities to subvert conventional gendered divisions of labour.[3] Prevailing understandings of
femininity and what constituted feminine behaviour were brought
into particularly sharp focus by the demands of combatant work.
In order to remain at liberty to undertake their clandestine role,
the SOE agents had to pass as civilians. 'Passing' is the term used
to refer to the process whereby individuals attempt to appropriate
the characteristics of the 'Other' and desire not to be recognised
as different. Passing is essentially about undermining the scopic
and the specular, showing the visible to be an unreliable signifier
of authenticity. Moreover, so as to pass as civilian women, female

agents had consciously to undertake particular types of performances as the first quotation suggests. My conception of performance is informed by Judith Butler's theory of performativity.[4] She argues that gender acts, which produce the effect of an internal core, are inscribed on the body and thus the actions that profess to express the identity actually constitute the identity itself. Gender identities therefore do not pre-exist practices of femininity but emerge from performances that conceal their constitutiveness. Hence, gender is an enactment that masks the mechanisms of its own status as performance and erases the means by which it is produced. The display so seamlessly imitates 'reality' that it goes undetected as performance and is read as authentic and original. To understand gender in terms of performance and to recognise identity as a process of becoming through action, rather than the expression of an already fixed identity, is particularly fruitful in an exploration of femininity in my study of the Second World War. I will argue that female agents deliberately enacted and embodied various modes of femininity to enable them successfully to undertake their combatant role in the traditionally masculine arena of war.

One prominent feature of female agents' narratives is their accounts of the ways in which femininity was knowingly employed to deceive German soldiers on guard at checkpoints and controls. Women used their clothing and other accessories to conceal incriminating material, embodied disguises and undertook displays of flirtation and fragility to facilitate passing. This chapter will first explore testimonies that narrate the ways that female agents employed conventional forms of temporally specific attractiveness in order to assist passing. Second, it will discuss accounts that record the effectiveness of enactments of traditional feminine conduct. It is my contention, borne out by reference to the literature about the SOE, that female agents mobilised locally and historically specific forms of femininity as appropriate to their situations and that these gender performances usually made it possible for them to fit into civilian society, passing as noncombatant women. Furthermore, I note that the performances of female agents can be read very differently: although at the moment of undertaking the performance, they appeared to be maintaining conventional understandings of what it was to be a woman, in retrospect female combatants can be seen to be destabilising these understandings. Historian Joan Tumblety asserts that 'French women during the Occupation were able to subvert sexual stereotypes under the guise of fulfilling them.'[5] Female agents operational in France, as well as in Holland and Belgium, were able to destabilise traditional norms of femininity while ostensibly conforming to them by undertaking performances revolving around specific feminine codes of appearance, hair, clothing, flirtation and fragility. Not only did these enactments give them the freedom to undertake their work; they also masked the masculine connotations of working in the Resistance. Their performances can therefore be interpreted as having dual meanings.

Displays of femininity, however, were only employed when necessity arose, and accordingly the last section of the chapter will explore what the 'reality' was for female agents when they were not performing femininity in order to pass. Using the example of Nancy Wake, who herself occasionally performed various modes of femininity while operational in France, I will suggest that the everyday experiences of female combatants were much more in keeping with what is conventionally perceived as masculine behaviour.

This chapter is thus an exploration of textual accounts which narrate how femininities, which were strategic and empowering, could be mobilised and how the necessities of war impacted upon femininity. I shall be referring to a wide range of texts, including published auto/biographies of SOE agents, secret SOE files written during the war, oral history interviews, television documentaries and films. Considering this range of written, oral and filmic accounts will facilitate a broad scrutiny of how the performance of femininity was, indeed, 'the best disguise'.

Ungentlemanly warfare

The Second World War organisation the Special Operations Executive was the brainchild of Winston Churchill, who exhorted it to 'Set Europe Ablaze' in sabotage and subversion. Formed in July 1940, during Britain's 'darkest hour', the SOE was a break with tradition. M. R. D. Foot, the official historian of the organisation, notes that the 'SOE represented an acknowledgement by the British government that war was no longer entirely a gentleman's affair.'[6] Ungentlemanly conduct was envisaged as taking the form of sabotaging factories, cutting telephone cables and derailing trains. Perhaps it was the ungentlemanly nature of the organisation that facilitated the recruitment of women – as non-gentlemen – into the ranks of the SOE. Hitherto, women were excluded from the organisation because lawyers in the SOE believed that by recruiting female agents, it would be contravening the Geneva Convention, which stated that women could not bear arms.[7] However, the SOE was able to circumvent the combat taboo by seconding its female recruits to the First Aid Nursing Yeomanry,[8] whose independent, voluntary and civilian status placed them beyond the remit of the Geneva Convention. Consequently, women began to be conscripted and trained. Thirty-nine women were infiltrated into France, three into the Netherlands and two into Belgium.

The gendering of courier work

F section, which directed operations in France, built up a network of independent *reseaux* or circuits, incorporating an organiser, an arms instructor, a wireless operator and a courier. Each circuit was given a name, usually that of a masculine occupation, such as FOOTMAN or SALESMAN. Some tasks, however, were explicitly denied to women as a gendered division of labour was developed within the SOE with women being sent into France only as wireless operators and couriers. (In the Netherlands and Belgium, couriering was the only role undertaken by women.) The SOE files state that women were allocated the role of courier in resistance networks for very gender specific reasons: it was believed that women possessed skills and attributes that made them more suitable for this work. The following is an excerpt from an SOE file from the period on operations in the Netherlands which offers a number of explanations as to why this was the case:

> Girl couriers were used extensively, because it was a fact that women were rarely stopped at controls; and only during the period immediately before the Liberation − and even then rarely − were they searched. They were seldom picked up in mass arrests. They provided excellent cover for their movements about the country by visiting friends, carrying out shopping expeditions and, later, foraging the country for food.[9]

The author of this SOE file claims that female couriers possessed several distinct advantages over men which resulted in less frequent searches at controls in the Netherlands. One asset alluded to is the statement that women were unlikely to be suspected of being engaged in the Resistance. This did not pertain solely in the

Netherlands. Groups of men of any nationality who were not engaged in work looked suspicious. This was partly because it was generally assumed that 'terrorists' were male and it was a few years into the war before it was recognised that women were agents as well. German soldiers were slow to realise that young, attractive women were politicised and involved in the Resistance and, moreover, that they were exploiting this misconception.

Assumptions about the supposedly natural affiliation of women with domesticity protected them: women who were ostensibly fulfilling housewifely duties while undertaking resistance work, were able to go about undetected. The private, domestic tasks traditionally performed by women offered female agents immunity and provided them with a cover for their clandestine work. Feminine identity was closely linked to domesticity and this could be taken advantage of, enabling women to move freely under the pretence of performing domestic chores. Under the guise of the domestic and/or maternal figure, female agents could easily pass as civilians and negotiate controls without being searched. Women thus made use of the gender tags of activities such as shopping and childcare to cover their clandestine activities. By undertaking these domestic chores, the female combatants reproduced the gendered division of labour of that time and setting. Performing these domestic functions for a military cause altered their meaning in that they became quasi-military acts in themselves. But due to the importance of the clandestine nature of these tasks, it was necessary to maintain their feminine identification, and it is this that made them so successful. In this sense, women were, in effect, protected from being read as suspected 'terrorists' because of the very fact that they were women and also because of the conventional tasks assigned to women. It was the miscalculation by German soldiers that women were unlikely to be involved in clandestine operations that was so effectively exploited by the SOE, which employed female couriers.

In certain circumstances, the trappings of femininity, usually associated with oppression, can be used as levers of power and agency. Hence the feminine masquerading undertaken by agents, while being conformist in terms of contemporary norms, has, from a retrospective perspective, a disruptive dimension. Thus, their performances can be interpreted as having dual meanings. A retrospective evaluation of female agents' activities unfolds the irony about their displays of conventional enactments of femininity. At the moment of their performances, traditional understandings of femininity were upheld and played out: what constituted femininity was not challenged. But, subsequently, their daily enactments of traditional gendering can be seen to have different meanings. In retrospect, their feminine performances can be viewed as a subversion of traditional notions of femininity. Hence, although the activities female combatants were engaging in *were* transgressive of traditional gender norms, this was not evident at the time of their performances and the clandestine nature of their work was concealed under a mask of locally and historically specific femininity.

The dual meanings of female agents' performances can be seen in the following example of FREELANCE courier, Nancy Wake. She undertook an arduous bicycle ride in search of an SOE wireless operator who could transmit a message to London for her. She cycled over 500 km in 71½ hours through enemy lines in France. In her autobiography, Wake recalls one trip into a small village to purchase vegetables: 'I cycled to the local markets and filled my string bag with all the fruit and vegetables I could buy without food coupons, hoping that I would pass for a housewife out shopping'.[10] Although most food products were rationed and coupons were needed to purchase them, some items, such as fruit, vegetables and nuts, were more readily available and could be obtained without vouchers. Buying food was a task undertaken more or less exclusively by women, and Wake hoped that she would be mis/taken for a French housewife undertaking her domestic chores. During this trip, numerous trucks passed her packed with waving soldiers. She returned the gesture despite the fact that, as she recalled, she 'longed to break their fucking necks'.[11] Wake also encountered numerous German-patrolled checkpoints: 'I would just look over to the officer, flutter my eyelashes and say "do you want to search *moi*?" And they would laugh flirtatiously, "No, Mademoiselle, you carry on".'[12] This example illustrates that there is a fissure between Wake's performance that affirmed gendered divisions and the significance of her enactment for the accomplishment of the clandestine tasks in which she was engaged. It was in her mobilisation of dominant gender norms that her resistance to them becomes apparent.

Not only did childcare and shopping give female agents a reason for being out of the home, but also prams and shopping baskets could hide weapons and radio parts, as this contemporary document suggests: 'Messages and packages were concealed in bicycle-frames, shopping baskets, hand-bags, the lining of clothes or round the waist under the clothes.'[3] Testimonies of SOE agents reveal that women did indeed conceal incriminating material upon their person and in their baggage. Jos Mulder Gemmeke, a courier who worked in the Netherlands, carried microfilms in the shoulder pads of her coat and behind the mirror of her powder compact;[14] the bag belonging to Yvonne Cormeau, a wireless operator for the WHEELWRIGHT circuit in the south of France, had a false bottom under which she secreted documents and radio parts;[15] and courier Lise de Baissac, who also operated in France, strapped radio parts underneath the belt on her dress.[16] The masculine connotations of the Resistance materials they conveyed were thus literally cloaked in femininity. Evidence from both written and oral testimonies suggest that female agents routinely used both clothing and the trappings of femininity to smuggle documents and equipment in order to conceal their role as couriers.

In addition to this, until the latter stages of the war, German soldiers on guard at checkpoints were male,[17] and female agents frequently record consciously and deliberately performing femininity in their presence. Female agents' appearances and behaviours could contribute to images of civilian femininity that would place them beyond suspicion. They strategically used their knowledge of conventional gender relations and their awareness of the potency of feminine performances.

Jos Mulder Gemmeke, the Dutch agent who concealed messages in her shoulder pads, reflected upon the methods that she employed to deceive German soldiers:

> You could change your hair, your clothes, you could charm a lot of people, flirt and I was then young so you could easily do that. Sometimes with a red hat I think, but it always worked... When I arrived at a station, if I had luggage which was heavy and dangerous, I looked for a German soldier and asked him to carry my luggage and it always worked. He did it![18]

Mulder Gemmeke undertook a specifically feminine performance by mobilising a conventionally attractive appearance and appropriate conduct. In the rest of this chapter, I shall examine specific accounts of the mobilisation of the signifiers of femininity in order to explore further the gendered performances undertaken by female agents.

Femininity as appearance

Signs of femininity take different forms in different cultural settings; there is no one ubiquitous and unified pattern. Consequently, gender practices change over time as they can be contested and reconstructed as circumstances alter. However, despite these shifts, prevailing notions of what constitutes femininity are surprisingly continuous, inflexible and resistant to change. Femininity is almost always bound up with physical appearance and seen as oriented towards male pleasure. In these respects, stereotypes of femininity have remained largely intact. That particular forms of physical appearance are often crucial signifiers of femininity can be illustrated in the quotation above, in which Jos Mulder Gemmeke recalls that hair and clothing could enable her to pass through train stations unchallenged. She notes that as key markers of gender difference, they could assist in the performance of femininity. Long hair, for example, has generally been constructed in Western culture during the nineteenth and twentieth centuries as feminine and is perhaps one of the most durable and visible signifiers of femininity. By changing the style and length of her hair, as well as varying her clothing, she was able to present a different image of civilian femininity.

Testimonies of female agents illustrate the effectiveness of changing clothing for implementing a particular disguise and affecting different identities. They assumed the dress of ordinary housewives, rural peasant women or aristocratic socialites according to their circumstances. In each case, female agents either assumed the disguise in order to blend in, be inconspicuous and pass unnoticed or purposely to stand out and be observed. Clothing could thus be utilised as a tool for concealment or, conversely, for exposure. There were therefore numerous strategies that they could pursue. Different circumstances called for performances of different types of femininity. On some occasions, urban glamour was opted for; during others, understated displays of rural femininity or even unglamorous, peasant femininity were considered more appropriate. Several positive and negative effects beset each, and the women had to select which they thought would increase the likelihood of continuing freedom. I will examine testimonies that emphasise various modes of feminine appearance which female agents often consciously employed as part of a strategy to avert discovery. I shall begin by exploring glamour.

Clothing can provide a repertoire of status symbols, signifying, as well as distinguishing, between classes. However, in the 1940s, clothing was rationed in most European countries and items were perpetually recycled. In this context, Jos Mulder Gemmeke's red hat was even more likely to catch the attention of German soldiers. Her smart, elegant appearance may have implied that she was of a high social standing, given that sophistication and poise have class connotations. The interaction between gender and class meant that glamorous, attractive women were often read as middle class.[19] Indeed, agents were advised by SOE staff to use class-specific signals. An SOE file commented that 'it was found an advantage for couriers to travel first class as this gave them more prestige with train controls.'[20] Passengers seated in first class were less likely to have their luggage subjected to thorough searches. This was perhaps because German soldiers were unlikely to perceive first-class travellers as 'terrorists'. Agents' accounts testify to the respect for social status that was instilled within German soldiers. Reflecting on her treatment by German officials, Odette Sansom, courier to the French SPINDLE circuit, asserted: 'In those days I called them a "race de valets". I think if you treated them in a certain way, as if they were almost your servants, they had a type of respect for you.'[21] Sansom believed that the observance of social hierarchy was fundamental to German national identity. Consequently, invoking a middle-class identity could be an effective passing strategy. This was useful not only because conventionally attractive, respectable-looking women were generally regarded as middle class, but also because displays of femininity were seen as indicative of inner character. On both counts, glamorous women were unlikely to be suspected of being involved in the Resistance.

This miscalculation was exploited mercilessly. An excerpt from a recent biography of Nancy Wake emphasises her consciousness about the potency of sexual allure:

> Nancy's past experience had taught her that not only does sexual attraction not recognise national borders nor political divisions – meaning she had often been ogled by the very guards meant to check her – but the innate warmth and intimacy of that attraction was a great soother of possible suspicions. If she got it right, it had to seem beyond the range of possibilities for the Germans between her and her destination, that such an attractive young woman could be on a

mission specifically devoted to bringing them carnage and destruction in the very near future. That, at least, is the factor Nancy intended to play to the hilt and she spent the twenty-four hours before departure rustling up the most attractive outfit she could get.[22]

Narrative accounts, then, suggest that female agents found it productive to accentuate their physical appearance. These women presented themselves so as to appear attractive to men. These were heterosexual performances in that they were oriented towards male pleasure and were dependent upon male soldiers' sexual approval in order to be successful. However, in addition to various beneficial effects of performing glamour, this could undoubtedly lead to some negative consequences. Such appearances did not always protect these women from discovery: although female agents were afforded some protection, there was no safeguard against capture and some women were arrested despite such strategies. Indeed, the performance of feminine glamour could be highly ambiguous in that, although it might protect women from suspicion, it could also draw *too much* unwanted attention to agents as they worked. The attention they attracted as glamorous women made them more suspect than they would otherwise have been. Deliberate performances of femininity were, then, by no means unproblematic.

Occasionally, female agents attracted a different kind of attention, which was most unwanted. Shortly after parts of France had been liberated, Sonya Butt, a twenty-year-old courier and weapons instructor for the HEADMASTER circuit in France, embarked upon a new role with her organiser, going back and forth across the lines and providing the Americans with intelligence. Butt, who carried American papers in a secret pocket in her girdle, was sexually assaulted by two German soldiers:

> I heard this marching behind me and I turned around and there were these two guys so I just smiled at them and went on my way and they followed me in and they raped me. One held me down. My first instinct was to put up at fight and then I thought no, I can't. I've got these papers. If I put up a fight, they're going to overpower me and then they'll probably strip me and we'd be in a worse mess than we already are in. I've just got to let them do it and get on with it … Anyway, it was quite an experience! But they didn't get my papers![23]

Although being female and conventionally attractive have been recognised in both contemporary and post-war accounts as advantageous, as I have shown, it was not *necessarily* a major benefit since these qualities could induce unwanted attention. Sonya Butt's experience shows that female agents were as liable to assault and rape as were other young women.

In some instances, a less glamorous performance meant that female agents were not noticed and they merged into the background. If glamour is correlated with visibility, mundaneness resulted in relative concealment. For those who wanted to be comparatively invisible, it may have been necessary to downplay femininity in order not to attract attention. In order to be as inconspicuous as possible, Yvonne Baseden, WT operator to the SCHOLAR circuit in France, wore a very casual, plain grey skirt and a blue blouse: 'the idea was to blend in somehow'.[24] She didn't wear any make-up and styled her hair in a very simple way in order not to invite attention. When Diana Rowden, courier for the ACROBAT circuit, was concerned for her safety following the circulation of an accurate description of her by the French authorities, she changed her hair colour and style, disposed of all the clothing she possessed and borrowed clothes in a more modest fashion in order not to be recognised.[25]

Displays of ordinariness were only successful in specific contexts, and agents had to select carefully the correct style for the situation. Upon visiting a larger town, WHEELWRIGHT courier Anne-Marie Walters realised that her appearance was unsuitably casual. In her autobiography, she notes: 'I discarded my beret, it was all right in a small town like Condom, but in Agen women wore high, complicated hair styles and even more complicated ear-rings'.[26] There were, therefore, fashion differences between cities, towns and country villages, and agents had to be aware of these variations in order to blend in, to look as inconspicuous as possible and be mis/taken as civilians.

Undertaking performances that totally lacked glamour was another strategy employed by some agents. On one occasion, when Nancy Wake needed to adopt a disguise in order not to be recognised, she chose to dress in antiquated and outmoded clothing and to pass as a middle-aged peasant. In her autobiography, she writes:

> I borrowed a long white piqué dress which must have been fashionable before World War I ... I was ... looking like a real country bumpkin, wet hair pulled back tight, no make-up, an old-fashioned dress, and

wearing a pair of the farmer's old boots ... Our cart and the produce
were inspected several times by the Germans as we entered Aurillac;
they did not give me a second look, even their first glance was rather
disdainful. I did not blame them. I did not look very fetching.[27]

Wake's performance of unglamorous femininity was successful in
that her drab appearance meant that she was comparatively invisible. Her one-off performance as a peasant farmer's daughter, which
effected obscurity, contrasts with the attention that performances of
middle-class femininity received. For many of the agents, the codes
of middle-class femininity became associated with visibility, while
those of working-class femininity were linked to invisibility. In her
peasant attire, with her hair deliberately lank and without any trace
of make-up, Wake was read as unrefined. Her lack of glamour held
no fascination for the guards on duty at the controls, and as a result
she was less noticeable, enabling her to pass successfully.

Stereotypes of the alluring female spy seducing her enemy, epito-
mised by Mata Hari,[28] might suggest that performances of glamour
would always work and were the key to passing, as the cases of
conventionally attractive women who were not suspected of engaging
in paramilitary tasks suggest. Although this was sometimes the case,
there is also evidence to indicate that in some instances glamour
would have been inappropriate and unsuccessful. Indeed, auto/
biographical evidence suggests that almost every type of femininity
was employed by female agents to pass: glamour, quotidian, lack of
glamour, chic/urban and peasant/rural femininities are just some
of the different stagings of femininity that I have discussed here.
Agents had to decide what they felt would be the most suitable
performance of femininity for the specific circumstances in which
they were working, because choosing inappropriate modes of femininity could have led to capture. Appearance was thus crucial in
constructing different identities, and, although the objective was to
pass as a law-abiding civilian woman, the strategies to effect this
were diverse.

Femininity as conduct

Crucial to these heterosexual performances, which hinged upon
the effect of the physical appearance of female agents on German
soldiers, was both heterosexual flirtation and physical frailty. These
were tactics that Jos Mulder Gemmeke employed to turn situations

to her advantage. Theorist Susan Brownmiller asserts that 'Feminine armour is never metal or muscle but, paradoxically, an exaggeration of physical vulnerability that is reassuring (unthreatening) to men.'[29] Memoirs, biographies and oral histories of veterans overflow with tales of female agents who stimulated chivalrous behaviour in German soldiers, who unknowingly transported suitcases containing radio sets and weapons across borders or past checkpoints. The slight physique and attractive appearance of Sonya Butt enabled her to take advantage of the conventional correlation of femininity with physical weakness. On numerous occasions German soldiers assisted her from trains and carried her suitcase through controls:

> Ask for help if you want to bring your suitcase down. Don't try and do it by yourself if there's a German chap there. Ask him 'would you mind bringing down my heavy suitcase for me'. It just seemed the natural thing to do.[30]

There is an interesting tension between the performance of physical frailty and the mental strength that such performances required in order to be successful. The agents' performances of fragility suggested that they were exactly what they were not; they *did* fragility when it was thought to be necessary or useful in order to accomplish their tasks in relative safety and not because they *were* fragile. Hence there is a contradiction at the heart of such performances. Female agents' power was, therefore, ironically vested in performances of physical weakness. Duping German soldiers into assisting with bags was made possible by female agents' invoking of traditional feminine behaviour by demonstrating helplessness and reliance on others, combined with a feminine appearance. By asking a German soldier to carry her baggage, a female agent elicited traditionally masculine behaviour from the soldier, while enacting femininity. Paradoxically, the much-used strategy of requesting assistance from German guards overturned conventional gender norms, despite seemingly reinforcing them.

Flirtation was a further strategy employed by Jos Mulder Gemmeke. Her flirtatious behaviour was consolidated by the signifiers of ideal femininity mentioned above – hair, clothes and appearance. Sociologist Beverley Skeggs asserts that flirtation involves an amalgam of the reproduction of conventional femininity, in particular passivity, helplessness and reliance on others; the stretching of traditional femininity, exemplified by the direct engaging in conversation; and the reproduction of heterosexuality.[31] Mulder Gemmeke's display of physical weakness, her active seeking of assistance and her hetero-sexual appearance and behaviour facilitated her flirtation with German guards. Many performances involved the projection of convention-ally feminine appearance and heterosexual flirtation that could turn precarious situations to women's advantage. A friendly disposition coupled with an attractive appearance could disarm soldiers much more effectively than the strategies employed by male agents, as Sonya Butt explains:

> You just react to the moment and think 'I'll get by alright with a nice smile'. I just sort of smiled and waved to them. All the time. Women could get by with a smile and do things that men couldn't and no matter what you had hidden in your handbag or your bicycle bag, if you had a nice smile, you know, just give them a little wink. It just happened constantly, all the time. So I got away with it. It becomes sort of second nature … You did that [flirted] automatically. Absolutely. That was just par for the course. Just sort of went into the role auto-matically, just quite naturally.[32]

Written accounts of SOE agents' wartime experiences relate epi-sodes of flirtatious encounters with German soldiers, as the following extract from the biography of courier Nancy Wake illustrates:

> 'I played the part of a giddy Frenchwoman who didn't give a bugger what happened in the war', Nancy recalls frankly. 'I was a *good-time girl*. I used to give Germans a date sometimes, sometimes three or four if I was away on a long trip and give them a little bit of hope. I played the part – I should have been an actress.'[33]

Nancy Wake was not the only agent to arrange meetings with German soldiers in order to negotiate checkpoints successfully. Beryl Escott illustrates the successful use of flirtation in her narration of an episode involving Patricia O'Sullivan, wireless operator to the French FIREMAN circuit. She was cycling down a country lane with her radio set in her bicycle basket when she observed two German soldiers at a checkpoint:

> Putting on her most sunny and beguiling smile, she rode boldly up to the two men, one of whom liked the look of her advanced some way up the road to meet her. She stopped and leaning on her bike, chatted animatedly with him. Flattered by her friendly attitude, he asked her to meet him for a drink … the other German awaited her,

and while he examined her papers, she laid herself out to be just as delightful to him, consequently so bemusing him also that he completely forgot to examine her case, while excited by the notion of making his own assignation with her for that same evening ... It had been a very close shave, only carried off by consummate acting and the brazen use of her charms.[34]

The exchange between the German soldiers and O'Sullivan illustrates the powerful and effective use of conventionally feminine appearance, coupled with appropriate feminine behaviour. Escott's couching of the episode in terms of 'putting on', 'carried off', 'consummate acting' and 'brazen use' emphasises the performative nature of femininity and illuminates O'Sullivan's agency. This show of femininity was an acting out of a performance that protected her from a potentially dangerous situation. O'Sullivan took the initiative by cycling confidently up to the German soldiers and actively seeking their attention. She played on the soldiers' heterosexual interest in her, permitting her to avert their gaze from her basket containing the wireless set and enabling her to outwit them.

The tactic of accepting engagements with German soldiers when in precarious situations has also been captured in filmic accounts of agents' experiences. The film *Carve Her Name with Pride*, chronicling the wartime activities of Anglo-French agent Violette Szabo, depicts the heroine accepting two dinner invitations with an Obstführer, a high-ranking German official, neither of which she keeps.[35] The treatment of feminine performances in *Now It Can Be Told*, a documentary filmed in 1944 starring ex-SOE agents Harry Rée and Jacqueline Nearne as Felix and Cat, is quite different to that in *Carve Her Name with Pride*:

Cat – The police were searching luggage at the station and made me open my suitcases.

Felix – What did you do?

Cat – I tried sex appeal.

Felix – Did it work?

Cat – No, it was a complete flop! I had to open it.

Felix – What about the WT set?

Cat – I told him with a sweet smile that it was an X-ray machine.

Felix – Must have been a very sweet smile for him to swallow that![36]

In contrast to other related texts, such as SOE documents and auto/biographies, which identify successful performances of femininity, this documentary downplays their effectiveness. The audience does not witness Cat's performance; rather we hear her reconstruction of the event when she informs Felix. This serves to de-emphasise her strategy, which is further dismissed by her claim that her performance was unsuccessful – she was compelled to open her suitcase despite her feminine performance. Nevertheless, it could be argued that her enactment of femininity was successful in that her smile stimulated a reaction and she was able to persuade the policeman that her suitcase contained a piece of medical apparatus. There is, then, ambivalence to this aspect of the SOE image in *Now It Can Be Told*. The documentary offered a down-to-earth, unglamorous account of the SOE which also omitted the romance between the two central characters that later audiences of *Odette*,[37] *Carve Her Name with Pride* and, more recently, *Charlotte Gray*[38] have come to expect. That *Now It Can Be Told* was the official, government-sanctioned documentary of the SOE's F section might suggest that acknowledgement of feminine performances was considered unsuitable for public consumption. Yet the performance of Cat's flirtation was evidently too central to the construction of a female agent for the documentary to dismiss it altogether.

Both filmic and personal accounts, then, suggest that female agents found it productive to flirt and be responsive to German soldiers' advances in an attempt to avoid potentially dangerous situations. However, undertaking a flirtatious performance was not infallible and, on some occasions, female agents were arrested in spite of their enactments. Courier Sonya Butt, who had found flirting highly productive on numerous occasions, discovered that her flirtatious manner did not save her from imprisonment. As she was walking down a country road in mid-1944, she was stopped by two German soldiers, who demanded to see her papers. Despite 'flashing her most charming smile',[39] she was taken to a cell while her papers were checked. After several hours, she was released without an explanation. This episode indicates that a smile was not *necessarily* a safeguard against arrest and suggests that the heightened sensitivity on the part of Germans, due to the increasing possibility of defeat, meant that by 1944 women were no longer entirely beyond suspicion: the 'natural' cover they possessed had ceased to be an unqualified advantage by this point.

Non-feminine reality

Female agents selected from these various strategies to assist their passing as civilian women. These particular enactments were intermittent and transitory, only undertaken when situations necessitated. As Yvonne Baseden asserted, 'it only came to the fore when it was necessary. I didn't live like that all the time. I popped in and out of it when I had to, which wasn't very often.'[40] So what was the 'reality' when female agents were not performing femininity in order to pass?

Nancy Wake, who on different occasions performed both drab peasant femininity and glamour, lived among seven thousand male comrades on the hillsides of the Auvergne, wearing khaki trousers, shirt, tie and beret, as well as army boots. Evenings were spent sitting round the fire, swigging whisky, participating in drinking competitions (which, she asserted, she always won), swearing, raucously singing and playing cards with her male colleagues. This was certainly no place for femininity. During the daytime, she would go on reconnaissance, ambush German troops or train men in weapons. On one occasion, Wake attacked the local Gestapo headquarters at Montluçon, running into the room throwing her grenades before retreating.[41] Wake also played a prominent role in the blowing up of a bridge over the Allier river. With the explosives strapped to them, she and four men climbed down the struts of the bridge to set the explosives in place.[42] Wake also participated in sabotaging an armaments and munitions store in Mont Mouchet. When she went to disable a sentry, he heard her and a struggle ensued. His bayonet penetrated her arm, but this did not impede her as she used her bare hands to kill him.[43] In an interview, Wake told me:

> Tardivat [a Resistance colleague] said 'she is the most feminine woman I have ever met in my life, but in battle she's worth ten men'. So I changed. I was feminine, but fighting. All I wanted to do was to kill Germans. I didn't give a bugger about them, to kill Germans. Didn't care about it. I hated, I loathed the Germans. I loathed them. As far as I was concerned, the only good one was a dead one and I don't care what anybody thinks of me. A dead German![44]

Wake's assertion that she was 'feminine but fighting' emphasises that femininity could also be belligerent. She dispels the myth that women are innately pacifistic by asserting that she relished killing

German soldiers, and experienced no remorse for doing so. Her admission of hatred and loathing for the Germans and the manner in which it was said were quite startling. The unequivocal remark 'the only good one was a dead one' was spoken without passion, in a cool, calculated manner. From 'I hated, I loathed the Germans' to 'I don't care what anybody thinks of me', Wake's voice remained dispassionate and deliberate. The short, emphatic 'a dead German!' at the end of this statement, accompanied by a decisive nod of the head, gave closure to the topic of conversation. She appears to have had no moral compunction about ending the lives of dozens of Germans, and states that other people's assessment of her ruthlessness had no effect upon her. Wake's lived reality was thus more in keeping with what is conventionally regarded as masculine behaviour.

Although Wake was by no means representative of the female agents, her experiences illustrate that while enactments of femininity were infrequent performances contrived to facilitate passing, the everyday reality was quite different. The actuality for female wireless operators, such as Yvonne Baseden and Patricia O'Sullivan, was much more mundane than the tense excitement provoked by performing femininity: hours sat at their radios coding, decoding, receiving and transmitting messages was more typical of their daily work. Feminine performances were thus infrequent interludes between days of tedious technical work. Female agents' everyday experiences were thus quite different to the sporadic displays of femininity that I have discussed above.

This chapter has examined both written and oral testimonies of men and women veterans, as well as analysing the SOE files and filmic accounts, for the purpose of exploring some of the crucial strategies employed by female agents to avert discovery and to facilitate passing. As I have shown, in certain circumstances, some female agents courted danger for the greater protection it might offer: drawing attention to their chic, urban appearance and flirtatious behaviour, and thereby inducing the attention of German soldiers in order that the enemy would unwittingly give protection and safe passage. However, in other situations, some female agents deliberately performed a quotidian, rural femininity and occasionally even unglamorous, peasant femininity in order to blend into the surrounding scene and be less visible.

The gendered performances enacted by female combatants were not deconstructive, challenging or parodic, but had life and death consequences. These feminine performances were enacted out of necessity, not out of choice or for entertainment – they were intentional and strategic. However, many derived pleasure from the successful negotiation of such encounters. Patricia O' Sullivan, a wireless operator, reported that she felt 'elated' after safely negotiating checkpoints when she travelled with her radio set.[45] These women were extraordinarily conscious of the power that feminine performances could render, and undertook them for their own protection. Moreover, it was their knowledge of the effectiveness of particular feminine performances that enabled them to choose from a repertoire of modes of femininity and embody that which was suitable to the situation. Female agents therefore had to be very adept at choosing the guise of femininity that they would display: how they comported themselves, their posture, accent, behaviour, clothing and hairstyle, were all crucial in the performance of specific modes of femininity, but were not necessarily appropriate to all situations. Female combatants consciously made use of heterosexual, feminine appearance and realised a range of behaviours suitable for the circumstances. Their performances required a consciousness about the effects of their actions. This doubleness (or consciousness), the seeing of oneself through the eyes of others, was crucial in facilitating passing. Female agents had to undertake an ongoing self-surveillance or circumspection that ensured an awareness of the performative effectiveness of bodily gestures. Their performances denied the work that went into producing a specific mode of civilian femininity and concealed the performative nature of their enactments. Performances such as these erased, rather than exposed, their dissimulation and it is this concealment of work which not only produced the illusion of interiority in the effects of their feminine performances but also facilitated passing.

The conventions of femininity can be simultaneously seen as being maintained and undermined. On the one hand, there was the seemingly apparent upholding of the customs of femininity by female agents in their performances. However, conventional understandings of what it meant to be a woman were put to extremely unconventional and unfeminine purposes, which resulted in an undermining of gender norms incurred by the kind of military activity in which the SOE was engaged.

Women's involvement in combatant work suggests that there were opportunities for a subversion of traditional gender relations, given the signification of war as a masculine enterprise. Seen in a longer-term perspective, women were breaking down established Western divisions of male and female tasks in war by participating actively at the 'front line'. However, the fact that women were allocated the very gender-specific task of courier and because of their daily re-enactments of localised and historically specific forms of femininity, this potential to undermine gender norms was never fully realised and there was little conflict concerning women overstepping traditional gender delineations. In the Second World War, women were involved in undercover work but they were concentrated in particularly female-appropriate positions. This is in direct contrast to more recent conflicts, such as the Gulf War, in which there were great instabilities with women undertaking traditionally masculine tasks, including being in charge of men in the combat zone.[46] Rather than challenging the gendered division of labour, female SOE agents' performances of femininity resulted in the production and rehearsal of conventional gender acts; the irony is that they were challenging gendered notions about what tasks women should undertake in wartime, but in a way that was not explicit.

Notes

I would like to thank Professors Penny Summerfield (University of Manchester) and Maureen McNeil (Lancaster University) for their unstinting support and the Economic and Social Research Council for funding my postgraduate research.

1   B. Escott, *Mission Improbable: A Salute to the RAF Women of SOE in Wartime France* (Sparkford: Patrick Stephens, 1991), p. 232.

2   P. Schwartz, 'Partisanes and Gender Politics in Vichy France', *French Historical Studies*, 16:1 (Spring 1989), p. 131.

3   Much has been written on gender instabilities in wartime. See Schwartz; G. DeGroot, '"Whose Finger on the Trigger?" Mixed Anti-aircraft Batteries and the Female Combat Taboo', *War in History*, 4:4 (1997), 434–53; P. Summerfield, *Reconstructing Women's Wartime Lives: Discourse and Subjectivity in Oral Histories of the Second World War* (Manchester: Manchester University Press, 1998); G. DeGroot and C. Peniston-Bird (eds.), *A Soldier and a Woman: Sexual Integration in the Military* (Harlow: Pearson Education, 2000).

4   J. Butler, *Gender Trouble: Feminism and the Subversion of Identity* (New York: Routledge, 1990).

5   J. Tumblety, 'Review of M. C. Weitz's *Sisters in the Resistance*', *Women's History Review*, 6, 1997, p. 147.

6   M. R. D. Foot, *Resistance* (St Albans: Granada Publishing, 1978), p. 141. The term 'gentleman' has class connotations and Foot suggests that the men who fought and died in battles were upper-class men. Yet this was never the reality of war.

7   The British women's services preserved the noncombatant status of women as

enforced by the Geneva Convention; the ATS women who staffed the anti-aircraft batteries, for example, could aim the guns but not load or pull the trigger. See G. DeGroot, '"I Love the Scent of Cordite in Your Hair": Gender Dynamics in Mixed Anti-aircraft Batteries during the Second World War', *History*, 82:265 (1997), 73–92.

8 The FANYs, which was the first women's service, was established in 1907 by Captain Edward Charles Baker. See H. Popham, *FANY: The Story of the Women's Transport Service, 1907–1984* (London: Leo Cooper, 1984). I. Ward, *F.A.N.Y. Invicta* (London: Hutchinson, 1955).

9 PRO HS 7/66, Public Records Office, Kew.

10 N. Wake, *The Autobiography of the Woman the Gestapo Called the White Mouse*, (Melbourne: Macmillan, 1985), p. 134.

11 P. Fitzsimons, *Nancy Wake: The Inspiring Story of One of the War's Greatest Heroines* (London: Harper Collins Entertainment, 2002), p. 239.

12 Fitzsimons, p. 239.

13 PRO HS 7/66.

14 Mulder Gemmeke featured on *Timewatch: Secret Memories*, broadcast on BBC 2 on 11 March 1997.

15 Escott, p. 116.

16 Personal interview with L. Villameur (née de Baissac), 17 April 2002.

17 As the war progressed, German women began staffing checkpoints in France and as a consequence more female resisters were searched, incriminating evidence was found and many were arrested. An SOE file records: 'During the later part of the Occupation, controls and searches by women attached to German C.E. [counter-espionage] became more and more rigorous.' PRO HS 7/66.

18 Gemmeke, *Timewatch*.

19 In this context, femininity is more transportable across class than masculinity. This may not be true for all other instances, however.

20 PRO HS 7/66.

21 O. Sansom (1986), interviewed by Imperial War Museum Sound Archive, classification code 9478.

22 Fitzsimons, pp. 236–7.

23 Personal interview with S. d'Artois (née Butt), 19 June 2002.

24 Personal interview with Y. Burney (née Baseden), 11 April 2000.

25 R. Kramer, *Flames in the Field: The Story of Four SOE Agents in Occupied France* (London: Penguin, 1995), p. 81.

26 A.-M. Walters, *Moondrop to Gascony: An Account of the Author's Experiences in France during 1945 as a Member of the French Resistance* (London: Macmillan, 1947), p. 52.

27 Wake, pp. 132–3.

28 Mata Hari was a Dutch-born exotic dancer and courtesan who became embroiled in espionage by accident at the behest of her German lover. She was suspected of being a double agent working for both the French and the German authorities, and was finally captured, tried and executed by the French in 1917. See J. Keay, *The Spy Who Never Was: The Life and Loves of Mata Hari* (London: Michael Joseph, 1987). More recent analyses judge her spying capacities as non-existent.

29 S. Brownmiller, *Femininity* (London: Hamish Hamilton, 1984), p. 51.

30 Personal interview with S. d'Artois (née Butt), 19 June 2002.

31 B. Skeggs, *Formations of Class and Gender: Becoming Respectable* (London: Sage, 1997), p. 128.

32 Personal interview with S. d'Artois (née Butt), 19 June 2002.

33 Fitzsimons, p. 111; author's emphasis.

34 Escott, pp. 169–70.

35 *Carve Her Name with Pride*, film, directed by Lewis Gilbert and produced by Daniel M. Angel, starring Virginia McKenna, 1958.

36 *Now It Can Be Told*, film documentary, RAF, 1944.

37 *Odette*, film, produced and directed by Herbert Wilcox, starring Anna Neagle and Trevor Howard, 1950.

38 *Charlotte Gray*, film, directed by Gillian Armstrong and produced by Sarah Curtis and Douglas Rae, starring Cate Blanchett and Billy Crudup, 2002.

39 Escott, p. 211.

40 Personal interview with Y. Burney (née Baseden), 11 April 2000.

41 Wake, p. 148.

42 Fitzsimons, p. 265.

43 Fitzsimons, p. 270.

44 Personal interview with N. Wake, 28 August 1999.

45 Escott, p. 176.

46 See C. Stabile, *Feminism and the Technological Fix* (Manchester: Manchester University Press, 1994).

8

The war at home:
family, gender and post-colonial issues
in three Vietnam War texts

Marion Gibson

In June and July 2002 four wives of soldiers serving with US Special Forces were murdered by their husbands, three of whom had recently returned from service in Afghanistan. A major's wife, too, has been arrested in Fort Bragg, North Carolina (home of the Special Forces), for killing her husband. Two of the men subsequently killed themselves, and twelve children were thus bereaved of one or both parents. In each case, marital difficulties and the stresses of raising children were cited alongside experiences in Afghanistan, Haiti, Bosnia, Somalia and the Gulf as factors leading to the tragedies. 'The context of each marriage' was important, suggested one expert, whilst the chairwoman of the Defense Department's Task Force on Domestic Violence implicated 'husbands who craved control'.[1] 'This is not something they [the US military] can blame on the Taliban' noted *The Times*; 'family life in the Special Forces is becoming so dysfunctional ... that the killings are going to continue.'[2] Meanwhile, other voices blame the military profession itself, seeing the victims as 'a casualty of war', or Fort Bragg as a 'dumping ground for the problems of the American century of war and empire'.[3] The events highlight the analogies between domestic and foreign battles, and require a subtle response. One local woman offered a unifying theory: 'if you can't control it, you kill it.'[4] Yet, is it possible for academics to theorise about such events, which we know only through stories, without unethically oversimplifying the 'real'?[5] Reading this tragic story and writing simultaneously about gender, post-colonial issues and war, I was struck by the persistence of interrelations between family relationships and war (both 'real' and rhetorical), especially in narratives complicated by the rhetoric of colonialism as a familial relationship. Is it possible to say that such stories offer insights into the geopolitics of rhetoric, or will help us understand and avoid oppression and violence, martial or marital?

As if it were a warning, J. M. Coetzee's story 'The Vietnam Project' is an extreme illustration of the folly of stereotyping perceptions of any conflict, particularly in simple terms of gender and familial relationships. In it, suburban mythographer Eugene Dawn reports to America's military strategists, gathering threads of Vietnamese myth to weave his own crude pattern. He theorises that in order to win the war psychologically, American propaganda and military strategy must fuse to destroy the mother earth of Vietnam. The Vietnamese 'child' will then allow the father voice of American authority to triumph. 'The voice of the father utters itself ... out of the sky ... from the B52s', Dawn clarifies. What he proposes is total war between 'heaven and earth, father and mother', based on the fatherly admonitions of bombers and the air cavalry, already mythologised as the war's decisive force, Fort Bragg's 'soldiers from the sky'.[6] Coetzee ensures, however, that the reader is suspicious of Dawn's reading of familial psychology. The character begins his narration by stating and apologising for his name: 'My name is Eugene Dawn. I cannot help that.'[7] Readers may want to connect his name with a fear of effeminacy, with eugenics, and the false dawn of manifest destiny/white supremacy. 'Married life has taught me that all concessions are mistakes', he opines, adding 'Believe in yourself and your opponent will respect you. Cling to the mast, if that is the metaphor.'[8] It isn't − demonstrating, as it does, helpless desire for the love of the opponent rather than authoritative rejection enforcing respect. Dawn's wife/opponent is Marilyn, surely named after America's favourite domestic goddess/siren.[9] Yet Dawn does not desire Marilyn. The physical repugnance of their relationship is obsessively documented: Dawn's penis is for him just a 'length of gristle', whilst 'my seed drips like urine into the futile sewers of Marilyn's reproductive ducts'. Meanwhile his country is given over to those 'who no longer feel the authentic American destiny crackling within them and stiffening their marrow'.[10] Laden with *double entendre*, Dawn's sickened meditations in the Harry S. Truman library lead seamlessly from his war-torn marriage to Vietnam. When he kidnaps and tries to kill his son at the novella's end, thinking he has 'saved the child' from Marilyn, the reader notes the correspondence between his 'jettisoning of his wife and capture of his child' and his 'mythographic prescriptions for Vietnam'.[11] Immediately, Coetzee has inverted the 1970s stereotype of the Vietnam veteran who brings the war home with him.[12] Instead, Dawn is exporting his domestic troubles to Vietnam.[13]

Susan Jeffords, writing in the late 1980s, said that 'Vietnam [war] representation is only topically "about" the war in Vietnam … Its true subject is the masculine response to changes in gender relations in recent decades, its real battle that of the masculine to dominate and overpower its "enemy" – the feminine.'[14] Coetzee's story makes a similar point: the war is represented as a battle of the sexes over children. He links this analysis with a post-colonial reading of the war, stressing the incompatibility of 'domination and benevolence', an imperialist contextualisation later popularised by the adaptation of Joseph Conrad's *Heart Of Darkness* into *Apocalypse Now* in 1979.[15] His setting announces this at once: if the Truman Library is the presidential library at Independence, Missouri (and it is never made entirely clear), then it was once the spot where pioneer wagons massed on their Great Trek west, an image full of resonances for Afrikaners and Americans alike. Home of the independent, true man, it is a perfect location for Dawn: beset by foreign influences and tempted to savagery, he is linked with Kurtz and with Coetzee himself.[16] Both *Dusklands* stories feature avatars of J. M. Coetzee: the Coetzee whose 'Narrative of Jacobus Coetzee' accompanies 'The Vietnam Project', and the Coetzee who has 'asked [Dawn] to revise [his] essay' are both projections of aspects of a coloniser's identity. Jacobus approvingly promotes the murder and rape of the 'Hottentots', stating flatly that 'a bullet is too good for a Bushman' and that their women are 'completely disposable'. The Coetzee of Dawn's narrative, although incapable of the crude racism of his literary ancestor, is nevertheless unconcerned with 'the substance' of Dawn's report, focusing on tone: 'I want you to rewrite your proposals so that people in the military can entertain them without losing self-respect'.[17] As Dawn is consumed by his family's wretched present, Coetzee burdens himself with literary versions of his South African family's 'real' history. Author and characters are thus trapped in identities within family, gender and nation, and Coetzee's books are partly about an escape.[18] By exploring the dangers inherent in seeing political conflict simply as a power struggle centred on a patriarchal family, he here provides aversion therapy to the reader.[19]

It was Lyndon Johnson who described Vietnam as 'a member of the Free World family' in need of rescue.[20] But the family metaphor was one shared by the Viet Cong. Vietnamese autobiographer Le Ly Hayslip quotes Viet Cong cadres' view of the war, designed for broadcast to the peasantry: 'A nation cannot have two governments any more than a family can have two fathers.'[21] For Hayslip, too, the family is an instinctive point of reference. Her books *When Heaven and Earth Changed Places* and *Child of War, Woman of Peace* (known collectively as *Heaven and Earth, Parts One and Two*) recur continually to the metaphors Dawn sees as characteristic of Vietnamese thought, but with a difference. Hayslip titles her chapters 'Fathers and Daughters', 'Sisters and Brothers', 'Daughters and Sons', 'Finding a Family', but where Dawn sees only psychoanalytic concepts and the Viet Cong slogan offers a falsely simple choice, it is the particularities of real families that shape Hayslip's rhetoric. As a developing member of an extended family (the last of six children, a younger sibling, an unmarried mother, a third wife), Hayslip produced a subtly nuanced reading of war as a family affair. Where the Freudian Dawn has only father, mother and child as static models, Hayslip often speaks of the process of ageing and growth, of brothers and sisters, uncles and aunts, cousins, second wives and husbands, step children. Ho Chi Minh is 'Uncle Ho ... a kindly grandfather'. Saigon is 'both saving mother and painted, jealous sister', and the view from an airliner of the earth falling away beneath suggests 'the way a mother dwindles in the eyes of her growing daughter'.[22] Speaking from within such an evidently complex family identity, she, unlike Dawn, does not often claim to speak for a people, or even from a single viewpoint, 'exposing', as Rebecca L. Stephens suggests, 'the artificiality of a homogeneous national "we"'.[23] In dreams and apparitions her ancestors offer opinions that often contradict her own, so that she embodies the voices of not just 'daughter' or 'wife' but also 'father', 'husband' and 'brother'. Within her colonised nation and threatened culture, as within her family, she thus stresses a spiritualised multiple identity, and it is a divided society in civil war (not foreign invaders) that is her main concern – something masculine-oriented political polemic is incapable of imaging in its binary parental tropes. Hayslip's often explicitly feminised, fluid rhetoric allows her to rewrite the notion of war as a family quarrel.

When Hayslip discusses America's role in the war, her imagery initially seems to echo Dawn's. As he suggests, the earth and the natural world are seen as embodying parental virtues. Whilst Vietnam is sometimes described as 'our fatherland', when Phung Thi Le Ly (Hayslip) sees her first American helicopter she falls down to 'hold fast to mother earth', and in a chapter titled 'Open Wounds' she describes the aftermath of a battle between the Republicans and the Viet Cong in graphically maternal terms:

> The paddies would be littered with rubble – upturned trees, shattered rocks and charred craters where bombs or artillery rounds went astray. Those crops that weren't pulverised were scorched by the blast and lay withering on stalks like embryos cut from the womb.[24]

But, as it develops, her imagery of family says something very different from Dawn's:

> It was as if the American giant, who had for so long been taunted and annoyed by the Viet Cong ants, had finally come to stamp its feet ... It meant that a generation of children would grow up without fathers to teach them about their ancestors or their rituals of worship. Families would lose records of their lineage and with them the umbilicals to the very root of our society ... Our ties to the past were being severed, setting us adrift on a sea of borrowed Western materialism, disrespect for the elderly and selfishness ... It was as if I was standing by the cradle of a dying child and speculating with its aunts and uncles on what the doomed baby would have looked like had it grown up. By tugging on their baby so brutally, both parents had ended up killing the seedbed of us all. This, to me, was the highest crime – the frenzied suicide of cannibals. How shall one mourn a lifeless planet?[25]

Family roles and the natural order are disrupted. The giant crushes the ant parents, who in turn cripple their children. The past, both lineage and land, is destroyed along with the symbolic umbilicals. Infanticide becomes suicide. The anarchy among those images suggests both the richness and destruction of Vietnamese familial culture, but is reduced to a crudely gendered, anti-maternal simplicity by patriarch Dawn. Unlike his rigid concepts, Hayslip's mixed and flexible metaphors of war as family strife are helpful in dealing with its dangers and overcoming its after-effects. She blames no father figures: America is not linked with 'Ong Troi ... Mr. Sky, the god of all'.[26] But Hayslip's tumbling images also suggest unfixed readings, the impossibility of reducing complex physical experience to a coherent image or narrative.

Hayslip's descriptions of the Vietnam War contrast starkly, then, with Dawn's neurotically neat reading, and with Johnson's simple image of family that stands behind it. This is unsurprising: Coetzee designed Dawn as a fallible narrator making an anti-war point through irony. But Hayslip's position also differs from some of the conclusions that Coetzee seemingly invites us to draw from *Dusklands*. 'The Vietnam Project' relies on a stark opposition between America and Vietnam, and Coetzee's reader is outraged by the viewpoints put forward by Dawn as 'an archetypal American'. Coetzee felt that 'the war ... was welcomed ... I think people were given the kind of opportunity they've never been given before to participate by identification with massive acts of violence'.[27] Therefore, Dawn's society seems irreparably sick. His wife is wretched, a 'mental patient with hair in rats'-tails', Dawn finishes the story in a psychiatric hospital, even the Library's stack attendant is a 'microcephalic', as Dawn puts it, and is cared for at a convent.[28] There seems no escape from a binary opposition forcing us to despise American psycho-political dysfunction and brutality. America appears as oppressor and tyrant, its 'pacification' strategies companioned in *Dusklands* with the eighteenth-century massacres of the repulsive Jacobus Coetzee. Similarly, Dawn's enjoyment of his role as patriarch ('the father cannot be a benign father until his sons have knelt before his wand') and his murderous indifference to the sufferings of his wife and child ('Marilyn floats face down through my nights', 'I push the knife in. The child kicks and flails') force the reader to hate him as a man.[29] But as any good feminist, anti-racist or peace campaigner should know, the most effective and ethically satisfying way to challenge a binary opposition is not simply to reverse it.

One of the most surprising things that Hayslip's books do is to displace the fatherly Americans from the centre of their Vietnam story, the one blaming them for the war, and encouraging them to 'bring it home' as guilt. In fact, in Hayslip's eyes, the Americans are almost irrelevant in what she calls 'our war'. They are certainly unwelcome, but the war was really about 'Vietnamese on both sides who were making our country not just a graveyard, but a sewer of corruption and prison of fear'. Le Ly's father takes her through a litany of alternative culprits for the war:

who's to blame? If you ask the Viet Cong, they'll blame the Americans. If you ask the Americans, they'll blame the North. If you ask the North, they'll blame the South. If you ask the South, they'll blame the Viet Cong. If you ask the monks, they'll blame the Catholics, or tell you our ancestors did something terrible and so brought this endless suffering on our heads. So tell me, who would you punish? The common soldier who's only doing his duty?

He concludes:

when you see all those young Americans out there being killed and wounded in our war – in a war which fate or luck or god has commanded us to wage for our redemption and education – you must thank them, at least in your heart, for helping to put us back on our life's course.[30]

One might expect conciliatory logic from Hayslip's authorial voice, since her books are intended to promote understanding between Vietnam and America. But when she places these words in the mouth of her father they carry massive weight. Her father is portrayed as the personification of Vietnamese wisdom, advising his daughter in life and death, and his final word on the subject of the war, followed closely by his suicide, is uniquely privileged for her. Hayslip's focus is on an attempt to regain ownership of the war for the Vietnamese. They are not children to be fought over by feuding parents, but a family in their own right.

In Hayslip's account, the Vietnam conflict is not an American war, or a war in the world 'family', free or not (Hayslip barely mentions China or Russia, the possible Communist 'parent'). It is a Vietnamese war: 'We were what the war was all about'. She characterises the civil war which led to American involvement in the country as 'a family feud … A spat between brothers.' Leslie Bow notes her own brothers' and sisters' affiliations on different sides, and adds that Le Ly is transformed from 'prodigal daughter', seen as a traitor for marrying an American, to the 'maternal' builder of the 'Mother's Love' clinic. Although he says her return as American citizen and benefactor begs questions of US economic policy towards Vietnam and 'who will step in as 'saviour' to Vietnam within the global family', he adds that Hayslip's rhetoric 'remains on the level of extolling decent human interaction and the strength of family bonds as a means of forging alliances'.[31] Thus, for Hayslip, the war is a private matter for the Vietnamese family and the Americans are misunderstanding outsiders, 'barbarian saints' who intrude in support of one sibling against another. The feuding brothers are all too human and unsaintly: as a teenaged child Phung Thi Le Ly had been tortured by one side in the civil war, sentenced to death and raped by the other. In fact it is within the wider Southeast Asian context that stereotyping is hardest for her to root out: Korean and other Asian soldiers are likened to Japanese soldiers of the Second World War as 'ruthless killing machines'; whilst in contrast, at a defining moment, Le Ly upbraids a Vietnamese interpreter for not translating her request to a GI: 'Come on – give the American a chance to speak for himself!'[32] If he can speak for himself, then the Vietnamese can judge for herself, and thereby take some control over her life. This is a stage of her development from 'child of war' to 'woman of peace', as her second book's title implies, and presents her and thus her country as adult.

One effect is to destroy the binary relationship locking America and Vietnam together as guilty parental oppressor/protector and hapless child victim, a relationship documented in many texts on the war. In *The Green Berets* villagers and Americans come together when the 'white men' treat an injured little girl, and her killing by the Viet Cong justifies their hatred of the 'commies'. Meanwhile, an orphaned boy represents his country ('You don't have anybody else in the whole world, do you?' asks surrogate father Petersen) and is led off into the sunset by fatherly Colonel Kirby (John Wayne) at the film's end with the words (like, but so unlike, Hayslip's) 'you're what this is all about'.[33] Anti-war films explore the same familial territory: the idea of patriarchal rule by the American military as a workable policy was exploded by *Apocalypse Now*'s Colonel Kurtz (Marlon Brando), brutal godfather to his tribe ('these are all his children'), and his surrogate son and heir Willard (Martin Sheen). Killing the father figure and abandoning the 'children', together with a refusal of the army's mythography of itself as 'Almighty' (the codeword for a final, apocalyptic airstrike) is all Willard can do – essentially paralleling America's withdrawal from Vietnam. This patricidal iconography had developed further by the time Martin Sheen's son Charlie took a similar role. Surely in part cast because of the generic generational implications of his character, Charlie Sheen as Chris Taylor in *Platoon* is offered 'two fathers' in Sergeants Barnes and Elias – one of whom kills the feminised other 'father', and is then oedipally fragged by Taylor. As the ruthless patriarch, Barnes

is seen, Kurtz-like, chastising Vietnamese villagers, killing a woman
and holding a child at gunpoint.[34] American audiences were thus
used to thinking about the war in parental terms, and, in order to
create space for her own story, Hayslip breaks and reconfigures that
family relationship. As part of this process, she shows herself becoming a parent, not just of Vietnamese-American children but of her
'daughter', the East Meets West Foundation, and her 'literary child',
the two-volume autobiography, which goes on to have 'children of
its own'. She moves from 'the kid's end of the table' in her American
mother-in-law's home to 'sitting down at my kitchen table' realising
that she is a householder and restaurateur. In seizing control of the
imagery of family, she concludes: 'We are all brothers and sisters.
We must all repay our mother's love.'[35] Like her conflicted imagery,
however, this unexpectedly anti-binary representation incorporates
its own problems.

Her view of American foreign policy – 'It was not your fault' she
states in her prologue addressed to former GIs – prompts Lynette Tan
to criticise Hayslip for 'absolving the Americans'. Leslie Bow adds that
she 'ends up supporting American interests by refusing to hold either
side accountable for the war'.[36] Tan and Bow see her story as structured by – perhaps sold out to – American myths of 'making it', and
several critics have also been troubled by her willingness to assume
traditional subject roles in forgiving America. Viet Thanh Nguyen,
for example, describes Hayslip's echoes of the classic Vietnamese
poem *Truyen Kieu* (*The Tale of Kieu*), where the protagonist (representing
both woman and nation) sacrifices her happiness in submission to
others, as a pure but self-denying heroine accepting injustice.[37] If
Hayslip rewrites the American familial stereotypes of the war, she
substitutes others that are differently problematic. Vietnam must be
both adult and able to deal with the consequences of 'his' or 'her'
(freely made?) decisions. But metaphors and similes, useful as they
are to mythographers and essayists, cannot fully represent Vietnam's
history or Hayslip's life, her 'crucial act of witnessing' as Nguyen
puts it.[38] Unlike the fictive Coetzees and Dawns with their shadowy
flesh and blood ancestry, experienced reality of war and gendered
conflict was and is an important component in her narrative. To accuse her of 'jaded fatalism', just as to accuse Vietnam veteran Oliver
Stone, the director of *Heaven and Earth* (the film of Hayslip's books),
of turning her/his war story into a 'wacky, liberal guilt trip', is to
privilege criticism of representation over respect for a (lost but still

meaningful) reality, and ignores the explicit attempts made by such
war survivors to create, through their rhetoric, connections with a
wider 'family' of those who did not experience the war.[39] The need
for a nuanced response to autobiographical accounts is evident if
one looks at the relationship between Hayslip's books and the film
Oliver Stone made from her story, *Heaven and Earth*.

Stone said that he made the film, the third of his 'Vietnam
trilogy', to challenge revisionist filmic versions of the war in which
America 'won', whilst 'hundreds of nameless, faceless Vietnamese
are casually shot, stabbed and blown to smithereens'. Commendably,
Stone wanted to know 'who were they?'[40] He had already replied to
these films in *Platoon* (which in fact helped inspire Hayslip to write
her account), but the Vietnamese version of events remained, for
him, untold.[41] Perhaps he was also thinking of recent portrayals of
Vietnamese women in the war in films such as *Full Metal Jacket*, in
which a young female Viet Cong fighter is captured and reluctantly
killed by American troops, or the ugly, emotive *Casualties of War*,
which deals with the abduction, rape and murder of a Vietnamese
village girl.[42] Both films, whilst examining the (im)morality of
such acts, leave their female victims effectively voiceless. Hayslip's
books promised a voice related to these characters' experiences, but,
essentially, it offered too complex an answer to Stone's question.
His film, therefore, exemplifies the problems of responding to a
text like Hayslip's, complicated by his own status as a combatant
in Vietnam. Oliver Stone, said Robert Stone, ended up wanting 'to
be a vet and a protester, to be for the GIs and the Viet Cong, an
American and a Vietnamese'. [43] He also, it seems likely, wanted to
be both man and woman, but was unable to do so, perhaps in
part because Hayslip accompanied him each day during filming.[44]
Even if he were capable of androgynising his own experience, he
was concerned to replicate hers faithfully, and – more problematically – saw their stories as complementary. Like Coetzee, Stone was
burdened by history and nation, and by gender and family, on
public display during the film's making and release as his second
marriage broke up. He was at the time involved in relinquishing
custody of his children.[45] Hayslip's story surely attracted him because it offered an opportunity to examine such issues, but, unlike
her, Stone did not move on generically in response to this complex
life-writing. In particular, her multiplicitous imagery of family gets
lost in *Heaven and Earth*.

Instead, Stone seemed beset by his own personal circumstances. His difficulties are made clear in his interview for *Entertainment Weekly*, in which he fragmentedly links his family life with *Heaven and Earth*:

> the tension surrounding the release of *Heaven and Earth*, going through a divorce, my assets are depleted – I don't mind because it's going to my family – all these factors combine to put a tremendous amount of stress on me. *Heaven and Earth* is going out into the world – its my baby.[47]

Stone, known for personal engagement with issues in his films, made *Heaven and Earth* as a soldier, a father and a man, something elliptically recognised in Hayslip's lionising of him: 'Oliver has given us many strong "sons" ... I am pleased and honoured that, with *Heaven and Earth*, he has now also raised a daughter worthy of his warrior's heart.'[47] Although, therefore, he had made two films about American men in Vietnam and on return home, he still had something to say and it was not quite what Hayslip was saying. In particular, by conflating four men in Hayslip's life into 'Steve Butler', Vietnam veteran and a character whom Bryan Marinelli calls 'Oliver Stone/Butler', Stone's film returns to the gendered imagery of family created by Eugene Dawn in Coetzee's post-colonial context. He re-imagines Dawn's parental battle over a distressed child, this time with the added complications that both mother and child represent the desired/feared colonial subject, and both have come 'home' to the coloniser's land.[48] As I suggested in analysis of *Dusklands*, this strategy is a dangerous one.

As Dominic Head says of 'The Vietnam Project', the issue in *Heaven and Earth* is 'not only the paternal imperialism of the U.S., but the nation's role as the sometimes inhospitable host to a complex migrant multi-culturalism'.[50] In *Heaven and Earth*, as in Hayslip's book, her husband Steve/Dennis Hayslip's response to her as unwanted migrant mother is to kidnap her children and attempt to enforce her obedience with threats that she will lose them. Le Ly describes Dennis's fears that she and her Vietnamese-American friends (whom he refers to as heathens and 'dinks') are plotting against him and their host nation: 'you Vietnamese really stick together, don't you? Still taking advantage of the Americans.'[50] This supposed plotting of family members or nations traditionally figured as dependent motivates his violent 'response', and Stone's film creates a connection with America's role in Vietnam not present in his source. His

Steve Butler is a Black Ops assassin, torn between desire to protect his Vietnamese family and, brutally yet fearfully, to dominate them. When he first meets Phung Thi Le Ly, he has a nightmare recalling experiences in the field, in which he sees her bleeding face staring at him in submission. Waking, he believes she is an attacker, and draws a knife. But fully conscious he offers her and her children protection and a home in America – which will itself become a battleground over divorce and custody. All the elements of Dawn's analogy of family and war are re-created. In fact Hayslip's two husbands, Ed Munro and Dennis Hayslip, were not Vietnam veterans, but their story is mapped on to Steve's to create 'Oliver Stone/Butler', with additions from the lives of two other partners, veteran Dan DeParma and fantasist Cliff Parry.[51] In addition, Stone rewrites the relationship between man and wife: Steve's first wife Beverly (whom we never meet) 'gets half my pay check, plus support for the kids, and she's still pissed', and Steve and Le Ly have stand-up rows instead of the masculine explosions depicted in the book. A connection is made between these set pieces and a scene early in the film, expanded from a brief dialogue-less passage in Hayslip, in which her parents argue and her father hits her mother, who weeps because she has made her husband 'lose face'. In the film 'Hayslip's' voice-over echoes this guilt after a row with Steve: 'I was starting to behave like an American, yelling back at my husband, frowns, scowls'. *She* hits *him* when he opposes her, and thus the vision of the childlike foreign wife as attacker is validated, in a way that Hayslip's books never allow.[52] Stone's own life as former GI and family man seems to inform the rewriting in multiple painful ways, and Hayslip's more complex portrayals of woman, child and colonial subject fuse into uniformity in the film in part because of its binary structure, the other half of which is 'Oliver Stone/Butler'.

Stone has been criticised for telling either his own story, or the stereotypical veteran's story, in *Heaven and Earth*. Even favourable reviews ('his voice is just as powerful when expressed through a woman') suggested Hayslip had been bypassed, or had become merely 'an icon of womanhood' set against (literally) Steve Butler.[53] It has been pointed out that the actress playing Hayslip (Hiep Thi Le) received only fourth billing, whilst Steve Butler (Tommy Lee Jones) came first, and that 'it seems as if [Butler's] and Le Ly's story hardly intersect'.[54] Marinelli, surveying the process of Stone's transformation of Munro, DeParma, Hayslip and Parry into Steve Butler/Oliver

Stone, refers to his highlighting of Butler's story as 'when man and woman changed places'. He finally suggests that 'Stone has appropriated Hayslip's ... texts as vehicles to once again exhibit his own personal and political agenda'.[55] It is certainly true that Stone focuses on the conventional story of the soldier who brought the war home with him and tore his innocent family apart, rather than the real experience of the woman who built and rebuilt her family during and after the war. He erases, too, Hayslip's contrasting imagery of an inclusive family, including 'my American "brothers and sisters"', deployed in direct response to the claustrophobic notion of family incarnated in her menfolk and Butler.[56] Stone's vision of family is the Western one, with a small parent–child nucleus surrounded by relatives who are at best minor characters, and he sites all the tensions of the war inside that central bad marriage. But one reason for Stone's rewriting is probably Hayslip's own attitude to veterans as fellow-sufferers, and her lack of investment in Western feminist notions of gender. Despite her very different construction of the idea of family, her appalling marital experiences, and what Bow calls her 'gendered pacifism' based on motherly love, she does not explore the gendered implications of relationships.[57]

In part this may be because the Vietnamese culture whose virtues Hayslip is eager to remember, and whose destruction she earnestly mourns, was also – from her adult Americanised viewpoint – one where women were oppressed throughout their lives. Phung Thi Le Ly grew up in a world where the suggestion of the midwife had been 'Suffocate her!', the first words of Chapter 1. 'I was a girl', she explains, 'Everybody wanted sons and brothers, not daughters and sisters.'[58] She was expected to marry, entering a period of subjection to her new family. As for other female East Asian writers, such as Amy Tan and Maxine Hong Kingston, there was an alternative myth of woman warriors[59] (Le Ly's ancestor Phung Thi Chinh), but whilst her father told her this story, he added that her duty was 'to stay alive ... to find a husband and have babies'.[60] Bow argues that Hayslip's decision to fulfil this command by flouting Vietnamese conventions of patriotic chastity (prostituting herself, marrying an invader to give herself and her child safety) contradictorily 'indicates' for her 'a true Vietnamese nationalism' in its assumption of the role of 'feminine nurturing', whilst allowing survival and independence – but it also still represents a rejection of Vietnamese traditions.[61]

I understood the choices I had made – and the things that resulted from them. What happened had been as much my doing as theirs. For a Vietnamese woman, realising this was like emancipation to a slave.[62]

In Hayslip's view (and it is a hotly contested one) war and male American invaders have helped to free her in a way that her own society would not have done.[63] This belief, and her ethos that 'you were only a victim – truly a victim – when you felt like one', has enraged some critics, but it is a viewpoint that Bow suggests requires in response the development of 'a concept of complex agency' incorporating (in Lata Mani's words) 'the ways in which women negotiate oppressive, even determining social conditions' as well as offering more obvious resistance.[64] Cooperation, in other words, is not automatically submission. The same reformulation could also be applied to Hayslip's view of Vietnam's future, and her sympathy for American veterans. Stone's film builds on this stance, and, although the film has been accused of succumbing to its 'hyper-masculine' genre, Hayslip's own views at least partly validate Stone's interpretation.[65]

Only once does Hayslip speak bitterly about her treatment by American men:

All the American men I had known – in Vietnam or America – became narrow-minded, petty and vindictive when they were angry. They didn't know about women and didn't respect them. I couldn't believe such men had ever known a mother's love ... They considered children – even their own – as no more than weeds in a garden ... They were men who loved their hunting dogs and guns more than their ancestors ... they were nothing but dogs themselves.[67]

Even here, the passage moves swiftly from male attitudes to women back to their attitude to family, always the books' touchstone. Children were the focus of the battle between Le Ly and Dennis Hayslip, as between the film's Le Ly and Steve Butler. In trying to force her to dismantle her altar ('that stupid shrine') and so lose contact with her ancestors, one attack is being made on her family, but the more important one for her is that made through her children. The monk to whom she turns for guidance asks her, if she could save only one person, her child, husband or mother from a fire, who would she save. 'Thinking like a Westerner', she chooses her child, and although on his advice she returns to Vietnam to seek out her mother, leaving her children behind, it is to them that she returns.[67] The husband as fire victim does not receive a moment's consideration, for her gendered troubles are not the focus of Hayslip's text.

When Oliver Stone's Steve Butler appropriates separate fragments of the speeches of Hayslip's husbands ('My first wife taught me a real lesson ... I'm serious. I need a good Oriental woman like you'),[69] he does however change her emphasis. Steve's desire to avenge the implied wrongs of his 'first wife' shades into the desire to begin again with a supposedly submissive 'good Oriental woman' through the word 'need'. In articulating Steve's viewpoint so bluntly, Stone returns to the classic Western stereotype of the insecure, dominating, male colonialist, not present in Hayslip's books, of which Eugene Dawn is the most extreme representative. Describing attempts at total war and rapes perpetrated in the hope of a 'miracle' ('if you will prove yourself ... you will prove us too, and we will love you endlessly'), Dawn concludes 'when we came back we were still alone'.[69] The sense of lacking and the desire for loving contact is in permanent co-dependence with the desire to dominate, something Stone stresses in adapting Hayslip's experiences to incorporate the classic veteran's story. As with his patriarchal colonist predecessors, Mr and Colonel Kurtz and Eugene Dawn, Butler ends alone with his horror. As Roger Ebert notes in a review of one of the first 'coming home' Vietnam war films, Travis Bickle's famous line 'Are you talkin' to me?' is followed by 'Well, I'm the only one here.' He calls this aggressive reformulation of 'utter aloneness' ' the truest line in the film', and sees it as characteristic of the portrayal of the violent returning veteran.[70] In inserting it into *Heaven and Earth*, Stone has placed an extremely negative masculine response to war alongside Hayslip's feminised optimism. Reinforcing a message of tragic despair, instead of Hayslip's proffered forgiveness, it dominates the end of the film. Where Hayslip was finally able to image America and Vietnam as lovers, a husband and wife who 'fight in order to communicate better' and then 'make love after they make up', the film's image of that marriage is one of failure.[71]

In his *Utopia*, the English humanist Thomas More told of an exotic land in which, when it went to war,

> just as no man is forced into a foreign war against his will, so women are allowed to accompany their men on military service if they want to – not only not forbidden, but encouraged and praised for doing

so. They place each woman alongside her husband in the line of battle; and in addition they place around him all of a man's children,
kinsmen, and blood- or marriage-relations, so that those who by
nature have most reason to help one another may be closest at hand
for mutual aid. It is a matter of great reproach for either partner to
come home without the other.[72]

Whether More intended his philosophical rationale to be taken
seriously or mocked is unclear (as so often with More), but his situation of the family at the heart of battle, as the key unit of survival
in and after war, is striking. In this he resembles Hayslip, whose
home and battlefield are identical, and identically an important test
of family life. She refashions the story of the interaction between
family and war in a way that stresses continuity, relativism and familial identity. On one hand her texts construct war as being about
families – both metaphorically (for her brother and sister Vietnamese
and Americans), and in real terms (the danger families experience in
war zones and the importance of their mutual strength to survival).
On the other, she chronicles families at war in peacetime, portraying conflict, especially when centred around children, as at least as
damaging as the trauma of a military campaign. Viet Thanh Nguyen
says that she 'literally brings the war home'.[73] It is this conceptual
continuity that is important to her, empowering her own voice
with the imagery of family itself, strong enough to survive and
articulate even divorce or death. In these images, she finds security
in a sometimes contradictory feminised inclusiveness – a peace
that is never available to those whose essentially binary imagery
of family conflict (husband/wife, father/child) is used to promote
colonialism and violence at home and abroad. With the prospect of
another Gulf War as part of the War Against Terrorism, her unifying
un-American but pro-American approach to the spiritualised family
network and to the familial rhetoric of colonialism seems especially
relevant. Such a balanced view contrasts terribly with the kind of
domestic tragedies associated with returning Vietnam veterans but
repeating themselves today. 'No matter what they say, Special Forces
is not about family values', says one Green Beret's wife.[74]

We may not be qualified to comment in detail on what happened at Fort Bragg in summer 2002, but the picture that emerges
from an examination of these three literary texts about war and
family suggests that an understanding of the way the two discourses

intersect is vital to practical attempts to prevent such strikingly clustered tragedies. The texts are especially relevant in that after 11 September 2001 America is in a position curiously reminiscent of the Vietnam era – traumatised by the effectiveness of an assault by underestimated forces, who are driven by cultural imperatives only semi-comprehensible to traditional military strategists. The resultant patterns of military-familial life and the rhetoric of protection and domination are thus also similar, and the tragic conjunction between foreign aggression and domestic violence once again engages our attention.

Notes

1   Jim Martin, quoted in Dave Moniz, 'Connection Probed in Fort Bragg Killings', *USA Today*, 28 July 2002, at www.usatoday.com/news/nation/2002-07-28-fort-bragg-killings-x.html, and Fox Butterfield paraphrasing Deborah D. Tucker in 'Wife Killings at Fort Reflect Growing Problem in Military', *New York Times* 29 July 2002, 9. The film from which I take my title, *The War at Home* (directed by Emilio Estevez and starring himself and his father, Martin Sheen), deals with the violent homecoming of a Vietnam veteran and his relationship with paternal authority (Touchstone, 1996).

2   Tim Reid, 'What They Can't Control, They Kill', *The Times*, T2, 2 August 2002, p. 2.

3   Reid, 4, and Catherine Lutz, quoted in Manuel Roig-Franzia, 'A Base Rocked by Violence', *Washington Post*, 2 August 2002, p. A3.

4   Reid, p. 3.

5   On 'what is at risk when cultural critics … depend upon realist discourses and notions of authenticity to theorise personal and political agency', see Wendy S. Hesford and Wendy Kozol (eds.), *Haunting Violations: Feminist Criticism and the Crisis of the 'Real'* (Urbana and Chicago: University of Illinois Press, 2001), p. 1 and *passim*.

6   J. M. Coetzee, 'The Vietnam Project', in *Dusklands* (Harmondsworth: Penguin, [1974] 1996) pp. 21, 26; *The Green Berets*, film directed by John Wayne and Ray Kellogg, Warner, 1968.

7   Coetzee, p. 1.

8   Coetzee, p. 2.

9   David Attwell, '"The Labyrinth of My History": J. M. Coetzee's *Dusklands*', in Sue Kossew (ed.), *Critical Essays on J. M. Coetzee* (New York: G.K. Hall, 1998), p. 38.

10 Coetzee, pp. 7–9.

11 Coetzee, p. 38; Peter Knox-Shaw, '*Dusklands*: A Metaphysics of Violence', in Graham Huggan and Stephen Watson (eds.), *Critical Perspectives on J. M. Coetzee* (Basingstoke/ New York: Macmillan/St. Martin's Press, 1996), p. 113.

12 See for example, *Taxi Driver*, film, directed by Martin Scorsese, Columbia, 1976; *The Deer Hunter*, film, directed by Michael Cimino, Universal, 1978.

13 As Philip R. Wood puts it, it is 'a continuation of his relations with his family … and *vice versa*', 'Aporias of the Postcolonial Subject: Correspondence with J. M. Coetzee', *South Atlantic Quarterly* 93:1 (Winter 1994), 182.

14 Susan Jeffords, *The Remasculinisation of America: Gender and the Vietnam War* (Indianapolis: Indiana University Press, 1989), p. 49.

15 See Derek Maus, 'Kneeling Before the Father's Wand: Violence, Eroticism and Paternalism in Thomas Pynchon's *V* and J. M. Coetzee's *Dusklands*', *Journal of Literary Studies* 15 (June 1999), 198; Joseph Conrad, *Heart of Darkness* (London: Penguin, [1899] 1973) and *Apocalypse Now*, film, directed by Francis Ford Coppola, Zoetrope, 1979.

16 Dawn also has an office at the Kennedy Institute, presumably in Boston, as he remarks on 'the boys from M.I.T', Coetzee, p. 33.

17 Coetzee, pp. 1, 60–1, 2–3.

18 As Stephen Watson sums up, Coetzee wants to 'escape the warped relationships that colonialism fosters', 'Colonialism and the Novels of J. M. Coetzee', *Research in African Literatures* 17 (1986), 390; quoted in Debra A. Castillo, 'Coetzee's *Dusklands*: The Mythic Punctum', *PMLA* 105:5 (October 1990), 1109. Rosemary Jolly argues that Coetzee sees history as a prison which must be escaped, 'The Gun as Copula: Colonisation, Rape, and the Question of Pornographic Violence in J. M. Coetzee's *Dusklands*', *World Literature Written in English*, 32:2 and 33:1 (1992–93), 44.

19 A number of writers have disputed Knox-Shaw's contention that Coetzee's fiction is implicated in the violence it describes. Dominic Head sums up: Coetzee called characters by his own name because he felt himself to be 'tainted' – 'with the intellectual and privileged withdrawal of supervisor Coetzee', for example (Dominic Head, *J. M. Coetzee* (Cambridge: Cambridge University Press, 1997) pp. 47–8. David Attwell adds that *Dusklands* is 'an agonising encounter with colonialism's violence, and with the discursive legacy it leaves to its heirs', one of whom is J. M. Coetzee. Attwell, p. 29.

20 In 1965. Quoted in Lynette Tan, '*Heaven and Earth*': Oliver Stone's Vietnamese Frontier (Sheffield: Sheffield Hallam University Press, 1999), p. 6.

21 Le Ly Hayslip with Jay Wurts, *Heaven and Earth Part One: When Heaven and Earth Changed Places* (London, Sydney, Auckland: Pan, [1989] 1994), p. x.

22 Hayslip, *Part One*, pp. 53, 83, 129, 147.

23 Rebecca L. Stephens, 'Distorted Reflections: Oliver Stone's *Heaven and Earth* and Le Ly Hayslip's *When Heaven and Earth Changed Places*', *Centennial Review*, 41:3 (Fall 1997), 661.

24 Hayslip, *Part One*, pp. xii, 55, 102.

25 Hayslip, *Part One*, pp. 255–6.

26 Le Ly Hayslip with James Hayslip, *Child of War, Woman of Peace: Heaven and Earth Part Two* (London, Sydney, Auckland: Pan, [1993] 1994), p. 49.

27 Rosemary Gary, 'J. M. Coetzee's *Dusklands*: Of War and War's Alarms', *Commonwealth Essays and Studies* 9:1 (Autumn 1996), 35. Gary quotes Peter Temple's interview with Coetzee.

28 Coetzee, pp. 11, 6.

29 Coetzee, pp. 26, 34, 42.

30 Hayslip, *Part One*, pp. 260–2.

31 Leslie Bow, 'Third-World Testimony in the Era of Globalisation: Vietnam, Sexual Trauma and Le Ly Hayslip's Art of Neutrality', in Hesford and Kozol, pp. 178–9.

32 Hayslip, *Part One*, pp. xvi, 42, 264, 405, 255, 247, 259, 258.

33 *The Green Berets*, film, directed by John Wayne and Ray Kellogg, Warner, 1968. The boy refers to Petersen (Jim Hutton) as 'my Peter-sen', an echo of 'papa san'.

34 *Platoon*, film, directed by Oliver Stone, Orion, 1986. Although Taylor refers to Elias

(Willem Dafoe) and Barnes (Tom Berenger) as 'two fathers' warring 'for possession of my soul', the nurturing, sometimes camp Elias is actually motherly.

35 Hayslip, *Part Two*, pp. 370, 16, 216, 362.

36 Hayslip, *Part One*, xvi; Tan, p. 16; Bow, p. 184.

37 Viet Thanh Nguyen, 'Representing Reconciliation: Le Ly Hayslip and the Victimised Body', *Positions* 5:2 (Fall 1997), 630–4.

38 Nguyen, p. 636.

39 *Heaven and Earth*, film, directed by Oliver Stone, Warner, 1993; Tan, p. 16; James Vermiere, review of *Heaven and Earth* in the *Boston Herald*, quoted in Norman Kagan, *The Cinema of Oliver Stone* (New York: Continuum, 1995), pp. 224–5.

40 Kagan, p. 209.

41 Le Ly Hayslip, 'Heaven and Earth', in Robert Brent Toplin (ed.), *Oliver Stone's USA* (Lawrence: University of Kansas Press, 2000), p. 180.

42 *Full Metal Jacket*, film, directed by Stanley Kubrick, Warner, 1987; *Casualties of War*, film, directed by Brian de Palma, Columbia, 1989.

43 Robert Stone, 'Oliver Stone's U.S.A', review in the *New York Review of Books*, quoted in Kagan, p. 224.

44 'Oliver Stoned', interview by Gregg Kilday in Charles L. P. Silet, ed., *Oliver Stone Interviews* (Jackson: University of Mississippi Press, 2001), p. 212.

45 Silet, p. 114.

46 Silet, p. 121.

47 Kagan, p. 225.

48 Bryan Marinelli, 'When Man and Woman Changed Places', in Don Kunz (ed.), *The Films of Oliver Stone* (Lanham and London: Scarecrow, 1997), p. 244.

49 Head, p. 30.

50 Hayslip, *Part Two*, pp. 149, 154, 163.

51 Marinelli, p. 244.

52 Michael Singer, working from Stone's screenplay, explains that this scene is meant to show them 'not like a couple but like enemies from opposite sides of the world'. Michael Singer, Oliver Stone, Le Ly Hayslip, Jay Wurts and Hiep Thi Le, *The Making of Oliver Stone's 'Heaven and Earth'* (London: Orion, 1993), p. 81.

53 See for example Todd Doogan at www.the digitalbits.com/reviews2/stonedvds. html; and Augustin K. Sedgewick quoting David Denby at www.wm.edu/CAS/ ASP/faculty/Lowry/Amst2000/projects%202000/Stone/public_html/heaven_ earth2.html.

54 Mark R. Leeper at http://reviews.imdb.com/Reviews/23/2343, and Marjorie Baumgarten at www.auschron.com/film/pages/movies/1885.html.

55 Marinelli, p. 244.

56 Hayslip *Part Two*, p. 304.

57 Bow, p. 171.

58 Hayslip, *Part One*, pp. 1–2.

59 Amy Tan, *The Bonesetter's Daughter* (New York: Flamingo, 2001); Maxine Hong Kingston, *The Woman Warrior* (New York: Alfred A. Knopf, 1976).

60 Hayslip, *Part One*, pp. 16, 37, 41.

61 Bow, p. 178.

62 Hayslip, *Part One*, pp. 338–9, 388, 425.

63 See for example Lynette Tan, p. 9.

64 Bow, 185.

65 Sedgewick.

66 Hayslip, *Part Two*, pp. 296, 174.

67 Hayslip, *Part Two*, pp. 140, 232–3.

68 Adapted from Hayslip, *Part One*, pp. 429, 435; Hayslip, *Part Two*, p. 109.

69 Coetzee, pp. 17–18.
70 Roger Ebert, review of *Taxi Driver* at www.suntimes.com/ebert/ebert_reviews/1999/12/taxidriver.html.
71 Hayslip in Toplin, p. 185.
72 Thomas More, *Utopia*, ed. and trans. Robert M. Adams (New York and London: W.W. Norton, [1516] 1992), p. 70.
73 Nguyen, p. 625.
74 Reid, p. 4.

9

Chicken or hawk?
Heroism, masculinity and violence in Vietnam War narratives

Angela K. Smith

We come to stand behind him against the wall – we ghosts – as flat and pale as a night-light, easy on the eyes...[1]

Vietnam was a war of ghosts.

Since the earliest days of Western civilisation, soldiering has represented the ultimate in manliness. Prowess on the field of battle, successful action carried out against an enemy, has been an integral part of the way masculinity has been constructed for generations. A simple paradigm, perhaps, but complicated when viewed from the early twenty-first century. Discussing this, the helicopter pilots in Robert Mason's Vietnam War memoir Chickenhawk (1984) articulate an interesting paradox.[2] They call themselves 'chickenhawks'. The metaphor, a hybrid of bird of prey and flightless domestic fowl, seems to emblematise not only the conflicting emotions of the pilots as they face the daily routine of death and boredom in the combat zone, but the experience of soldiers everywhere, in any war. For them, it works literally. Grounded, with the time to think about what they must do and watch others doing, they feel themselves to be cowards, not quite 'men' enough to be soldiers. But in the air, where they have the unique power of skilled flight, they know that the adrenaline rush of battle will give them the courage they need to face the danger.

It is a paradox that is repeated in countless war memoirs and other writings of the twentieth century and beyond. Soldiers continually try to find ways to articulate both the fear and the power of the combat experience. The need to be a 'man', to exhibit the characteristics of a traditional heroism that will confirm individual success, so often tainted by the fear, or, as society terms it, the 'cowardice' that brings conventional notions of masculinity into question. The 'extraordinary exultation'[3] expressed by Wilfred Owen at the experience of going over the top in the First World War is remarkably similar in inference to Philip Caputo's much later response to a successful infantry action: 'When the line wheeled and charged across the clearing, the enemy bullets whining past them, wheeled and charged almost with drill-field precision, an ache as profound as the ache of orgasm passed through me.'[4] But, equally, expressions of fear and doubts about masculinity can be found across the broadest spectrum of war literature.

Samuel Hynes has argued that 'war writing ... is a genre without tradition to the men who write it',[5] suggesting that these narratives do not alter over time; nor do they reflect the events of their own time. Each writes the experience of war as though it is the first such narrative, yet each adopts the characteristics of the war text, employed countless times before. Embedded within many war narratives are explorations of masculinity, the complexities of conforming to being soldiers. The narratives of Vietnam appear to be no different, the same issues of 'being men' are explicit. Yet located as it was, in the second half of the twentieth century, the soldiers seem to have acquired a certain freedom of articulation. The passage of time allows Caputo to be much more explicit regarding these paradoxical emotions than Owen might have chosen to be. Caputo's memoir, *A Rumor of War*, consciously debates issues such as heroism, masculinity, violence and sexuality, identified and linked by Freud at the beginning of the twentieth century, but more confidently verbalised in the aftermath of Vietnam than after any previous war.

This chapter seeks to explore this verbalisation, through an examination of a range of textual representations of Vietnam: novels and memoirs by both men and women from both the West and the East. How do these narratives differ from those representing other wars? Does Vietnam bring to a climax the crises of masculinity first identified in the trenches of the Western Front? To what extent does the honesty about violence, and in particular sexual violence, influence the way that we perceive warfare at the beginning of the twenty-first century?

So why was Vietnam different? There are a number of obvious, publicly acknowledged reasons. It was a major war that Western powers lost. It was extremely unpopular on the home fronts particularly in the United States. It was fought between 'enemies' that were not only politically different but also 'racially' so. Vietnam itself offered the added complication of being a combat zone that, by the time the Americans arrived, had been in the grip of colonial and civil wars for decades. Many of the civilians they encountered there had never known peace. All this problematises the process of writing the Vietnam War. How do you present heroic failure, especially for an unsympathetic home audience? What role has the textual representation played in rewriting the Vietnam War in historic and cultural as well as literary terms? What can we learn from the ghosts that haunt all these records and testimonies?

Men's stories

When the most famous narratives of the First World War were written, they played a significant part in creating the impression of the war that was passed down to subsequent generations. Soldier poets such as Owen, whose poetry, full of pity and compassion, can be read in conjunction with prose writers such as Henri Barbusse, Robert Graves, Erich Maria Remarque and Siegfried Sassoon to create the still familiar picture of this war. They argued against the popular image of patriotic glory, asserting a different kind of heroism, that of the common soldier whose interests were not represented by the state, but by his devotion to his comrades and his dedication to duty despite the questionable motives behind the war. In a sense these were soldiers who lost the battles but won the war. By demonstrating the complete lack of heroism in First World War combat, they, perhaps paradoxically, created the 'heroic' image of the suffering trench soldier that has travelled across the generations.

Heroism is a difficult concept in the twentieth century. John Onions has devised three different ways of defining heroism.[6] The first he labels 'cultural heroism', which 'accords primacy to heroic action and posits rewards for successful heroes. The second is 'social heroism', which is inspired by a particular cause or belief. The third is 'existential heroism', illustrated by men who 'risk their very existence and this risk cannot be measured solely by culture or cause'.[7] While Onions is able to identify examples of this third category in the writings of the First World War, it is very difficult to find any of them in the memoirs of Vietnam. Combative action in Vietnam often appears in terms of graphically violent representation, focusing on the victim of the violence or on the act itself, distilling the way in which the soldier is perceived. We are shocked, and presumably the writers intend us to be. These texts are anti-war; the soldiers themselves, by their own actions, are prevented from being heroic. Thus the age-old connection between heroism and masculinity is severed, leaving masculinity adrift – the spectre-like role of the 'man' becomes much more difficult to define.

Samuel Hynes suggests:

> You can see the effects... in the ways the narratives use the traditional language of military values, the Big Words like 'courage' and 'duty' and 'heroism.' Those words survive, but without a clear moral base; they are simply words for extra-ordinary kinds of behaviour.
>   ... for example, in Caputo's *A Rumor of War* ... Though the war was over and lost, it was still possible for a teller to bootleg a Big Word like 'hero' into his narrative; it just wasn't possible to tell a heroic story heroically all the way through. The consequent fluctuation of tone, in and out of irony, is not uncommon in Vietnam memoirs.[8]

Arguably, this is what Graves gives us in *Goodbye to All That*. But for all his ironic detachment, he wants us to believe in the heroic actions of his friend, Siegfried Sassoon:

> Siegfried's platoon went to support the Cameronians, and when these were driven out of some trenches they had won, he regained the position with a bombing-party of six men. Though shot through the throat, he continued the bombing until he collapsed.[9]

The problem for Caputo and his contemporaries is that the nature of warfare in Vietnam makes 'heroic action' in a conventional sense even more difficult to identify. Fighting for a cause they did not understand, against an enemy that they could not see, American soldiers in Vietnam seem to recall violent actions rather than heroic ones. And generally it is a violence without gain: the victims could as easily be civilians as soldiers.

Yet it is the way that this violence is represented that is most disturbing. There is confusion as to the identity of the enemy, suspicion of all Vietnamese as they may be harbouring the enemy, and resentment at being there at all. The result is a new slant on the 'extraordinary exultation' of war that leaves the combat soldier 'soaring high, very high in a delirium of violence'.[10]

In the Vietnam War there is a high emphasis on body count. Caputo emphasises that this was the way in which the American military determined their success rates, by counting 'enemy' bodies. The continuing horror of the wounded and the condition of the dead are all reminiscent of earlier war narratives; although the weaponry in Vietnam was more sophisticated, it was no less destructive. But these texts are full of different impressions of violence – for example, the mutilation of enemy corpses. It was not uncommon for British trench soldiers to pick up German helmets as souvenirs, but some American soldiers developed a taste for much more macabre keepsakes, leading Samuel Hynes to coin a new literary term to describe these narratives:

> Soldiers dishonoured the enemy dead, cut off their ears and strung them on strings for souvenirs, spit on them, urinated on them, preserved their skulls as ornaments. These degradations are told in detail in the narratives; they make the story barbaric and the Battlefield Gothic horrible. But they also make it commonplace.[11]

'Battlefield Gothic' is an interesting stylistic term, and one that applies specifically to the writings of Vietnam. For example, the ghost narrator of Larry Heinemann's *Paco's Story* tells us: 'Jones had thirty-nine pairs of blackened, leathery, wrinkly ears strung on a bit of black commo wire and wrapped like a garland around that bit of turned-out brim of his steel helmet.'[12] But what is perhaps most disturbing, and in keeping with Hynes's assertion of the commonplace nature of such practices is the fact that no action is taken against marines such as this one.

Joanna Bourke argues that this mutilation of bodies, the trophy collecting, can be read as an assertion of masculinity which enabled the soldiers to wear badges of their 'manhood'. It is part of the carnivalesque of combat:

> Killing itself could be seen as on set of carnival: combat gear, painted faces, and the endless refrain that men had to turn into 'animals' were the martial equivalent of the carnival mask; they enabled men to invert the moral order while still remaining innocent and committed to that order.[13]

Bourke goes on to argue that these carnival rites provided a way for men to carry out aggressive acts without having to take responsibility for them, knowing that although disapproved of by the authorities no action was taken against them. This behaviour was, in some ways, necessary to enhance 'effective combat performance'[14] – that is, make them better soldiers, and make them better 'men'.

'Performance' is an interesting term. Paul Fussell devoted a whole chapter of *The Great War and Modern Memory* to the discussion of warfare as theatrical experience as a way of distancing and therefore dealing with it.[15] Many critics have pointed out that for the soldiers of Vietnam, their war was cinematic rather than theatrical, but nonetheless performative. Philip Caputo is in no doubt about his motive for joining the Marines: '⸱ ° ¹ fi ᶜ ⟩ ʳfl ¹   ᶜ ffi⟩ fff   ᵈ ˋ ʳffi ˆ   MEN'[16] lured him in, the need to learn the roles of masculinity. He was inspired by the films of his childhood, what Tobey C. Herzog has called 'the John Wayne Syndrome':[17] 'I wanted the romance of war, bayonet charges, and desperate battles against impossible odds. I wanted the sort of thing I had seen in *Guadalcanal Diary* and *Retreat, Hell!*'[18] This identification with Hollywood films remains with Caputo throughout his tour of duty, but becomes tainted by an ironic bitterness. Towards the end of fierce battle, spurred on by the 'extraordinary exultation' of combat, Caputo offers himself as a decoy to draw sniper fire and thus give his men a target. His own narrative record of the event admits to delirium; he is out of control. But at the same time it also seems to be performance rather than reality:

> I was John Wayne in *Sands of Iwo Jima*. I was Aldo Ray in *Battle Cry*. No, I was a young, somewhat immature officer flying on an overdose of adrenalin because I had just won a close-quarters fight without suffering a single casualty.[19]

The fantasy of being the all-American hero is powerful: powerful enough to distract even at the climax of battle. It is also a way of distancing, of displacement, a way of not having to deal directly with the realities of the violence surrounding him. It is about performance rather than determined action. To play that role properly, to be a man, violence is prerequisite. Retrospectively, however, Caputo sees himself for what he was, a delirious young man carried away by the battle: the myth of 'John Wayne Syndrome' shattered.

A Rumor of War explores this new approach to violence as Caputo analyses his own loss of control:

> I had my first violence fantasy then, a hint that I was breaking down under the strains and frustrations peculiar to that war. In my mind,

the red liquid in the woman's mouth was blood, not betel-nut juice. In my mind, I had slapped her across the mouth with the back of my hand, and blood was pouring out from between her lips as she told me all I wanted to know. I had beaten the truth out of her.[20]

Caputo's confession is interesting. What he describes is a 'fantasy' involving an assault on a civilian. Although the woman he is trying to interview may be connected with the Viet Cong, she may not, this uncertainty feeding the fantasy itself. It is part of the complexity of the war, the being unable to identify the enemy. The habit of chewing betel nuts, common to Vietnamese women, was one which seems to have repulsed many American soldiers. For Caputo it almost operates as an incendiary act. The imaginary leap from juice to blood symbolises his frustration not only with the people, but with the war itself. Perhaps most important, while Caputo admits to the 'fantasy', he also locates it within the sphere of mental instability. It is war neuroses that causes these violent actions, not war itself or duty or heroism.

Whereas for soldiers in the First World War the 'extraordinary exultation', the adrenaline rush that makes killing possible, seems to have been channelled into legitimate acts of warfare, in Vietnam, where cause and motivation were much less clear, it can also be held responsible for the atrocity stories that seem to recur within the narratives. Mutilation, rape, murder: such acts can be performed by the unstable mind that believes violence is synonymous with manhood. Most war narratives from Vietnam feature some kind of breakdown. Caputo's takes the form of an escalating desire for violence, leading to the threat of court martial before his eventual return to the United States. For Robert Mason it is nightmares and sleepless nights that destroyed his post-Vietnam career and drove a descent into drug and alcohol addiction and convictions. Bobbie Ann Mason's veteran, Emmett Smith, cannot settle into civilian life a decade after the end of the war in *In Country*.[21] The problem is not only a Western one. Kien, Bao Ninh's protagonist in *The Sorrow of War*, uses drink as a way to forget despite being on the 'winning' side.[22] And in *When Heaven and Earth Changed Places*[23] Le Ly Hayslip describes her father's breakdown under the pressure of having his family torn apart as they struggle to survive between the Viet Cong and Republican forces, leading to his eventual suicide. All are haunted by the ghosts of Vietnam.

Of course it is too simplistic to connect the urge to kill, the pleasure of killing, so distinctly with war neuroses, particularly given that veterans of Vietnam were much more likely to suffer breakdown after their return home. Arguably it is a pleasure that has always been there. Joanna Bourke has suggested that in the past many men have been reticent about telling their war stories as much because of the pleasure of war as of the horror.[24] In many such stories the two blend. What war gives to masculinity is the power over life and death; a power not dissimilar to that of childbirth except with a focus on death rather than life.[25] This power can be intoxicating, a notion that leads right back to the consequences of the 'extraordinary exultation'.

As well as details of such atrocities as the taking of trophies and mutilation, the narratives of Vietnam are filled with sex-related war crimes. While this is a practice that is probably as old as warfare itself, it is not one commonly found recorded in earlier narratives. During the First World War there were, of course, sex-related atrocity stories – for example, associated with the German invasion of Belgium and publicised through the media and popular press. But, in fact, sex in any form rarely enters into the soldiers' narratives of that war. Robert Graves acknowledges homoerotic attachments and comments on the provision of army brothels.[26] Paul Baumer seeks solace in the arms of a French peasant girl forced to prostitute herself for a loaf of bread in Remarque's *All Quiet on the Western Front*.[27] But in contemporary texts the violence remains squarely on the battlefield and is never intentionally directed towards women or civilians.

In Vietnam, however, sexual violence seems to have been commonplace. While it is not an activity practised by men like Caputo or Robert Mason, it is one that was witnessed and recorded nonetheless. Samuel Hynes suggests:

> The ubiquity of sex is one reality that distinguishes this war from the others. There is another: that those sexual acts – so cheap, so casual, and often so violent – should be reported in the war narratives, that the sexual story should be felt to be a necessary part of the whole truth of Vietnam.[28]

Sexual violence in wartime may be about power and conquest. Arguably, American soldiers in Vietnam, unsure of why they were there, insecure in the face of that unseen, unknown enemy, may have felt the need to find alternative ways of asserting power and dominance. But Joanna Bourke tells us:

> Numerous servicemen admitted that they had been told by their instructors that 'we could rape the women' and they were taught how to strip women prisoners, 'spread them open', and 'drive pointed sticks or bayonets into their vaginas afterwards.' ... the fact that Marines were allowed to rape women was 'an inducement to encourage Marines to volunteer for Vietnam.'[29]

Such ideas are deeply disturbing, and there seems to be textual evidence to back them up. Certainly the rape of Vietnamese women by American men is well documented both in written texts and in film – for example, Larry Heinemann's *Paco's Story* and Brian De Palma's 1989 movie *Casualties of War*.

Yet sexual violence is not confined to Western narratives. Bao Ninh's *The Sorrow of War* explores the experience of the war and its aftermath through the eyes of a veteran of the North Vietnamese Army. It is a novel about the processes of writing war. Chronologically disjointed, the novel works around a series of combatant and non-combatant incidents concerning the war service of Kien/the narrator (who may or may not be the same person), and his relationship with his pre-war girlfriend Phuong. Kien's life and war have been shaped by certain events that are hinted at throughout the novel. The revelation of these events towards the end of the novel helps to explain the pattern of his war and his war neurosis. Both events hinge on shocking acts of sexual violence.

The first (but chronologically the second) involves Kien witnessing the gang rape, by American soldiers, of a teenage Vietnamese army scout, Hoa. Hoa's name echoes through the text, a ghostly voice that stands out from the polyphony of ghostly voices, because of the appalling circumstances of her death. Kien recalls a retreat following the 1968 Tet Offensive. He and a party of wounded are led by Hoa, who manages to lose the way through her inexperience. Kien's response is one of anger, but turns to despair when they see an American patrol with a sniffer dog pick up the trail of the wounded. Hoa, on the other hand, reacts, first shooting the dog, then using herself as a decoy to draw the Americans away from the trail. Although Kien is sickened, there is a deadpan inevitability about the narrative of Hoa's fate. Kien is helpless to save her;

drawing attention to himself would mean his own death and the discovery of the wounded.

Hoa's action, which redeems her from her crime of losing the trail, is perhaps the single heroic act recorded in the entire novel. Other combat scenes are bloody and brutal in a way that resembles the combat scenes of *All Quiet on the Western Front* and others. Kien himself, the 'sorrowful spirit', although occasionally wounded, has a charmed life, and is at times presented as a fierce opponent in battle. But his battle violence is tinged with the delirium acknowledged by Caputo:

> Kien saw himself holding a rifle, shooting at someone's head; the sub-machine-gun bullet, as powerful as a bomb, hit him right in the mouth and his face exploded taking his left eye, his cheek-bone and his lower jaw. 'Ahaaaahhaha,' he had cried. The sound was like laughter, more likely a wail. How frenzied and aggressive this generation of his had become! [30]

Kien's gratuitous involvement in the violence is reminiscent of the infantry charges in *All Quiet*, but for Remarque this involvement never becomes enjoyment. For Kien, 'the killing had become obsessive, all-devouring.'[31] It is no longer just about survival, but about something more primal. The result for the reader, however, is perhaps even more shocking. Kien the soldier, whose story intersects with that of Kien the post-war alcoholic, is seen as variously deranged, hysterical, vicious or a victim. But the message is anti-war, anti-heroic, from whichever angle you approach it.

Hoa is quite different. At her moment of crisis she is described thus:

> She was a magnificent portrait of courage; she stood against the setting sun, her lovely slim body erect, arm outstretched firing at the dog, and the dog only. The final rays of the setting sun silhouetted her against the Crocodile Lakelands, tingeing her skin copper colour, giving it the appearance of a bronze statue. Her long hair swirled around her shoulders and below her shorts Kien saw that her legs were newly scratched and bleeding. The dog, which had never baulked at going for her, was finally dropped in his tracks by her last two shots.[32]

This paragraph is unique. Here Hoa is described through the romantic rhetoric of conventional heroism. She is a 'magnificent portrait of

courage' that Bao Ninh goes on to draw in vivid and emotional detail.
Her femininity is stressed through her slim body, her hair, her legs.
But at the same time she is erect, highlighting the masculine elements
to this heroic sacrificial act. The setting sun is glorious, symbolising
her own end, and almost consuming her within it. She is bronzed,
as a statue, giving her the authority of an ancient god.

Hoa will be the victim of sexual violence and murder, but before
that happens she achieves a kind of warrior status that none of the
men in the text comes close to. Conventional notions of heroism
as a way of expressing 'manhood' are problematised here. Indeed,
the presence of large numbers of women soldiers fighting for the
North in the Vietnam War make it additionally difficult to examine
from the viewpoint of Western values. But the way in which Hoa
and her actions are represented, juxtaposed against the silent, mind-
lessly repeated rape, serves to make the sexual violence even more
shocking than it would otherwise be, raising further questions about
the nature of this war.

There is, perhaps, something of the 'chickenhawk' paradox about
women like Hoa. Portrayed as vulnerable and frightened, Hoa weeps
at her own helplessness to lead the wounded to safety. At the same
time, when real action is needed, she displays a determined courage. Kien's childhood sweetheart, Phuong, is represented as a similar
double. She is the driving force behind Kien's life, the woman he
should return to after the war. Indeed she is there in his post-war
life, yet inexplicably they are not together. The ghost voice of Phuong
is even stronger throughout the text. Their story, told gradually in
flashback, is inextricably linked to the war, but we do not learn
why until the final pages.

Hoa's rape, shocking though it is, has a heightened resonance
for Kien. At the end of Kien's war we learn about the beginning.
After a final leave, Phuong accompanies him as he tries to join his
unit. Having missed the troop train, they join another. During the
confusion of an air raid upon the train, Kien is thrown from the
carriage by a blast; the last image he sees is Phuong being attacked
by a man. When he finds her again, she has become a sailor's possession. Ignoring Kien, the man tells her, 'I'd hoped you'd stay with
me until Vinh. Otherwise I'll be bored, …What's up? Don't you
fancy a bit from me? That's not fair. I stopped those other turds
lining up for you again. It's my turn now. I've not had my turn.
I want some reward.'[33] Kien kills him as they try to escape with

the onset of further bombing. Both innocent teenagers have been tainted together.

Although they are teenagers, it is clear that Phuong has always been the dominant personality. Indeed she has been trying to persuade Kien to make love to her up until the air raid. Following the rapes, although she is not physically dead like the other women in the novel, she is spiritually dead. Phuong has no voice in the text; nevertheless, that of Le Ly Hayslip, in *Heaven and Earth*, seems to register the horror of being raped:

> What had been saved a lifetime for my husband had been ripped away in less time that it takes to tell ... What Loi had killed in me could not be buried; yet I already felt its weight – like a shoulder pole or tumour – on my soul ... I felt filthy and wanted only to bathe in the river and pray at the ruined pagoda that loomed darkly above the trees outside Tung Lam.[34]

The day after the attacks, Kien wakes to find Phuong missing. He discovers her doing what Hayslip describes, bathing in the river. Considering herself dead to her former love, Phuong, like her namesake phoenix, reinvents herself to go on living. As she washes away her experience, she uses a soldier's helmet to pour the water onto her body, sensually described as Kien sees it. It is a symbolic union with the war, heralding the birth of her wartime and post-war self, a self that will use whatever means she can find to survive, including prostitution.

Phuong is not raped by Western men. But she is a woman in the wrong place, in the war zone and therefore vulnerable to the sexual violence that seems to permeate this war. Yet she seems to deal with it, or at least to accept it in a way that Kien cannot. The subtext of the novel is built around the psychological trauma that he experiences as a result of this event. All his subsequent relationships with women are coloured by it. It makes Kien both the chicken and the hawk, releasing his uncertainty and vulnerability at the same time as his aggression. There is also the sense that his manhood has been reduced by this act. The manhood that he would have found during the act of love with Phuong is forever deferred, leaving him emasculated even as a soldier. The violence that might have secured that 'manhood' is condemned, diminished by the delirious frenzy of the war and deplored in comparison with the innocent courage of Hoa.

These women are fascinating figures. They bring to the text a strength that the men are denied. In *The Sorrow of War*, violence, machismo, the badges of masculinity do not signify heroism. Equally lacking is the ironic detachment of Caputo. Perhaps the real irony is that Kien, like Bao Ninh, himself a former soldier, is allegedly on the winning side. Le Ly Hayslip's narrative puts forward a similar argument. There are no winners in this war. For the Vietnamese, there will be a further three years of civil war following the withdrawal of the Americans. Hayslip's writings of her return to Vietnam years later illustrate a shaky peace. The ghost voices that continue to haunt Kien indicate that the war will never be over in a state that has lost so much.

There are similar ghosts on the other side of the Pacific. As Samuel Hynes argues, 'It [the Vietnam War] lingers in American minds like the memory of an illness, a kind of fever that weakened the country until its people were divided and its cause lost.'[35] It is a troubled memory and there are many reasons for it: the politics surrounding the war, the opposition to it, the successful recruitment of former soldiers into that opposition, being on the losing side, the unwelcome reception of Vietnam veterans back into American society. In the next section I shall examine some civilian responses to the war. How are issues such as heroism, masculinity and violence in the Vietnam War addressed by the women who stayed at home?

Women's stories

Just as the experience of combat in Vietnam differed from previous wars in many ways, so the noncombatants, the civilians on the home front, had different issues to confront. Geographically isolated and self-sufficient, the United States has traditionally fared well in international war situations. Vietnam did not even bring threats such as those presented by the German submarines in the Atlantic during the Second World War;[36] nor were there nuclear threats. Civilians did not have to do battle with hardships such as rationing and air raids. Life could, on the surface at least, continue as normal for the duration of the Vietnam War.

What was different, of course, was public response to the war and its psychological impact. Rick Berg and John Carlos Rowe argue:

> No community in the United States was unaffected by the Vietnam War. The Pentagon and Congress invaded not only Southeast Asia but the

American family, forcing ordinary citizens to reconsider conventional responsibilities to their families and local communities. Honest and civic-minded citizens served on local draft boards and their review panels, forced to decide which neighbors' children would go to war.[37]

This, they go on to suggest, ensured that the rhetoric of patriotism infiltrated the whole community, legal 'conscientious objection' was made almost impossible, and, as a result, the average age of the drafted combat soldier was just nineteen, tearing into the heart of the nuclear family in which American culture was rooted. The family structure was further threatened by the migration across borders of young men who wanted to avoid the draft. Either way, absence hit communities hard.

Jayne Anne Phillips's *Machine Dreams* explores this social impact of the war through the lives of the Hampson family. It is a wide-ranging novel that deals with war by proxy. Mitchell Hampson serves in the Far East in the Second World War; despite not actually fighting – he is a construction engineer – the experience scars him and traumatises his relationship with his wife, Jean. Twenty-five years later, his son Billy refuses to avoid the draft and goes to Vietnam. This time it is his sister, Danner, the woman left behind, whose trauma we experience. The collective memories and letters of these four characters make up the narrative strands of the novel.

Mitch and Billy share the machine dreams of the title. An innate identification with different types of machinery, a kind of mechanised masculinity, draws both men towards the military, and arguably imprisons both of them there permanently. After the war Mitch runs a concrete plant; 'He wore khaki shirts and work pants, the same kind of clothes he wore in wartime photographs when he was building airstrips in New Guinea and teaching Papuan natives how to operate steam rollers.'[38] It is when this business goes wrong and Mitch loses his sense of identity that his life falls into alcoholic decline. Without the machines he is somehow less of a man, no longer able to keep his wife and his family together. Billy grows up surrounded by the technology of 'Mitch Concrete', but takes the machine dream further, developing a love of aeroplanes. It is this passion that leads him, like Robert Mason, towards the military and the helicopters in Vietnam, where he serves as a door gunner.

These machines have a particular significance; they seem to lend the body power in wartime, the machines themselves become the invulnerable body that will win. This power, and its identification with masculinity and, by extension, conventional notions of heroism, lead to the eroticisation of the machine. The body and the machine become one, thus Robert Mason, in the air, becomes the hawk, sleek, powerful and predatory. Susan Jeffords argues, 'To link the body and technology through the erotic locates that object for control in an external frame – the display and beauty of technology – that enables the disavowal of the body's own vulnerability.'[39] Within this imagined space, courage may be realised. Billy articulates a similar feeling:

> My choice is ground or air, and I know I feel less like a sitting chickenshit in the air … My real feeling is that I'm not so scared of being dead, if it's fast – I'm scared as shit of lying in some jungle all fucked up, waiting for a dustoff that can't get in because the zone is too hot … If I go down in a chopper there will be another chopper in fast, to get me and to protect the machine.[40]

Even if the man isn't worth saving, the machine is. Together they are stronger. Phillips has Billy express the same attitude to combat and courage explored by Robert Mason. He exudes a security and confidence as a result of the machine. However, when his helicopter is brought down by enemy fire and he is declared 'missing in action' this mythology of the machine is shattered. Despite going in after the machine, his fellow soldiers can find no trace of the missing men. It is the ambiguity of this disappearance – Billy is never found – that resonates through the text and beyond.

Billy's few letters aside, it is Danner who translates the Vietnam War for the reader. She is profoundly anti-war, taking steps to prevent her brother from entering it, even offering him the money to pay for his defection to Canada. Danner is bewildered by his resistance, and her internalised anxiety and fear take material form in her own life: she is arrested for possession of narcotics just as Billy is about to leave for the army. Danner's relationship with Billy has a closeness that resembles the brother–sister bonds of an earlier age.[41] After his disappearance, she cannot believe in his death; she does anything she can to get close to him, bombarding the military with questions, dating Vietnam veterans, going into therapy. Overwhelmingly, it is the 'not knowing' that leaves her fragmented. Without the closure of death, her war cannot end.

Danner's confused response to the war seems to embody that of her community and country. Michael Clarke suggests:

> Associating that memory [of Vietnam] with a woman who never left the United States internalizes Vietnam within American society as a dislocation in the usual mechanisms of order and significance rather than as a threat from the outside, and representing those ideological mechanisms as a literal machinery of personal desire and family continuity dramatizes the constructed nature of both memory and history.[42]

The pastiche of Hampton voices crystallises in Danner the voice of the American people, articulating all the anger and frustration about Vietnam, pointlessness, uncertainty and loss. Her demands for answers echo the public questioning in the aftermath of the final evacuation, but are endorsed by a respect for the men who fought, which is in line with the 1980s' revisions. The absent Billy is a victim, brought up in a belligerent society, lured to danger by the power of the machine.

There is a sense in which Bobbie Ann Mason's *In Country* picks up the story a decade or so later. Here we have another woman asking questions, Danner's youthful heir, Sam[antha] Hughes. For Sam, the absent Vietnam soldier takes the ghostly form of her father, killed in action a month before her own birth. Much of the novel is built around her search to know him, in a world that appears to have forgotten. Like Danner, Sam is surrounded by Vietnam veterans, most significantly her Uncle Emmett Smith, who joined the army after the death of his brother-in-law. Clearly suffering from some kind of post-traumatic stress disorder and possibly from the effects of Agent Orange, Emmett finds it impossible to settle in 'normal' society, unable to hold a job or sustain relationships beyond those with his fellow vets and his family, particularly Sam, with whom he lives.

Sam's quest to 'know' her father takes her through the experiences of Emmett and his friends, particularly Tom, to whom she is attracted. It takes her through countless written accounts of the war and through every episode of the television series M*A*S*H. As Sam searches, so Bobbie Ann Mason demonstrates the imprint of Vietnam on all aspects of post-war American society. Sam is a teenager, living through a normal teenage rites-of-passage experience, but she is constantly seen as a parallel with her father, who was approximately her age at the time of his death. Emmett's neuroses shape her life; she has made a conscious decision to remain with him instead of joining her mother and new family. Her discovery of Tom's impotence when they try to make love illustrates to her the literal and symbolic emasculation of the Vietnam soldier, unable to control his own destiny.

The turning point for Sam is the discovery of her father's brief war diary, kept, unread, for eighteen years by his parents. The diary of Dwayne Hughes illustrates the unglamorous, unheroic nature of the war and, as with other war narratives (fiction or otherwise), emphasises the tedium, the violence and the uncertainty that is left out of formal accounts. Sam is appalled by what she reads of his attitude to violence and death. 'We got two V.C. I think one of 'em's mine, but Jim C. claimed it too ... Joe's got five notches on his machety ... Two weeks out and finally we got two. We had cigarettes and felt wild.'[43] To his diary, he confesses violence fantasies that Sam cannot accommodate with her former impressions of her teenage farmer father; 'If I saw a gook and didn't have any ammo, I'd take a cig. And twist it in his eyes and burn 'em out.'[44] And he reports trophy hunting in a matter-of-fact way that inflates the horror for his young reader:

> July 17. Two days ago, we come upon a dead gook rotting under some leaves, sunk into a little swamp-like place ... Interesting to see the body parts broken down, like we studied in biology. It had a special stink. Dead gooks have a special stink, we know by now. Bobby G. poked a stick around in it and some teeth fell out. Darrel's carrying one for good luck. He says now he'll have special gook stink on him and that will protect him.[45]

Dwayne's own naivety is illustrated in this extract. The soldiers appear like a group of schoolboys around the corpse of a dead squirrel. Indeed, he automatically equates it to a biology lesson. A youth and innocence are emphasised here that sit very uncomfortably with the gratuitously violent world that surrounds him. Through this juxtaposition, Mason enables Sam to continue to identify with her father, even while she is repulsed by his apparent acclimatisation to the war. This identification leads her to question how she would have behaved and, indeed, how those she knows well, such as Emmett, behaved under the same pressures.

Sam's response is to try to go 'in country' herself, spending the night at a nearby dangerous swamp. It is the reaction of a child, yet once more emphasises the youth of the combatants. When Emmett finds her the following morning, it proves cathartic for him. Weeping, he recalls for Sam his own previously hidden traumatic experience, a purgative deed that sets him on the road to some kind of emotional recovery.

The novel is framed by a trip to the Vietnam Veterans Memorial in Washington, undertaken by Sam, Emmett and her paternal grandmother, 'Mamaw'. Here they locate the name of Sam's father on the wall and lay his ghost to rest. Emmett finds a certain solace in the names of his fallen comrades. And, in a final symbolic gesture, Sam finds a version of her own name, 'Sam Alan Hughes', reinforcing Mason's message of ubiquity. The Vietnam War has pervaded the American psyche: its effects are palpable to many as a result of the way it has been assimilated into the culture and experience.

The effects of the Vietnam War were double-edged for Le Ly Hayslip. Her narrative, *Heaven and Earth*, attempts to write the war from multiple perspectives. Hayslip grew up as a farm girl in southern Vietnam surrounded by conflict, with the French, the Americans and with her own countrymen locked in civil war. She is one of the Vietnamese peasants who all look alike in so many American narratives. She could be the woman who so frustrates Caputo; is she Viet Cong or not? Hayslip reveals layers of complexity that are not anticipated in the stories of the American soldiers. Some of her family fight for the North, others are employed by the South. She herself is drawn in to Viet Cong activity at a very young age, imprisoned and tortured by the southern police. However, what comes across most distinctly is that lack of trust between various factions. Le Ly and her mother both work for the Viet Cong, and support the cause of the North – her eldest brother is in the army there – yet both are almost executed by the Viet Cong, who appear to suspect betrayal in everyone.

Hayslip's mother escapes death because of the intervention of an influential villager. Hayslip herself is instead punished for her imagined misdemeanour by rape at the hands of two Viet Cong guards. The sexual violence so regularly associated with this war is again not confined to 'enemy' troops. Indeed, this text is full of atrocity stories told from the other side. The Vietnamese civilian is under threat from every quarter. As a woman, Hayslip is doubly threatened, with sexual violence (there are other instances of attempted rape) and with the violence of war as an informal member of a military organisation and as a civilian in a war zone.

Hayslip's representation of the Americans in Vietnam is much more positive, however. After the birth of an illegitimate child and numerous adventures, Hayslip marries an American civilian and flees to the United States. Thus the narrative holds twin strands, one dealing with her early life in her homeland, the other detailing her return to Vietnam in 1986, after fourteen years as an American citizen. Hayslip brings with her that culture of guilt and failure that has become ingrained in American society as she rediscovers her family, still living in an atmosphere of fear and distrust reminiscent of the war years. What she reveals, like Bao Ninh, is that there are no winners. While the 'losers' struggle to come to terms with the conflict, by the mid-1980s offering the veterans the kind of recognition usually given to returning soldiers, which was missing in the 1970s, the 'victors' continue to battle to come to terms with the aftermath of decades of war.

Heaven and Earth offers a different perspective on familiar material, but highlights the same themes as so many other Vietnam narratives. The violence is ubiquitous and detailed, fuelled by what appears to be an ongoing crisis in masculinity, men whose 'manhood' is threatened by their lack of control over their own lives and situation. And fear and confusion cripple notions of heroism; the chicken and the hawk link in a battle for survival that does not end with peace. The ghosts of the dead are always present.

Vietnam was a war of ghosts.

Le Ly Hayslip's family cling to the memory of her brother Sau Ban, killed in action but whose body was never found, and of her father, who killed himself rather than serve the Viet Cong one more time. Bao Ninh's Kien, part of the Missing In Action body-collecting team, searches the 'jungle of the screaming souls' in 1976. At night he is haunted by their ghostly voices as he carries with him memories that simultaneously define and destroy him. Ghosts cause Robert Mason to wake screaming from post-war sleep. They lock Emmett Smith in an alternative reality, unstable and alien to his hometown. The ghostly voice of a dead narrator tells us *Paco's Story*. The spectre of the missing Billy keeps Danner Hampson searching, replaying filmic memories of the past, trying to make sense of the future. The ghosts continue to rise, textually or otherwise, like a kind of allegorical representation of the war itself.

'Phantoms, I thought, we're fighting phantoms',[46] muses Philip Caputo after an early brush with the North Vietnamese army. On a literal level, they are fighting men that they cannot see. On an allegorical one, they are fighting a war that they cannot see, for an unclear cause, in a strange land. It is a phantom war even for those who do understand what is at stake territorially, politically. This is what sets Vietnam apart from previous wars. This phantom status draws with it a trail of violence that reflects the confusion. 'Heroism' in all its forms is as ghostly as the war dead, and the struggle to deal with this helps to shape the narratives that the war produced. The violence, the sexual violence, the psychological pain that runs through each of these textual representations, repeatedly emphasis this trauma. The imaginary hybrid, the chickenhawk, becomes a ghostly symbol for all. The telling of tales continues to attempt that all-important exorcism, but these are haunted tales linked by themes that threaten accepted notions of heroism and masculinity – notions that have historically offered solace to narrator and reader alike. In Vietnam, the ghosts seem to have the final word, with their backs to the wall, flat and pale, and they are voices that cannot easily be silenced.

Notes

1 Larry Heinemann, *Paco's Story* (London: Faber & Faber, 1987), p. 138.
2 Robert Mason, *Chickenhawk* (London: Corgi, 1984).
3 Wilfred Owen in a letter to his brother in May 1917, quoted in Paul Fussell, *The Great War and Modern Memory* (Oxford: Oxford University Press, 1977), p. 271.
4 Philip Caputo, *A Rumor of War* (London: Pimlico, 1999), p. 268.
5 Samuel Hynes, *The Soldiers' Tale* (London: Pimlico, 1998), p. 4.
6 John Onions, *English Fiction and Drama of the Great War, 1918–39* (London: Macmillan, 1990); see Introduction.
7 Onions, p. 5.
8 Hynes, pp. 212–13.
9 Robert Graves, *Goodbye to All That* (London: Penguin, [1929] 1957), p. 211. Graves goes on to explain that Sassoon was recommended for a Victoria Cross, but the recommendation was turned down because the action as a whole was a failure. The implication is that Graves believes this to be unjust.
10 Caputo, p. 269.
11 Hynes, p. 191.
12 Heinemann, p. 7.
13 Joanna Bourke, *An Intimate History of Killing* (London: Granta, 1999), p. 37.
14 Bourke, p. 41.

15 Fussell, Chapter 6, 'The Theater of War'.
16 Caputo, p. 7, emphasis added.
17 Tobey C. Herzog, *Vietnam War Stories: Innocence Lost* (London: Routledge, 1992), p. 16.
18 Herzog, p. 14.
19 Herzog, p. 269.
20 Caputo, p. 255.
21 Bobbie Ann Mason, *In Country* (London: Flamingo, [1985] 1990).
22 Bao Ninh, *The Sorrow of War* (London: Minerva, 1994).
23 Le Ly Hayslip, *Heaven and Earth* (London: Pan, 1994).
24 See Bourke, Chapter 1.
25 There are many critical works linking the experience of war to the experience of childbirth. For example: Nancy Huston, 'The Matrix of War: Mothers and Heroes', in Susan Sulieman (ed.), *The Female Body in Western Culture* (Cambridge, MA: Harvard University Press, 1986), and 'Arms and the Woman: The Con[tra]ception of the Text' in H. M. Cooper, A. A. Munich and S. M. Squier (eds.), *Arms and the Woman* (Chapel Hill, NC and London: University of North Carolina Press, 1989).
26 Graves.
27 Erich Maria Remarque, *All Quiet on the Western Front* (London: Picador, [1929] 1991).
28 Hynes, p. 187.
29 Bourke, pp. 190–1.
30 Bourke, p. 110.
31 Bourke, 111.
32 Bourke, p. 177.
33 Bourke, p. 192.
34 Hayslip, pp. 121–2.
35 Hynes, p. 177.
36 See G. H Bennett, 'Women and the Battle of the Atlantic 1939–45', Chapter 6 in this volume.
37 Rick Berg and John Carlos Rowe, 'The Vietnam War and American Memory', in J. C. Rowe and R. Berg (eds.), *The Vietnam War and American Culture* (New York: Columbia University Press, 1991), p. 4.
38 Jayne Anne Phillips, *Machine Dreams* (London: Faber & Faber, [1984] 1993), p. 297.
39 Susan Jeffords, *The Remasculinization of America: Gender and the Vietnam War* (Bloomington and Indianapolis: Indiana University Press, 1989), p. 10.
40 Phillips, p. 286.
41 For example Vera Brittain's relationship with her brother Edward. See Brittain, *Testament of Youth* (London: Virago, [1933] 1992).
42 Michael Clarke, 'Remembering Vietnam', in Rowe and Berg, p. 194.
43 Bobbie Ann Mason, p. 202.
44 Bobbie Ann Mason, p. 202.
45 Bobbie Ann Mason, p. 203.
46 Caputo, p. 58.

Elite women warriors and dog soldiers: gender adaptations in modern war films

Jeffrey Walsh

'I think I can handle it': women in war films

Wars represented in Western cinema are almost universally gendered as male, which corresponds to the battlefield history of twentieth-century warfare. As this situation changes, and more women join the armed services, especially in the United States, a more inclusive cinematic coding evolves through struggle. Three decades of film, from the Vietnam War to the present, will be considered in this essay.

Despite the growing US archive of women's writing about their overseas involvement in the Vietnam War, no such active American female presence is visible in US cinema treating the conflict. Women's writing signifies the contribution made by the serving 15,000 American women, equally divided between civilian relief workers and military-related personnel, whereas mainstream cinema excludes them entirely, apart from the token romanticised representation of a nurse as in Furie's *Purple Hearts* (1984).[1] The implications of cinema's exclusion of women is that the war experience of both American and Vietnamese females is only available from published sources, principally from oral history, memoir and fiction. Two novels written by Vietnamese women are especially interesting, Minh Duc Hoai Trinh's *This Side... The Other Side* (1980), and Duong Thu Huong's *Novel without a Name* (1995).

There is little doubt that some of the stories told by American women in Kathryn Marshall's oral history *In The Combat Zone* (1987) could have provided alternative narratives to the peripheral filmic

representations of women who participated in the Vietnam conflict.
As a general rule, women shown in films depicting the Asian war
draw upon the stock figure of the prostitute, usually a scantily clad
whore, olive skinned and desirable, a crude re-visioning of the
oriental geisha stereotype that may be traced back through earlier
Western representations. Films such as Irvin's *Hamburger Hill* (1987),
in its bath-house scene, replicate this sensuous bar-girl cliché of
promiscuous harlots with slit skirts and sloe eyes.

An antithetical image of the Vietnamese girl may be situated
within what I have called elsewhere 'the Miss Saigon syndrome'.[2]
This discourse conceives of the Vietnamese female through subliminal
allusions to Puccini's *Madame Butterfly*. The young woman's seductive
power over the American in uniform derives from her innocence
when it is linked to her willingness to submit. A line of Vietnamese
women pictured on screen during the war echoes this iconography, which retraces through *South Pacific* (1958), and *The World of Suzy
Wong* (1958) to the hegemonic post-colonial ideology categorised
by Edward Said as Orientalism. An early example is Phuong, the
Vietnamese trophy woman in Mankiewicz's film of Graham Greene's
The Quiet American (1959), who is portrayed as child-like, deferential
and willing to yield to the most successful of the two Western males
competing for her affections.

Phuong wants to accompany her man to the United States, unlike
Trinh, the chaste Vietnamese heroine of Levinson's *Good Morning Vietnam*
(1987), who is respectfully treated by Americans and chaperoned
by members of her extended family. Both of these representations
suggest that America intended Vietnamese women no harm in its
Vietnam enterprise. Only in one film, Stanley Kubrick's *Full Metal Jacket*
(1987), is the Vietnamese woman accorded respect as a revolutionary fighter out of the pages of Arlene Eisen's *Women and Revolution in
Vietnam* (1984). The deadly woman sniper, who kills three soldiers,
is an elite warrior who emulates the two legendary heroines of her
race, the martial Trung sisters, who inspired their people to throw
off the Chinese yoke in AD 40–43. There is no wish fulfilment in
Kubrick's symbolism, only an acknowledgement of her lethal skills
as a riflewoman.

Because of the ethnocentric character of American cinema, there
are very few credible fictional presentations of the lives of Vietnamese
women. Such women are usually portrayed as victims, stereotyped,
for example, as bewildered and unattractive mama-sans lost in the

chaos of battle. The reasons for such racist and prejudicial images are linked to the patriarchal institutions of Hollywood and to
the perceived exigencies of box office. The complex politics of a
Vietnamese civil war and nationalist struggle largely evaded the attention span of movie executives. When Oliver Stone attempted to
tell the story of Le Ly Hayslip, a brave Vietnamese woman, in *Heaven
and Earth* (1990), the film was not a commercial success.

An alternative discourse which addresses the experience of Vietnamese women during the war is that of fictional films made by
nationalist Vietnamese filmmakers. Despite their patriotic fervour,
Vietnamese films, such Dang Nhat Minh's woman-centred *When the
Tenth Month Comes* (1984) and Nguyen Xuan Son's adolescent love
story, *A Fairy Tale for Seventeen Year Olds* (1986), help to contextualise the
situation of women in the thirty-year revolutionary conflict. Recent
critical studies of Vietnamese cinema are also valuable in contribut-
ing to this project of recuperation.[3]

A feminist alternative to the phallocentric genre of the war film
has immense transgressive potential. War films, from *The Big Parade*
(1925) to *Saving Private Ryan* (1998), have always privileged the male
point of view, masculine initiation rituals, and male spectatorship.
Such dominance is threatened by cinematic narratives which devalue
male prowess in war and celebrate female skills; gender stereotyping is thus sabotaged, an important citadel of patriarchal ideology
challenged. Such a development accords women their rightful place
in war films, and thereby subverts codings of gender which natu-
ralise forms such as romantic melodrama for women and combat
narratives for male audiences.

Two recent films, Edward Zwick's *Courage Under Fire* (1997), and
Ridley Scott's *GI Jane* (1996), have posed such a threat to the masculine
language and form of the popular war film. Both films enunciate the
female soldier's inevitable fight to subvert male authority, and are
feminist films (although directed by men) rather than anti-militarist
and pacifist in character. They build upon imaginary figures of women
warriors in earlier films and written texts which adumbrated their
feminist concerns. The science-fiction genre, for example, unrestricted
by the tenets of realism, has created individual warriors, such as the
legendary Ripley in Ridley Scott's *Alien* (1979), or groups of women
fighters alongside men, as in Verhoeven's *Starship Troopers* (1996). Postmodernist fiction has also subverted the masculinist war myth by
symbolising the instability of gender, as in novelist Tim O'Brien's

story 'Sweetheart of the Song Tra Bong' from *The Things They Carried* (1990), which narrates the descent of a wholesome American girl into primitive violence through associating with degenerate Green Berets. More radical is the vituperative counterattack on sexual abuse carried out by male soldiers in the experimental stories of feminist writer Emily Prager, *Visit from the Footbinder* (1983). Her short story 'The Lincoln–Pruitt Anti-Rape Device' purports to be memoirs of a women's army in Vietnam.

A distinction needs to be made between what Yvonne Tasker classifies as films with action heroines and other works where women's participation in war is central.[4] Surrounding the problematical issue of women fighting in the front lines are satellite films which broach the problem but retreat from treating it seriously. Most notorious is Howard Zieff's cosily decorous *Private Benjamin* (1980), the bane of feminist critics struggling to attain recognition for women in the military. This comic evocation of the army as a benign and pleasurable institution confirms traditional representations of femininity, and contrasts with the harsh world of harassment and sexual abuse later registered in *GI Jane*.

A rhetorical move to exclude women from centre stage in war narratives is metaphorically to disarm them, leaving men to perform the heroics and thus protect their females from danger. This is the ruse adopted in Tony Scott's *Top Gun* (1988), where Charlie, the female flight instructor with a Ph.D. in astrophysics, is a wingless flyer confined to the classroom while the virile aviators burn up the skies. Another more subtle stratagem is employed in Jean Jaques Annaud's *Enemy at the Gates* (2001), which portrays the battle for Stalingrad in the Second World War. The decisive military significance of this campaign is reduced to a couple of implausible plot lines. Two alpha male snipers – Vasily, a Russian, and his German opponent, Koenig – duel to the death; on the outcome rests the city's fate, and ultimately victory over Germany. Running parallel is a love triangle, comprising a young woman, Tania, who has volunteered to help at the front by using her skills as a speaker of German, and two rivals, Danilov, an officer, and the mythical sniper, Zaitsev. The film is too schematic; although its visual setting and historical reconstruction are impressive, it distorts the bravery of the Russian people by portraying their heroic resistance through the metaphor of a comic-book shoot-out between two men. It also limits the potential of the woman character, Tania, who has learned to shoot well as a child. Despite these skills as a riflewoman, which could have symbolised the traditional role of women in the Russian army, she is virtually ignored as a sniper and is there simply for romantic reasons. Hence the film's potential for showing a resolute woman warrior is curtailed; Tania could easily have been constructed as a lethal woman fighter, to rival the Vietnamese woman in *Full Metal Jacket* or the Vietnamese female sniper in *Platoon* (1986), who tries to entice American soldiers into firing range. (There was an actual Russian woman sniper, documented in soviet archives, called Lyudmila Pavlichenko, who reputedly killed 309 German soldiers, and was awarded the accolade Hero of the Soviet Union in October 1943).

In the cinematic representation of women warriors the gender of the director, in theory, should be significant. It is perhaps only a matter of time before one of the leading women directors, such as Jane Campion, Jodie Foster or Kathryn Bigelow, makes a war film representing women in combat. (Bigelow has directed a masculine-centred submarine film *K19: The Widowmaker* [2002]) Of course, there is no guarantee that a woman director will produce a feminist war text; this is illustrated in *Charlotte Gray*, a British work directed by Gillian Armstrong (2001). In the tradition of earlier, 1950s' films which celebrated heroines of the French Resistance, such as *Odette* (1951), and *Carve Her Name with Pride* (1958), its genre is more female adventure or spy story than combat tale. The heroine, played with an unconvincing Scottish accent by Cate Blanchett, is a translator whose knowledge of French assists the war effort, initially in London. After a whirlwind romance with an RAF flyer, who goes missing in action, she volunteers to serve in France in order to discover his fate. While behind enemy lines, she performs undercover operations, and is involved in trying to prevent two Jewish boys from being deported to a concentration camp. She proves herself courageous, and capable of outwitting a Nazi agent sent to capture her. Despite the potential of this film to pay tribute to the heroism of female agents whose work has never been properly acknowledged, *Charlotte Gray* is marred by being a sentimental romance and period piece, and by caricaturing the Francophilism of the story's creator, the novelist Sebastian Faulks. It compares unfavourably with Apsted and Jagger's *Enigma* (2001), in which Kate Winslett plays an intelligence officer at the Bletchley Park code-breaking centre. The focus of the latter film is not on personal relations, but upon team effort, scientific rationalism and the values of Britishness.

The critical methodology of gender analysis calls for a knowledge of the actual gender composition of US forces if an informed critique of films such as Courage Under Fire, set in the Persian Gulf theatre, is to be attempted. A new book by Joshua Goldstein, War and Gender, which is likely to become a definitive reference work, supplies appropriate data.[5] Goldstein summarises the gender balance thus; 'in the Gulf War, nearly 40,000 US women participated – six per cent of the US forces deployed (i.e. almost half the proportion of women as the overall military had). About a dozen women soldiers died, of whom five were killed by hostile forces.' In addition to statistical analysis, Goldstein offers his own opinion of the outcome of the gender war when he describes it as 'a big victory for liberal feminism. Women participated in large numbers, and performed capably, and the public proved willing to accept women soldiers as casualties and POWs.'[6] One of the captured women soldiers was Rhonda Cornum, jokingly a self-styled 'Rambo Rhonda'.

Cornum, a Ph.D. and medical research scientist, who joined the army and became a flight surgeon, supplied the role model for the fictional woman helicopter pilot in Courage Under Fire. Cornum's own story of her shooting down and POW experience, told briefly in It's Our Military Too, and more fully in The Rhonda Cornum Story, is instructive.[7] Although both of Cornum's arms were broken, and she had a bullet in her back, she survived the experience remarkably well. Her account is humorous and understated. Cornum's motivation for joining the forces is expressed in similarly low-key fashion: 'I think women are just like men; women who are motivated to be in the military have the same range of reasons as men. In terms of performance, there's also that same range.' [8]

The plot of Courage Under Fire has dual focus. Nat Serling (Denzel Washington), a tank commander who has accidentally caused a comrade to be killed in battle, is ordered to rubber-stamp the posthumous award of a Medal of Honor to Karen Walden (Meg Ryan). Serling will not allow a cover-up of the friendly-fire incident, nor will he recommend the gallantry award without a thorough investigation. Eventually, after having informed the parents of Boylar, his dead friend, of the circumstances of their son's death and accepting the blame, Serling is discovered to have saved the lives of many other men by ordering all the tanks' lights to be turned on. Serling's inquiry into Karen Walden's death is more complex. Ignoring pressure from the Pentagon to reach a conclusion quickly,

Serling questions the crew of her downed Huey. Walden, the pilot, came to the rescue of a stricken Blackhawk chopper. In a firefight lasting the night, she was apparently killed by enemy fire, and her crew rescued. Monfriz, Elario and Altemeyer, the men under her command, are pressurised by Serling, who is unconvinced by their versions of the firefight and of Walden's death. The truth is eventually revealed, that a mutiny took place; Monfriz shot her, leaving her badly injured; the three men abandoned her, and Walden was killed by napalm as the retreating US helicopters blitzed the area. When Elario finally admits the truth in his second account, it is clear that Walden acted courageously, protected Wright, the injured man, prevented the mutiny, and provided cover for her escaping crew.

The intricate narrative of *Courage Under Fire* is a fascinating example of gender appropriation. It is the story of a dead heroine whose courageous actions were deliberately falsified, and whose death was in danger of being used for propaganda purposes. Eventually the truth about her gallantry emerges, but only because a man with a troubled conscience rescues her from the obscurity of history. She is constructed only through flashbacks, as if her very presence in war is disturbing. Like the stories of Vietnamese people that are told by well-intentioned American writers, such as Robert Olen Butler's *A Good Scent from a Strange Mountain* (1992), she is recovered from the memory of others by someone who did not know her. What is interesting in the screenplay of Zwick's film is the reflexive way competing fictions of her heroic actions are disclosed to the spectator. The men in her crew, to conceal their own cowardice, impede Serling's inquiry by telling devious untruths. Only the brutal honesty of the dominant male truth-teller or narrator can finally uncover reality, seeing through the fictionality of their versions.

A number of interesting questions arise from the errand of truth dramatised in *Courage Under Fire*. The film's narrative does not correspond factually with some of the military realities pertaining to women's role in the conflict; for example, its gung-ho presentation of Walden seems exaggerated, and women cannot receive combat medals. Critics have objected to its 'reverential feminism' which, it is suggested, capitalises upon the marketable images of women succeeding in combat. (In the USA a poll of women reported that 84 per cent of American women believe that they have the aptitude for combat.[9]) Some other criticisms are subconsciously linked to the nature of film semiotics. The choice of Meg Ryan, playing against type, may account for the unconvincingly macho way in which she barks out her orders in an implausible Southern accent. She tries too hard to replicate the male iconography of war through her voice, gestures and body language. Although it is easy to attack the film as falsifying the story of Cornum, the narrative is worth defending. The film received no support, for example, from the US military because it projected an unfavourable view of a cover-up over the sensitive friendly-fire issue. Army censors also objected to the 'butch' nature of Walden's conduct, clearly preferring a more feminine type of heroine.[10]

Zwick's film takes risks, despite succumbing to clichés at the end when the military is shown in a favourable light after acknowledging the cover-ups exposed by the heroic African-American officer. *Courage Under Fire* struggles, albeit unsuccessfully, both to integrate women into the foreground combat narrative and to explore the processes which hinder that integration. Because there is no established canon which codes women generically or semiotically as warriors, there are inevitably unresolved contradictions in trying to remedy this absence. This representational difficulty is best overcome when Walden is shown combining her roles as mother and soldier; for example, when she does press-ups while singing to her daughter, Ann Marie, or shouts at Monfriz, when, in pain, she sheds tears brought on by tension: 'I gave birth to a nine pound baby, asshole. I think I can handle it.'

GI Jane is generally regarded as a disappointing film from a celebrated male feminist director, Ridley Scott, whose track record includes *Alien* (1979), and *Thelma and Louise* (1992). Its narrative revolves around gender politics in the US military. Jordan O'Neil (Demi Moore), an intelligence officer, is selected as a test case for propaganda purposes by a deceitful senator, Lilian De Haven (Anne Bancroft), and is intended to fail an intensive course for entry into the Navy Seals, the United States' most elite fighting force. During her training O'Neil is patronised and taunted by a succession of men, yet her strength of character and defiance of all attempts to make her quit enable her to pass the punishing induction regime which causes six out of ten men to drop out.

Scott's film, which falsifies many of the realities about women serving in the US military, provides a copybook example of Sex Role Congruency theory, according to academic feminist Sheri Cowley Rooks, illustrated through the way the military continues to dichotomise men's and women's roles and capabilities and still holds to the concept of woman as military other.[11] O'Neil, out of frustration, protests against this gender typecasting when she exclaims, 'Why don't you just issue me with a pink petticoat?' The male commanding officer of the Seals training programme, irritated that his men are compelled to undergo sensitivity training to acculturate them to the presence of women, is himself committed to androcentrism, a male-centred practice which hinders women's careers through occupational exclusions and physical barriers. He pretends otherwise, and, like De Haven, ridicules her progress, likening her mental control and physical fitness to 'Joan of Arc meets supergirl'. O'Neil rejects his attempts to provide separate shower facilities, segregated sleeping accommodation and compensation (called gender norming) in drill exercises. In the film's later sequence, when she has successfully completed her training, O'Neil participates in an operation off the Libyan coast, and performs her combat role with distinction.

The most interesting aspect of *GI Jane* is the symbolic transformation of the heroine into a woman admired and befriended by her fellow trainees. This metamorphosis from female outsider to trusted comrade is crudely executed through a ritualised humiliation. Throughout the film she is humiliated both verbally as a 'split tale' or physically bullied. In addition to the spiteful tricks played on her by Cortez and the other recruits, she is stigmatised as a sexual object, and sexist jokes are made about her. More problematically, the film constructs her, in Laura Mulvey's theoretical model, through a process of scopophilia: she becomes a pleasure object for the male gaze, her breasts sexualised and the camera lingering voyeuristically over her body as she exercises. The apotheosis of this fetishising of the female occurs in a shower scene when she is leered at by the Master Chief (who, appropriately enough, often quotes from a primitivist poem by D. H. Lawrence).

O'Neil, who wryly observes that 'combat is impossible if you've got tits', sets out to emulate the 'cock-swinging commandos', as her fiancé calls the Seals. She shaves her head to look butch, to the soundtrack 'the bitch is gone', and metaphorically sheds her breasts. This ritual of defeminisation culminates in her being fully accepted into the male fight club. After being betrayed by one of her men when in command of a mission, she is severely punished in a disturbingly sadistic episode. She is bound and badly beaten, and then knocked to the ground by the Master Chief. However, in bloody-minded fashion she staggers to her feet and defiantly shouts 'suck my dick'. She is now fully self-masculinised. This implausible outcome signifies male revenge for the Freudian threat of castration that her presence poses.

Scott's film unintentionally defeats its own ostensibly feminist thesis. While its manipulation of facts is just about excusable in a libertarian cause, its dismissal of the Jungian idea of psychosexual duality is unacceptable. O'Neil cannot, the film suggests, be natu-ralised as a man without first subjugating her identity as a female. This confirms patriarchy as the working ideology of the state by demanding that a woman soldier must not only possess commen-surate physical attributes to a man but also reconfigure herself as culturally masculine. By concentrating too much on the physicality of exercise, GI Jane becomes propagandistic, and is therefore unable to explore intelligently the double standards and inequalities still prevalent throughout military culture. Fortunately these issues are being widely discussed by a range of female scholars, making it likely that women warriors will not, as in films representing Vietnam, again go 'missing in action'.[12]

'I didn't mean to sound so tough': masculinity at war

Representations of masculinity in war films are endlessly fluid and adaptable, such negotiations and generic inflections being related to the ways in which commercial film-makers have packaged images and narratives of men at war. Cinema as an institution is responsive to changing cultural contexts and socio-economic factors. Masculinity and its diaspora of core concepts such as patriarchy, manhood, paternalism, manliness and fatherhood are all problematical terms, their meanings cultural rather than strictly linguistic. These shifting signifiers of masculinity have mutated cinematically. Manliness, for example, now an unfashionable virtue, can equally be associated with John Wayne in Operation Pacific (1951) or Tom Hanks in Saving Private Ryan (1998): two contrasting role models, the patriarchal US tough guy or the sensitive captain whose hand is always shaking.

In the discourses of cinema, sub-generic signifiers may be observed in every war film. Some of these are self-evident, such as images of the enemy, fellow soldiers, the possibility of death or wound-ing. Other structural elements are less apparent and susceptible to moral ambiguity: in the latter category, we might include notions of leadership or of fighting for one's country. It is how the narrative sequence of events is treated that contributes to these more ideological resonances; for example in Allan Dwan's *Sands of Iwo Jima*, (1949), the sergeant who leads the platoon to glory refers to the Japanese as 'lemon coloured characters' or 'nips'. In the film they are mentioned only as distant adversaries who threaten danger and must be eliminated. Most war films similarly dehumanise, debase or 'feminise' the enemy, which makes those exceptions such as Eric Weston's largely ignored *The Iron Triangle* (1988) especially interesting. Based on the diary of an unknown National Liberation Front soldier, the film incorporates a story of Vietnamese troops, thus showing, like Remarque's *All Quiet on the Western Front* (1930), the common humanity of men on both sides. Far too often the Asian enemy, as in *Rambo* (1985) or *The Deer Hunter* (1978), is presented as an evil masculine other. American masculinity, in contrast, is constructed mainly through heroic and sympathetic signifiers.

It was not always like this, and a critical evaluation of British war films in the 1940s, 1950s, and 1960s offers an illuminating contrast with American texts of the same period. British constructions of masculinity are more hierarchically ordered, where men clearly know their rank and respect their officers; soldiers display a firm awareness of class position; officers are generally stoical, valuing the 'stiff upper lip'; they prefer understatement to articulation of feeling; British eccentricity is prized as a sign of individuality and often of genius; and the conduct of the gentleman is everywhere looked up to, even though such an aristocratic code is challenged by an immature, public-schoolboyish sense of flaunted class superiority; a genuine English officer is a true gentleman best represented by Kinross, played by Noel Coward in the film *In Which We Serve* (1942).

Masculinity is, therefore, best understood in war films as nationally constituted, which French films about the French Vietnam War or German ones about the First World War demonstrate. Vietnamese cinema typically shows a humane and tender NLF, or North Vietnamese army soldier, motivated by love for his family and country, fighting against a massively resourced American military. American war films can also be related usefully to other filmic discourses of masculinity from US cinema, especially the masculine-dominated Western genre or the action cinema of Schwartzenegger and Bruce Willis.

Over the last twenty years or so critiques of American war films have increasingly made reference to theoretically based analyses of masculinity. Popular films such as Cosmatos's *Rambo: First Blood, Part II* (1985), for example, have been extensively analysed not because of their intrinsic merit as films but because of what they communicate about the construction of masculinity. Such interpretations demonstrate the intellectual affiliations of their writers. A casebook on *Rambo* could easily be published which represented diverse gendered readings of the text. Extracts from Yvonne Tasker's formal discussion of *Rambo* as a male action movie, for example, could be set alongside Robert McKeever's political and ideological analysis of the narrative, which suggests Rambo is a hero whose story embodies myths of nationhood such as Manifest Destiny or American exceptionalism.[13] Among such eclectic critiques, encompassing also the work of semioticians and historians, two methodologies are dominant: the psychoanalytic and the feminist-orientated discourse of gender analysis. Psychoanalysis has focused prominently upon male subjectivity and desire, the narcissistic self-love which propels the hero to seek mastery over the enemy. Freudian theory, in particular, offers potential exegesis of combat narratives, for example by explaining aggression and violence as a manifestation of the masculine unconscious, or scenes of wounding and carnage as, at a hidden level, pleasurable because they confirm the hero's and the viewer's own bodily inviolability. Familiar motifs in war films such as the soldier's yielding to a kind of 'death wish' when he recklessly faces enemy fire, anxiety about castration, or the fetishising of weapons may also be illuminated by psychoanalytic interpretation. Michael Selig's essay 'Boys Will be Men: Oedipal Drama in *Coming Home*' (1978) and Antony Easthope's critique of *The Deer Hunter* are examples of psychoanalytic commentary on war films.[14]

Gender analysis of American war films has been largely written by women writers influenced by the critical discourses of US feminism. This line of enquiry is often challenging and complex, although it may on occasions be reductive. Both of these characteristics may be observed in a stimulating collection of essays, including work by male and female scholars, *Gendering War Talk* (1993), edited by Miriam Cooke and Angela Woollacott. A contributor to feminist debate about masculinity in war texts, including films, whose work is both cogently written and theoretically sophisticated, is Susan Jeffords. Her major work, *The Remasculinization of America* (1989), is a landmark study which argues that 'representations of the Vietnam war can be used as an emblem for the "remasculinization of American culture", the large scale renegotiation and regeneration of the interests, values and projects of patriarchy.'[15] By exploring the strategies that achieve this revitalisation of patriarchy as evident in film and other narratives, Jeffords offers a valuable set of categories, methodological practices and theoretical frameworks for other scholars, and her work is drawn upon throughout this chapter.

In his book on the masculine myth in popular culture, Antony Easthope identifies four distinctive structural elements in the mainstream Hollywood war film: defeat, combat, victory and comradeship.[16] He might also have added to this list of core signifiers four others: leadership, forefathers, transformation and competitiveness. Significantly, one of these themes, defeat, is absent in Dwan's *Sands of Iwo Jima*, which culminates in US marines raising the flag on Mount Suribachi. The film's narrative has two parallel trajectories: while celebrating an assured and confident military campaign, it also embodies a fable of masculine transformation. At the film's conclusion, the plot lines converge, and victory is attained through military solutions that are readily accessible and comprehensible, notably through superior discipline and fighting skills.

The relationship between the rebellious young man, Pete Conway, and the busted veteran, Sergeant Stryker, played by John Wayne, dramatises conflicting energies within warrior masculinity. Stryker, the formerly competitive ex-boxer, a heavy drinker and professional soldier who has devoted his whole life to the army, has lived too long apart from his wife and son and has repressed his fatherly feelings in the pursuit of duty. He belongs to an older military culture similar to that which shaped Conway's father, nicknamed Screamin' Sam. Stryker has named his own son after the late Colonel Conway, his former commanding officer, praising him as 'the best officer and finest man I served under'. The theme of forefathers, fathers and sons, encompassing filial obligation and paternal duties, is thus at the heart of Dwan's film, as it is in all masculinist war texts. The young man, Pete Conway, initially rejects the values of his father, 'the hard product of a hard school', yet admits that he is influenced by him, confiding to a comrade: 'I've got to prove something to someone who is dead.' When Conway later learns he is himself to become a father, he disowns his father's action-man priorities, wishing that his child will instead be 'intelligent, cultured and gentle'. The narrative of *Sands of Iwo Jima* negotiates a compromise between the 'soft' civilian, Conroy, who enlisted only because he was expected to do so, as his forefathers have always served in the Marines, and the rugged drill sergeant, Stryker. Masculinity is constructed as somewhere between these two conflicting subject positions. As the narrative progresses, Stryker is shown to be fiercely protective of his men. His punctilious adherence to discipline helps to save their lives, and his emotional and verbal restraint is shown to conceal tenderness towards his wife and son. He displays this family sensitivity when he visits the home of a bar hostess, and pays for baby food for her child, and also through his articulation of how a man feels about fatherhood: 'there's something inside of a guy; he's always proud of his kid.'

Interestingly all of the children in the film are boys, including Conroy's child and the prostitute's baby, giving ideological expression to Stryker's axiom that a father 'gets more kick outa a boy'. It only remains for Conroy to move beyond Oedipal rebellion and grow up to become his father's dutiful son. When Stryker dies heroically, having led his Marines to the summit of Suribachi, Conroy, his surrogate son, assumes temporary command, barking out in cavalry fashion the order to 'saddle up'. Stryker's unfinished letter to his son serves as an exhortation to all of America's sons: 'you gotta take care of your mother ... always do what your heart tells you is right.' Conroy has now also demonstrated that he will be a worthy soldier-hero, like Stryker 'in some things, not like (him) in others'. Masculinity, the film suggests, should include Stryker's physical resilience and leadership as well as Conroy's emotional literacy. *Sands of Iwo Jima* thus adumbrates later inflections of male conduct in war, encapsulated in Stryker saying to the prostitute, whom he treats with respect, 'I didn't mean to sound so tough.'

Not until Steven Spielberg's recuperation of the Second World War fifty years later in *Saving Private Ryan* (1998), was masculine identity presented so positively in a landmark war film. Other Second World War films of the 1950s tried to emulate the moral coherence and ideological unity of *Sands of Iwo Jima*, and by exploring also the atavistic side of men's behaviour in combat were often psychologically interesting; yet none was as influential in symbolising transcendent white masculinity. This value system is expressed principally in Dwan's film through linking the patriotic duty of safeguarding the Stars and Stripes to specific codes of male behaviour. The grainy black-and-white photography, as well as the film's squad format of Greek, Italian and Mexican boys under the command of the iconic Wayne, segues into a traditional male-centred landscape of the mind. Little boys, 'husky little brutes' as Stryker notes, are entrusted with the defence of the Republic. Women, the nurturers, are to be cherished, yet some of them, like Stryker's wife, who prevents his son from writing letters to his father at the front, hinder the male defence of freedom and liberty. This motif, of the faithless woman who either jilts her man or does not fully support him, is a recurrent sub-theme of American war films, signifying the disloyal women who do not comprehend the hardship their husbands or lovers are enduring on their behalf. It is found, for example, in the closing episode of perhaps the finest war film of the 1990s, Terrence Malick's *The Thin Red Line* (1998). Nearly twenty years after *Sands of Iwo Jima*, John Wayne sought to re-create the unambiguous war narrative of the earlier film when he co-directed *The Green Berets* with Ray Kellogg in 1968, ironically the year of American humiliation during the Tet Offensive. A commercial and critical failure, the film demonstrates the formal obsolescence and ideological inappropriateness of the traditional war genre to represent Vietnam, the 'dirty war'. The complex histori-cal, economic and political changes in the post-war world, most significantly the nuclear arms race, the Cold War, and the cultural revolution of the 1960s in the West, had rendered flag-waving films of men united in brotherly devotion gratuitous.

The reasons for the breakdown of a unified male subjectivity in later film texts are socially diverse, and are usually related to a perceived crisis in US masculinity. Lack of public trust in the American administrations of the 1960s and early 1970s, evident in the anti-war and civil rights movements, infiltrated the politics of masculinity. Discredited leaders, such as Johnson, Agnew, Nixon and Westmoreland, betrayed the Kennedy myth of an idealistic national father. The women's liberation, gay and lesbian movements, and stu-dent activism, also radically questioned patriarchal authority. Television pictures of atrocities at My Lai and of troops torching Vietnamese huts alienated large sections of the American public after 1968. This sense of a profound collapse of traditional patriarchal values, which undermined the ideology of a unified masculine sensibility, is retrospectively illustrated in the narrative of Oliver Stone's film *Platoon* (1986), which portrays feuding soldiers, loss of morale and the murder of civilians.

The three most distinguished Vietnam films of the 1970s, Scorsese's *Taxi Driver* (1976), Cimino's *The Deer Hunter* (1978) and Coppola's

Apocalypse Now (1979), all communicated an aura of loss and bitterness, which was inevitable perhaps after the war's futile ending for American foreign policy. The widespread imagery of trauma, moral taint and madness contributed to cinematic presentations of returned servicemen as victims, losers and unstable misfits. As Timothy Corrigan has argued in *A Cinema without Walls* (1994), 1970s' Vietnam films also exemplified a fascination for the 1960s as an era when utopian aspirations and the possibility of discovering 'active and unrestricted selves' coexisted.[17] The Vietnam War curtailed such idealism when utopian models of subjectivity collided with intractable political realities. Corrigan explains the thematic return to Vietnam in 1970s' films such as *The Deer Hunter* and *Apocalypse Now* as enabling audiences 'to appropriate and empty the meaning of a lost generation'.[18] What Corrigan and other critics have perceived as a crisis in subjectivity may be extended to cinematic discourses of masculinity.

As a cultural metaphor, the suffering veteran soon translated into a stereotypical avenger; as well as excluding women from the discourse of the Vietnam War, such hackneyed representations often misrepresented the facts about post-traumatic stress syndrome.[19] Images of troubled subjectivity and trauma recur through a range of 1970s' Vietnam War films, including Jaglom's *Tracks* (1976), Kagan's *Heroes* (1977) and Ashby's *Coming Home* (1978). The pain of the veteran is represented, though, most powerfully in Scorsese's *Taxi Driver*, which narrates how an insomniac former Marine, Travis Bickle, having repressed his memories of combat, finally regresses, killing a pimp and a brothel keeper in an outburst of violence. The film's narrative constructs Bickle's incipient breakdown initially through his failure to integrate with a male group; he lacks the ability to bond with his fellow taxi drivers. Masculinity as a value system has collapsed within Vietnam, and now, after the war, has also failed to offer Bickle a form of male collectivity that can rescue him from despair. He kills, like a vigilante, in order to clean the streets of corruption.

Masculinity is often presented in war films as profoundly enigmatic, consequent upon the nature of warfare involving what Michael Herr in *Dispatches* (1978) called 'a heart of darkness trip'. The male subject follows the dark river inside himself, rather like Willard and the crew of the boat who pursue the unknowable Kurtz in Coppola's *Apocalypse Now*. Willard's mission is not only to kill Kurtz, who is out of control, but to discover ancestral truths about himself. This idea that war releases men at some deep psychological level was articulated in a speculative commentary by William Broyles Junior entitled 'Why Men Love War':

> The love of war stems from the union deep in the core of our being, between sex and destruction, beauty and horror, love and death. War may be the only way in which most men touch the mythic domains in our soul. It is for men at some terrible level what childbirth is for women: the initiation into the power of life and death. It is like lifting off the corner of the universe and looking at what's underneath. To see war is to see into the dark heart of things, that no-man's land between life and death, or even beyond. [20]

Broyles fantasises that a man's rite of passage in war is close to a woman's mystical experience when giving birth.

Coppola's film exhibits more than a hint of the attitudes expressed in Broyles's essay, its technically impressive creation of spectacle envisioning war as mysterious, epic and thrilling, the ultimate experience for the male subject. Ever the *auteur*, Coppola's art-house direction, drawing upon the psychedelic and countercultural, registers innovative myths of warrior masculinity. Milius, the screen writer of the film, testifies to the enduring influence of this intoxicating formula of West Coast hipness and California cool. He was photographing Desert Storm for the Marine Corps, and a young soldier, through the smoke of burning oilfields, approached and ironically described his unit as 'First of the Ninth Cav Sir. You know First of the Ninth? Have you seen *Apocalypse Now?*'[21] (During the Persian Gulf War, American helicopters routinely played Wagner's 'Ride of the Valkyries' when flying combat missions, parodying the legendary aesthetics of Coppola's film). None of the war films of the 1980s came near to achieving the intellectual and literary complexity of *Apocalypse Now*, which has been analysed by Laurence Coupe as a text redolent with underlying allusions borrowed from *The Golden Bough*, the *Odyssey* and diverse fertility myths.[22] Such a reading of the film does help to elucidate the slaying of what the Montagnards see as the old god, Kurtz, by the new one, Willard, thus providing a symbolic variation on the 'father–son dynamic' theorised by Susan Jeffords as the axis of all male-centred war films.[23]

The nasty, brutish and destructive nature of all warfare generates extremities of violence, including atrocities and rape, documented, for example, in the My Lai massacre or the Winter Soldier investigation.

This mindless violence, when connoted in films is usually perpetrated by unexceptional soldiers supposedly acting under misguided orders. Representation of rape and murder in war are thus problematical for the viewer and for the film-maker. Perhaps more convincing social and psychic explanations of violent and extreme masculine behaviour need to be given diegetically, such as in the first half of Kubrick's *Full Metal Jacket* when fearful recruits are indoctrinated by inhumane military training to kill the enemy repeatedly, or the reason retrospectively hinted at in Adrian Lyne's *Jacob's Ladder* (1990) that soldiers were secretly drugged through a kind of CIA conspiracy. Susan Jeffords has theorised this cinematic representation of male violence differently as narrative 'excess', a matter of symbolic coding; 'it will be assumed that there will be no dominant narrative in a patriarchal system that does not include gender as excess, or, more typically, masculinity as excess.'[24] Such a mode of representation, she suggests, is therefore rhetorical and offers no material explanation of why men behave so violently.

The committing of atrocities in films such as *Platoon*, although visually and emotionally disturbing, is generally treated superficially. Little effort is made to explore such actions, perhaps relating them to institutional racism, fear, or, in the case of rape – for example, in De Palma's *Casualties of War* (1989) – to an individual's misogyny. The latter instance is especially concerning, over and above the standard scenes in American war films of men visiting prostitutes, as it provides no narrative exploration of extreme male conduct, only the cliché that men were previously under fire and had lost one of their comrades.

On the other side of the coin, masculinity in war films portrays trustworthy men, especially loyal to their male comrades, which is the theme of *The Deer Hunter* where men who touch and hug each other, whenever etiquette allows, are faithful unto death. The homoerotic tensions of this film are expressed in the narrative focus of Michael's platonic love for the poetic and charismatic Nick. The only time the words 'I love you' are used in the film, they are said by Michael to Nick. As Antony Easthope has suggested, the pain distilled from martial experience has earned Michael the right to speak of a taboo subject, the love of man for man.[25] The transcendent fraternal love of the three comrades in *The Deer Hunter* is paralleled elsewhere, often encapsulated in pre-war masculine ritual. In Cimino's film the first hunting trip is suffused with the frontier cadences of hunting, which is similar to how the mystique of surfing functions in Milius's *Big Wednesday* (1978) to signify lost-generation spiritual wholeness. Both of these ritualistic episodes of male communion nostalgically envision young men in touch with natural energies before they experience combat.

In 1980s' American war films images of the male body, often pumped up grotesquely, as in *Rambo: First Blood, Part II* (1985), should not always be taken too seriously. One way of reading films like Tony Scott's *Top Gun* (1986) is to draw upon the idea of carnival; the creator of *Rambo*, ex-university teacher David Morrell, referred to the film as a cartoon.[26] All those men in the shower room in *Top Gun*, or images of Stallone or Chuck Norris with their bodybuilder muscle rippling, are playful examples of what Lacan called 'the male parade', pleasurable male pin-ups dispensing *jouissance* for both the female and the male viewer. The faded swagger of Clint Eastwood in *Heartbreak Ridge* (1988), or the adolescent assertiveness of Tom Cruise, cannot disguise, as one critic noted, that the penis never lives up to the phallus. Yvonne Tasker has discussed these films as part of the male action genre, constituted by an influential muscle culture; Linda Bose explains them as exemplifying 'techno-muscularity', a performative stance.[27]

War films of the mid- to late 1990s supply a muted coda to the jingoistic war films of the previous decade by revisioning male soldiers in a less sexist, homophobic and confrontational manner. Steven Spielberg's epistemic *Saving Private Ryan* is a lament for and celebration of ordinary GIs who sacrificed their lives for what Studs Terkel has called 'the last good war'. The film captures end-of-century anxieties about the cultural absence of a confident male heroism in contemporary America, and elegises both a caring military and diffident men who are essentially unremarkable and family-loving. Like a spate of recent twenty-first-century war films, including Moore's *Behind Enemy Lines* (2001), Scott's *Black Hawk Down* (2001), and Wallace's *We Were Soldiers* (2002), Spielberg's patriotic film is fundamentally about masculine responsibility: brotherly comrades and dutiful senior officers will never leave their men behind whatever the cost and will be true to the mothers of America in looking after their sons.

An equally sensitive depiction of men at war also characterises perhaps most impressive American war film since *Full Metal Jacket*, Terrence Malick's *The Thin Red Line*, which turns James Jones's machismo-driven novel into an interrogative text, riddled with postmodernist angst and metaphysical doubt. Endlessly the soldiers pose unanswered questions or think aloud about being helpless men caught up in the confusion of battle: 'In this world a man is nothing, and there ain't no world but this one'; 'I seen another world ... I think its just imagination'; 'evil, where does it come from? How does it steal into the world?'; 'what's stopping us from reaching out, touching the glory?' War is thus depoliticised, and reified as an inexplicable cosmic aberration. Malick's visually sumptuous and verbose film codes masculinity through recurrent images of thoughtful, tormented men, the antithesis of Rambo, although they do commit atrocities in occasional scenes of hyperbolic violence. Unlike Spielberg's, Malick's film has no truck with chauvinistic myths of nation; its men are lost souls not good American citizens. As is likely in future war films, the dramatisation of masculinity in *The Thin Red Line* implies further fragmentation and loss of identity. Compared with Spielberg's paternalist iconography of male sacrifice, Malick's transcendentalist vision of the soldier's desire for the beauty of the natural world is hauntingly resonant.

Notes

1   A. Louvre and J. Walsh (eds.), *Tell Me Lies about Vietnam: Cultural Battles for the Meaning of the War* (Milton Keynes: Open University Press, 1988), pp. 17–20.
2   J. Walsh, 'Countering the "Miss Saigon" Syndrome: American Representations of Vietnamese Women', in P. Melling and J. Roper (eds.), *America, France and Vietnam: Cultural History and Ideas of Conflict* (Aldershot: Avebury, 1991), pp. 168–99.
3   S. Jeffords, 'Vietnamese Films of the American War', *Reflex*, 3:5 (1989), 13–14.
4   Y. Tasker, *Spectacular Bodies: Gender, Genre and the Action Cinema* (London: Routledge, 1993), pp. 14–34, 132–52.
5   J. Goldstein, *War and Gender: How Gender Shapes the War System and Vice Versa* (Cambridge:, Cambridge University Press, 2001).
6   Goldstein, p. 95.
7   J. H. Stiehm (ed.), *It's Our Military Too! Women and the US Military* (Philadelphia: Temple University Press, 1996), pp. 3–23. See also R. Cornum, *She Went to War: The Rhonda Cornum Story* (Novato, CA: Presido Press, 1992).
8   Stiehm, p. 20.
9   S. Churcher, 'Dangerous Myths behind Women Fighting on the Front Line', *Mail on Sunday*, 15 September 1996, pp. 41–4.
10 C. Goodwin, 'How Hollywood Gets its Marching Orders', *Sunday Times*, 14 July 1996, pp. 4–5.
11 S. C. Rooks, 'Looking at GI Jane through Lenses of Gender', http://acjournal. org/holdings/vol2/essays/rooks.html.
12 See list of feminist scholars in Goldstein, p. 37.
13 R. J. McKeever, 'American Myths and the Impact of the Vietnam War: Revisionism

in Foreign Policy and Popular Cinema in the 1980s', in J. Walsh and J. Aulich (eds.), *Vietnam Images: War and Representation* (London: Macmillan, 1989), pp. 43–68.

14 L. Dittmar and G. Michaud (eds.), *From Hanoi to Hollywood: The Vietnam War in American Film* (New Brunswick, NJ: Rutgers University Press, 1990), pp. 189–215. Also A. Easthope, *What a Man's Gotta Do: The Masculine Myth in Popular Culture* (London: Paladin, 1986), pp. 61–8.

15 S. Jeffords, *The Remasculinization of America: Gender and the Vietnam War* (Bloomington: Indiana University Press, 1989), p. xi.

16 Easthope, p. 63.

17 T. Corrigan, *A Cinema without Walls: Movies and Culture after Vietnam* (London: Routledge, 1991), p. 33.

18 Corrigan, p. 36.

19 M. Norden, 'Portrait of a Disabled Vietnam Veteran: Alex Cutter of Cutter's Way', in Dittmar and Michaud, pp. 217–25.

20 William Broyles Junior, 'Why Men Love War', in Walter Capps (ed.) *The Vietnam Reader* (London: Routledge, 1999), pp. 74–5.

21 John Milius, 'A Soldier's Tale', *Rolling Stone* (May 1996), pp. 272–7.

22 Laurence Coupe, *Myth* (London: Routledge, 1997), pp. 21–6, 82–9.

23 Susan Jeffords, 'Masculinity as Excess in Vietnam Films: The Father/Son Dynamic of American Culture', *Genre*, xxi (1988), 487–515.

24 Jeffords, *Masculinity as Excess*, p. 493.

25 Easthope, p. 66.

26 William Allard, 'The Man Who Made Rambo', *Knave*, 18:6 (1989), 60–3.

27 L. E. Bose, 'Techno-Masculinity and the "Boy Eternal": From the Quagmire to the Gulf', in M. Cooke and A. Woollacott, *Gendering War Talk* (Princeton: Princeton University Press, 1993), pp. 67–101.

Select bibliography

Alba, V. and Schwartz, S. (1988) *Spanish Marxism versus Soviet Communism: A History of the P.O.U.M.*, New Brunswick, NJ and Oxford: Transaction Books.

Aldington, R. (1915) *The Poems of Anyte*, London: The Egoist Press.

Aldington, R. (1948) *The Complete Poems*, London: Allan Wingate.

Aldington, R. ([1929] 1984) *Death of a Hero*, London: Hogarth Press.

Arendt, H. (1986) *The Origins of Totalitarianism*, London: Andre Deutsch.

Ash, E. L. (1919) *The Problem of Nervous Breakdown*, London: Mills & Boon.

Barker, R. (1984) *Goodnight – Sorry for Sinking You*, London: Collins.

Bedford, S. (1987) *Aldous Huxley: A Biography, Volume 1: The Apparent Stability*, London: Paladin.

Bennett, G. H. and R. (1999) *Survivors: British Merchant Seamen in the Second World War*, London: Hambledon Press.

Berry, P., and Bostridge, M. (1996) *Vera Brittain: A Life*, London: Pimlico.

Bourke, J. (1999) *An Intimate History of Killing*, London: Granta.

Braybon, G. and Summerfield, P. (eds.) (1987) *Out of the Cage: Women's Experiences in Two World Wars*, London: Pandora.

Brittain, V. ([1923] 1999) *The Dark Tide*, London: Virago.

Brittain, V. ([1933] 1979) *Testament of Youth*, London: Fontana.

Brittain, V. (1945) *Account Rendered*, London: Macmillan.

Brittain, V. (1953) *Lady into Woman*, London: Andrew Dakers.

Brittain, V. ([1957] 1979) *Testament of Experience*, London: Virago.

Brittain, V. (1960) *The Women at Oxford: A Fragment of History*, London: Harrap.

Brittain, V. (1981) *Chronicle of Youth: Vera Brittain's War Diary 1913–1917*, ed. Alan Bishop with Terry Smart, London: Gollancz.

Broué, P. and Témime, E. (1972) trans. T. White, *The Revolution and the Civil War in Spain*, London: Faber & Faber.

Buchanan, T. (1997) *Britain and the Spanish Civil War*, Cambridge: Cambridge University Press.

Buitenhuis, P. (1989) *The Great War of Words: Literature as Propaganda 1914–18 and After*, London: Batsford.

Calder, A. (1969) *The People's War*, New York: Ace Books.

Caputo, P. ([1977] 1999) *A Rumor of War*, London: Pimlico.

Carse, R. (1943) *There Go the Ships*, New York: Garden City Publishing.

Caulfield, M. (1958) *A Night of Terror: The Story of the Athenia Affair*, London: Frederick Muller.

Coetzee, J. M. (1996) *Dusklands*, Harmondsworth: Penguin.

Cohan, S. and Hark, I. R. (eds.) (1993) *Screening the Male: Exploring Masculinities in Hollywood Cinema*, London: Routledge.

Collecott, D. (1999) *H.D. and Sapphic Modernism*, Cambridge: Cambridge University Press.

Collins, J. et al. (ed.) (1993) *Film Theory Goes to the Movies*, London: Routledge.

Cooke, M. and Woollacott, A. (eds.) (1993) *Gendering War Talk*, Princeton: Princeton University Press.

Copp, M. (2002) *An Imagist at War: The Complete War Poems of Richard Aldington*, Madison, NJ: Fairleigh Dickinson University Press.

Dane, C. (1939) *The Arrogant History of White Ben*, London: Heinemann.

Dane, C. (1964) *London Has a Garden*, London: Michael Joseph.

Davison, P.,(ed.) (1998) *The Complete Works of George Orwell, Volume Eleven: Facing Unpleasant Facts 1937–1939*, London: Secker & Warburg.

DeGroot, G. and Peniston-Bird, C. (eds.) (2000) *A Soldier and a Woman: Sexual Integration in the Military*, Harlow: Pearson Education.

Dittmar, L. and Michaud, G. (eds.) (1990) *From Hanoi to Hollywood: The Vietnam War in American Film*, New Brunswick, NJ: Rutgers University Press.

Durham, M. (1998) *Women and Fascism*, London: Routledge.

Eatwell, R. (1995) *Fascism, a History*, London: Chatto & Windus.

Escott, B. (1991) *Mission Improbable: A Salute to the RAF Women of SOE in Wartime France*, Yeovil: Patrick Stephens.

Feinman, I. R. (2000) *Citizenship Rites: Feminist Soldiers and Feminist Antimilitarists*, New York: New York University Press.

Fitzsimons, P. (2002) *Nancy Wake: The Inspiring Story of One of the War's Greatest Heroines*, London: Harper Collins Entertainment.

Foot, M. R. D. (1978) *Resistance*, St Albans: Granada Publishing.

Frei, N. (1993) *National Socialist Rule in Germany: The Führer State 1933–45*, trans. S. B. Steyne, Oxford: Blackwell.

Freud, S. (1997) *The Interpretation of Dreams*, trans. A. A. Brill, Ware: Wordsworth.

Fuller, G. (ed.) (1998) *Loach on Loach*, London: Faber & Faber.

Fussell, P. (1977) *The Great War and Modern Memory*, Oxford: Oxford University Press.

Gilbert, S. M. and Gubar, S. (eds.) (1988) *No Man's Land: The Place of the Woman Writer in the Twentieth Century, Volume 1: The War of the Words*, New Haven: Yale University Press.

Goldstein, J. S. (2001) *War and Gender: How Gender Shapes the War System and Vice Versa*, Cambridge: Cambridge University Press.

Gregory, E. (1998) *H.D. and Hellenism: Classic Lines*, Cambridge: Cambridge University Press.

Graves, R. ([1929] 1960) *Goodbye to All That*, Harmondsworth: Penguin.

Grayzel, S. R. (1999) *Women's Identities at War: Gender, Motherhood, and Politics in Britain and France during the First World War*, Chapel Hill and London: University of North Carolina Press.

Gribble, L. R. (1944) *Heroes of the Merchant Navy*, London: Harrap.

Hanley, L. (1991) *Writing War: Fiction, Gender and Memory*, Amherst, MA: University of Massachusetts Press.

Hartley, J. (1997) *Millions Like Us: British Women's Fiction of the Second World War*, London: Virago.

Harvey, J. (1995) *Men in Black*, London: Reaktion Books.

Hawkins, D. (1969) *Atlantic Torpedo: The Record of 27 Days in an Open Boat, Following a U-Boat Sinking*, Bath: Cedric Chivers.

Hayslip, L. L., with Hayslip, J. (1994) *Child of War, Woman of Peace: Heaven and Earth Part Two*, London: Sydney, Auckland: Pan.

Hayslip, L. L., with Wurts, J. (1994) *Heaven and Earth Part One: When Heaven and Earth Changed Places*, London: Sydney, Auckland: Pan.

H. D. (1983) ed. Louis Martz, *Collected Poems: 1912–1944*, New York: New Directions.

H. D. ([1960] 1984) *Bid Me to Live*, London: Virago.

Head, D. (1997) *J. M. Coetzee*, Cambridge: Cambridge University Press.

Healy, D. (1993) *Images of Trauma: From Hysteria to Post-Traumatic Stress Disorder*, London: Faber & Faber.

Heinemann, L. (1987) *Paco's Story*, London: Faber & Faber.

Herzog, T. C. (1992) *Vietnam War Stories: Innocence Lost*, London: Routledge.

Hesford, W. S. and Kozol, W. (eds.) (2001) *Haunting Violations: Feminist Criticism and the Crisis of the Real*, Urbana and Chicago: University of Illinois Press.

Hibbert, C. (1965) *Benito Mussolini: The Rise and Fall of Il Duce*, Harmondsworth: Penguin.

Higonnet, M., Jenson, J., Micel, S., and Weitz, M. C. (eds.) (1987) *Behind the Lines: Gender and the Two World Wars*, Newhaven, CT and London: Yale University Press.

Higonnet, M. (ed.) (1999) *Lines of Fire: Women Writers of World War I*, New York: Penguin.

Hitler, A. (1969) *Mein Kampf*, with an Introduction by D. C. Watt, trans. R. Manheim, London: Hutchinson.

Howarth, S. and Law, D. (1994) *The Battle of the Atlantic, 1939–1945*, London: Greenhill Books.

Huggan, G. and Watson, S. (eds.) (1996) *Critical Perspectives on J. M. Coetzee*, London/New York: Macmillan/St Martin's Press.

Huxley, A. ([1920] 1946) 'Farcical History of Richard Greenow', in *Limbo*, London: Chatto & Windus.

Huxley, A. ([1921] 1967) *Crome Yellow*, Harmondworth: Penguin.

Huxley, A. ([1936] 1955) *Eyeless in Gaza*, Harmondsworth: Penguin.

Huxley, J. (1978) *Memories 1*, Harmondsworth: Penguin.

Hynes, S. (1992) *A War Imagined: The First World War and English Culture*, London: Pimlico.

Hynes, S. (1998) *The Soldiers' Tale*, London: Pimlico.

Jackson, A. (2002) *British Women and the Spanish Civil War*, London and New York: Routledge.

Jackson, G. (1965) *The Spanish Republic and the Civil War 1931–1939*, Princeton, NJ: Princeton University Press.

Jeffords, S. (1989) *The Remasculinization of America: Gender and the Vietnam War*, Bloomington and Indianapolis: Indiana University Press.

Kagan, N. (1995) *The Cinema of Oliver Stone*, New York: Continuum.

Kossew, S. (ed.) (1998) *Critical Essays on J. M. Coetzee*, New York: G. K. Hall.

Kramer, R. (1995) *Flames in the Field: The Story of Four SOE Agents in Occupied France*, London: Penguin.

Kunz, D. (1997) *The Films of Oliver Stone*, Lanham, MD and London: Scarecrow.

Laity, C. (1997) *H. D. and the Victorian Fin de Siècle*, Cambridge: Cambridge University Press.

Leed, E. J. (1979) *No Man's Land: Combat and Identity in World War I*, Cambridge: Cambridge University Press.

Leigh, J. (2002) *The Cinema of Ken Loach: Art in the Service of the People*, London and New York: Wallflower Press.

Loach, K. (director) (1995) *Land and Freedom*, film, Great Britain, Spain and Germany: Parallax Pictures, Messidor Films, Road Movies Dritte.

Lorentzen, L. A. and Turpin, J. (eds.) (1998) *The Women and War Reader*, New York and London: New York University Press.

Low, M. and Breá, J. (1937) introd. C. L. R. James, Red Spanish Notebook: The First Six Months of the Revolution and the Civil War, London: Secker & Warburg.

Mason, B. A. ([1986] 1990) In Country, London: Flamingo.

Mason, R. (1984) Chickenhawk, London: Corgi.

McKnight, G. (ed.) (1997) Agent of Challenge and Defiance: The Films of Ken Loach, Trowbridge: Flicks Books.

McLaine, I. (1979) Ministry of Morale: Home Front Morale and the Ministry of Information in World War II, London: George Allen & Unwin.

Mitchell, A. (ed.) (1990) The Nazi Revolution: Hitler's Dictatorship and the German Nation, Toronto: D. C. Heath.

Monnickendam, A. and Usandizaga, A. (eds.) (2002) Dressing Up for War: Transformations of Gender and Genre in the Discourse and Literature of War, Amsterdam: Rodopi Press.

Ninh, B. (1994) The Sorrow of War, London: Minerva.

Onions, J. (1990) English Fiction and Drama of the Great War, 1918–39, London: Macmillan.

Orwell, G. ([1938] 1989) introd. J. Symons, Homage to Catalonia, Harmondsworth, Penguin.

Orwell, G. (2001) ed. P. Davison, introd. C. Hitchens, Orwell in Spain: The Full Text of Homage to Catalonia with Associated Articles, Reviews and Letters from 'The Complete Works of George Orwell', London: Penguin.

Ouditt, S. (1994) Fighting Forces, Writing Women: Identity and Ideology in the First World War, London: Routledge.

Phillips, J. A. ([1984] 1993) Machine Dreams, London: Faber & Faber.

Plain, G. (1996) Women's Fiction of the Second World War: Gender, Power and Resistance, Edinburgh: Edinburgh University Press.

Preston, P. (1996) A Concise History of the Spanish Civil War, London: Fontana.

Preston, P. (2002) Doves of War: Four Women of Spain, London: HarperCollins.

Radosh, R., Habeck, M. R., Sevostianov, G. (eds.) (2001) Spain Betrayed: The Soviet Union in the Spanish Civil War, New Haven, CT and London: Yale University Press.

Raitt, S. and Tate, T. (eds.) (1997) Women's Fiction and the Great War, Oxford: Clarendon Press.

Rowe J. C. and Berg, R. (eds.) (1991) The Vietnam War and American Culture, New York: Columbia University Press.

Sheldon, S. P. (ed.) (1999) Her War Story: Twentieth Century Women Write about War, Carbondale and Edwardsville: Southern Illinois University Press.

Showalter, E. (1987) The Female Malady: Women, Madness and English Culture, 1830–1980, London: Virago.

Silet, C. L. P. (ed.) (2001) Oliver Stone Interviews, Jackson: University of Mississippi Press.

Skidelsky, R. (1975) Oswald Mosley, London: Macmillan.

Smith, A. K. (ed.) (2000) Women's Writing of the First World War: An Anthology, Manchester: Manchester University Press.

Smithers, D. W. (1988) 'Therefore, Imagine...', The Works of Clemence Dane, Tunbridge Wells: Dragonfly Press.

Stabile, C. (1994) Feminism and the Technological Fix, Manchester: Manchester University Press.

Stiehm, J. (ed.) (1996) It's Our Military Too! Women and the US Military, Philadelphia: Temple University Press.

Summerfield, P. (1998) Reconstructing Women's Wartime Lives: Discourse and Subjectivity in Oral Histories of the Second World War, Manchester: Manchester University Press.

Sutherland, J. (1990) Mrs Humphrey Ward: Eminent Victorian, Pre-eminent Edwardian, Oxford: Clarendon Press.

Tan, L. (1999) *Heaven and Earth: Oliver Stone's Vietnamese Frontier*, Sheffield: Sheffield Hallam University Press.

Tasker, Y. (1993) *Spectacular Bodies: Gender, Genre and the Action Cinema*, London: Routledge.

Thurlow, R. (1987) *Fascism in Britain, A History 1918–1985*, Oxford: Blackwell.

Toplin, R. B. (ed.) (2000) *Oliver Stone's USA*, Lawrence: Kansas University Press.

Tylee, C. M. (1990) *The Great War and Women's Consciousness*, London: Macmillan.

Waites, E. A. (1993) *Trauma and Survival: Post-Traumatic and Dissociative Disorders in Women*, New York: W. W. Norton.

Wake, N. (1985) *The Autobiography of the Woman the Gestapo Called the White Mouse*, Melbourne: Macmillan.

Watt, D. (ed.) (1975) *Aldous Huxley: The Critical Heritage*, London: Routledge & Kegan Paul.

Wheelwright, J. (1989) *Amazons and Military Maids*, London: Pandora.

Woollacott, A. (1994) *On Her Their Lives Depend: Munitions Workers in the Great War*, London: Berkeley & Los Angeles: University of California Press.

Woolf, V. ([1938] 1986) *Three Guineas*, London: Hogarth Press.

Woolf, V., Monk's House Papers/Three Guineas Scrapbooks, University of Sussex.

Zilboorg, C. (ed.) (2003) *Richard Aldington and H. D.: Their Lives in Letters*, Manchester: Manchester University Press.

Index

Aldington, Richard 5, 12–32,
    31n., 32n.
  Death of a Hero 21–4, 26–7, 29,
    32n.
Allen, Jim 78, 80–1, 86, 88–90,
    92, 94n.
Apocalypse Now 9, 156, 161, 210–11

Barbusse, Henri 176
Bloomsbury Group 56, 68, 72
Boer War 1–2
Braybon, Gail 4, 11n.
Brittain, Vera 5, 33–50, 50n.,
    51n., 52n., 72, 194n
  Account Rendered 49–50, 52n.
  Dark Tide, The 34, 48, 50n.
  Honourable Estate 48
  Lady Into Woman 50n.
  Not Without Honour 48
  Testament of Experience 51n.
  Testament of Youth 33–4, 36–8,
    40–7, 49, 50n., 51n., 52n.,
    72–3, 194n.
Butler, Judith 133, 151n.

Caputo, Philip 9, 175, 177–81,
    183, 186, 191, 193, 193n.,
    194n.

Rumour of War, A 175, 177, 179,
    193n.
Carve Her Name with Pride 146–7,
    153n., 199
Casualties of War 163, 172n., 182,
    212
Charlotte Gray 147, 153n., 199
Churchill, Winston 30, 111,
    134
Coetzee, J. M. 9, 155–7, 159,
    163–4, 170n., 171n.
  Dusklands 156, 159, 164, 170n.,
    171n.
Coming Home 206, 210
Communist Party 77–9, 83–5,
    88–91
conscientious objectors 56, 62
Courage Under Fire 9, 197, 200–2

Dane, Clemence 6, 96–102, 104,
    107–8, 109n., 110n.
  Arrogant History of White Ben, The 6,
    96–100, 109n.
Deer Hunter, The 170n., 205–6, 209,
    212

Einstein, Albert 96
Eliot, T. S. 12, 24, 56

Enemy at the Gates 198
ENIGMA 122

Fascism 6, 81, 83, 96–7, 99,
    103–6, 108
Feinman, Ilene Rose 8
First Aid Nursing Yeomanry
    (FANY) 6, 11n., 135, 152n.
Franco, Francisco 76, 81, 90, 92
Freud, Sigmund 29, 43–4, 51n.,
    59, 70, 96, 109n., 175
Ford, Ford Madox 24
Full Metal Jacket 163, 196, 199,
    212–13
Fussell, Paul 4, 68, 74n., 179,
    193n.

GI Jane 197–8, 202–4, 214n.
Gilbert, Sandra 53–4, 63, 66–7,
    72, 73n.
Goldstein, Joshua S. 11n, 200,
    214n.
Graves, Robert 3, 30, 42, 51n.,
    68–70, 72, 74n., 96, 176–7,
    181
Green Berets, The 161, 171n., 209
Greenham Common 8
Gubar, Susan 53–4, 63, 66–7, 72,
    73n.
Gulf War 8, 151, 169, 200

H. D. (Hilda Doolittle) 5, 12–21,
    24–31, 31n., 32n.
Bid Me To Live 20, 24–7, 32n.
Hartley, Jenny 3, 10n.
Hayslip, Le Ly 9, 157–69, 171n.,
    180, 185–6, 191–2, 194n.,
    197
Heaven and Earth 157–9, 162,
    166, 171n., 180, 185, 191–2,
    194n.
Heaven and Earth (film) 162–8,
    172n., 197
Heinmann, Larry 178, 182, 193n.
Paco's Story 178, 182, 193n.

Higonnet, Margaret 10n., 11n.,
    75n.
Hitler, Adolf 90, 98–9, 101–3,
    105–8, 109n., 117
Mein Kampf 98, 109n.
homosexuality 30, 71
Huxley, Aldous 5, 53–60, 63–8,
    72–3, 73n., 74n.
Brave New World 64
Crome Yellow 55
Eyeless in Gaza 54, 73, 73n.
'Farcical History of Richard
    Greenow' 5, 53–4, 56–65,
    66–8, 72, 73n.
Point Counter Point 64
Hynes, Samuel 4, 10n., 51n., 61,
    74n., 175, 177–8, 186,
    193n.

Jeffords, Susan 156, 171n., 188,
    194n., 206, 211–12
Joyce, James 12, 67

Land and Freedom 6, 76–83, 85–6,
    88–93, 93n.
Lawrence, D. H. 12, 17, 24–5, 56,
    203
Lawrence, T. E. 12, 30
Leed, Eric J. 51n. 74n.
Loach, Ken 6, 76–83, 88–91, 93,
    94n., 95n.
Lorentzen, Lois Ann 8, 11n.

Mason, Bobbie Ann 9, 180,
    189–91, 194n.
In Country 180, 189–92, 194n.
Mason, Robert 174, 180–1, 187–8,
    192, 193n.
Chickenhawk 174, 193n.
Mosley, Oswald 103–4, 110n.
Mussolini, Benito 90, 102, 104,
    106, 110n.

Ninh, Bao 9, 180, 182–6, 192,
    194n.

Sorrow of War, The 180, 182–6,
    194n.

Odette 147, 199
Orwell, George 78–83, 89, 93n.
    Homage to Catalonia 78, 94n.
Oudit, Sharon 3, 42, 51n.
Owen, Wilfred 3, 24, 71, 175–6

Pacifism 5, 61
Phillips, Jayne Anne 9, 187–9,
    194n.
    Machine Dreams 187–9, 192,
        194n.
Plain, Gill 3, 10n.
Platoon 161. 163, 171–2n., 199,
    209, 212
POUM (Partido Obrero de
    Unificación Marxista)
    76–83, 86, 89, 91–3, 94n.
Pound, Ezra 12–14, 17, 24
propaganda 7, 35, 56, 61, 67, 72,
    98, 113, 115–17, 119, 120,
    123, 126–8, 155, 201–2

Raitt, Suzanne 2, 10n., 67, 74n.
Rambo 205–6, 213, 215n.
Remarque, Erich Maria 176, 181,
    183, 194n., 205
Russian Women's Battalion of
    Death 6

Sandes, Flora 6, 11n.
Sands of Iwo Jima 9, 179, 205,
    207–8
Sansom, Odette 140
Sassoon, Siegfried 3, 42, 56, 59,
    69–72
Saving Private Ryan 197, 204, 208,
    213
Sheldon, Sayre, P. 4, 10n.
shell shock 33, 35–7, 39, 41,
    45–9
Showalter, Elaine 35–6, 45n., 47,
    49, 50n., 70

Smith, Angela K. 10–11n., 74n.
Special Operations Executive
    (SOE) 6–7, 132–8, 140,
    145–7, 149–51
Stalin, Joseph 80–1, 89
Stone, Oliver 9, 162–8, 171n.,
    172n., 197, 209
suffrage movement, the 5, 36,
    60, 66
Summerfield, Penny 4, 151n.

Tate, Trudi 2, 10n., 67, 74n.
Taxi Driver 168, 170n., 173n,
    209–10
Thin Red Line, The 209, 213–14
Top Gun 198, 213
Turpin, Jennifer 8, 11n.
Tylee, Claire M. 3, 10n., 74n.

Voluntary Aid Detachment (VAD)
    33, 35, 46

Women's Army Auxiliary Corps
    (WAAC) 6
Wake, Nancy 134, 137, 140–3,
    145, 148–9, 152n.
War Against Terrorism 169
Ward, Mrs Humphrey (Mary)
    54, 56–7, 59–61, 66–7,
    74n.
Wheelwright, Julie 11n.
Woolf, Leonard 96, 109n.
Woolf, Virginia 6, 66, 73, 96–7,
    100–2, 109n.
    Orlando 97, 109n.
    Room of One's Own, A 96
    Three Guineas 96, 100, 109n.
    Years, The 102, 109n.
Woollacott, Angela 4, 11n., 206
Women's Royal Air Force (WRAF)
    121
Women's Royal Naval Service
    (WRNS) 121–3

Zilboorg, Caroline 31n.